Understanding Governance

Series Editor
Rod Rhodes
Professor of Government
University of Southampton
Southampton, UK

Understanding Governance encompasses all theoretical approaches to the study of government and governance in advanced industrial democracies and the Commonwealth. It has three long-standing objectives:

1. To develop new theoretical approaches to explain changes in the role of the state;
2. To explain how and why that role has changed; and
3. To set the changes and their causes in comparative perspective.

The origins of the series lie in the renowned Whitehall Research Programme funded by the Economic and Social Research Council. Since 1997, it has published some 26 books by the best known names in the field including Colin Hay, David Marsh, Edward Page, Guy Peters, R. A. W. Rhodes, David Richards, Martin Smith and Patrick Weller.

Over the past twenty years the 'Understanding Governance' book series has constantly defined the state-of-the-art when it comes to the analysis of the modern state. From accountability to agencies, party politics to parliamentary power and from crisis-management to the core executive this book series continues to set the agenda in terms of world-class scholarship.

—**Matthew Flinders**, Professor of Politics and Director of the Sir Bernard Crick Centre at the University of Sheffield

More information about this series at
https://link.springer.com/bookseries/14394

Patrick Gibert • Jean-Claude Thoenig

Assessing Public Management Reforms

palgrave
macmillan

Patrick Gibert
University of Paris-Nanterre
Jouy-en-Josas, France

Jean-Claude Thoenig
University of Paris-Dauphine
Paris, France

Understanding Governance
ISBN 978-3-030-89798-7   ISBN 978-3-030-89799-4 (eBook)
https://doi.org/10.1007/978-3-030-89799-4

© The Editor(s) (if applicable) and The Author(s), under exclusive licence to Springer Nature Switzerland AG 2022

This work is subject to copyright. All rights are solely and exclusively licensed by the Publisher, whether the whole or part of the material is concerned, specifically the rights of translation, reprinting, reuse of illustrations, recitation, broadcasting, reproduction on microfilms or in any other physical way, and transmission or information storage and retrieval, electronic adaptation, computer software, or by similar or dissimilar methodology now known or hereafter developed.

The use of general descriptive names, registered names, trademarks, service marks, etc. in this publication does not imply, even in the absence of a specific statement, that such names are exempt from the relevant protective laws and regulations and therefore free for general use.

The publisher, the authors and the editors are safe to assume that the advice and information in this book are believed to be true and accurate at the date of publication. Neither the publisher nor the authors or the editors give a warranty, expressed or implied, with respect to the material contained herein or for any errors or omissions that may have been made. The publisher remains neutral with regard to jurisdictional claims in published maps and institutional affiliations.

This Palgrave Macmillan imprint is published by the registered company Springer Nature Switzerland AG.
The registered company address is: Gewerbestrasse 11, 6330 Cham, Switzerland

Contents

Part I	Introduction	1
1	Introduction	3
	References	7
Part II	An Analytical Perspective	9
2	A Conventional Assessment Agenda	11
	References	24
3	An Alternative Methodology	27
	3.1 The Foundations of an Assessment Framework	28
	3.2 A Test: Central Government Reforms in France	34
	References	37
Part III	Comprehensive Policies	39
4	Birth, Life and Termination of Comprehensive Approaches	41
	4.1 The Rationalization of Budgetary Choices	42
	4.2 The Renewal of Public Service Operation	45
	4.3 The Reform of the State and Public Service	47

4.4	The Revision of the Organic Law Governing Budgetary Laws	49
4.5	The Modernization Audits Reform	51
4.6	The Public Policy General Review	53
4.7	The Modernization of Public Action Operation	55
4.8	The Public Action 2022 Programme	57
References		61

5 A Recurrent Process of Fabrication 65
    5.1 Apparent Discontinuity 66
    5.2 The Same Tune 69
    Reference 78

Part IV The Appropriation of Toolkits 79

6 Dashboards and Cost-Benefit Analysis 81
    6.1 Tools That Reign but Do Not Govern: Dashboards and Indicators 82
    6.2 Cost-Benefit Analysis and Friends 95
    References 104

7 Evaluation and a Comparison 107
    7.1 A Chaotic Journey: Ex Post Evaluation 107
    7.2 A Comparative Assessment of Three Toolkits 117
    References 126

Part V Indirect Reforms 129

8 Well-tempered Agencification 131
    8.1 Productive Agencies 131
    8.2 Regulatory Authorities 139
    8.3 To Each Their Own Prism 144
    References 150

9	**From Espoused Theories to Theories in Use**	153
	9.1 Devolution	154
	9.2 The Public Health System	159
	9.3 State Field Agencies	163
	9.4 A Comparative Assessment of Theories in Use	164
	References	171
10	**Human Resources: A Keystone Structure**	173
	10.1 The Creation of the Basic Structure	173
	10.2 The Extension and Deepening of the Structure	180
	10.3 The Ineffective Quest for Flexibility	183
	10.4 A Challenge to the Structure?	191
	References	194

Part VI	**Conclusions**	197
11	**A Review of Developments in France**	199
	References	211
12	**Assessing Public Administration Reforms**	213
	References	217

About the Authors

Patrick C. Gibert, professor of management science, is an alumnus of Sciences Po Paris and the Northwestern Graduate School. He holds a master's degree in economics and one in public law, and a PhD in management science. He started his career as the head of the Institut du Management Public, a non-profit organization located in Paris. He then joined the University of Paris-Nanterre as a full professor. He also acted as dean of its Economics and Management School, and as the first vice president of the university. Most of his publications study the ways in which public organizations enact performance management and policy evaluation. As a consultant he has helped both central and local government institutions in France and in other countries to design and implement management control and policy analysis systems. He has also trained many junior academics, and is considered a pioneer of public management in France.

Jean-Claude Thoenig is a senior research director at the French Centre National de la Recherche Scientifique. Trained as a sociologist and a political scientist at the University of Geneva, he was appointed as a full professor at the Federal Institute of Technology in Lausanne. For several years, he was also an associate dean at INSEAD, a leading business school. A visiting scholar at Stanford, Harvard and Berkeley, he founded France's first research centre for policy analysis. He was the first chair of the European Group for Organizational Studies. He also headed the Conseil

Scientifique de l'Évaluation, reporting to the French Prime Minister. His academic contributions cover innovation management, policy implementation and evaluation, intergovernmental relationships, higher education, and research institutions. He was also a consultant for the European Commission and the French government.

Abbreviations

ENA	National school of public administration
IGF	Financial general inspection
INSP	National institute of public service
INET	National institute of territorial studies
MA	Modernization audits reform
MPA	Modernization of public action reform
NPM	New public management theory
OLGBL	Revision of the organic law governing budgetary laws
PA 2022	Public action 2022 reform
RBC	Rationalization of budgetary choices reform
RESP	Renewal of the State and public service reform
PPGR	Public policy general review reform
RPS	Renewal of public service reform
RSPS	Reform of the State and public service

List of Tables

Table 5.1   Major operations launched in France since 1968   67
Table 6.1   How bills should be justified. Organic Law, April 15 2019, art. 8   100
Table 9.1   Major developments in central government action:
             a comparison   165

PART I

Introduction

CHAPTER 1

Introduction

There is nothing more banal, on face value, than the topic of change in public management.

Its academic history began in the nineteenth century (Lynn, 2006). An uninterrupted succession of scholarly books, articles and accounts has followed, supplemented by the writings of practitioners about their experiences which enjoyed greater or lesser degrees of success. Professional gurus from the consulting world have offered one-size-fits-all recipes to enlighten public authorities on how to enhance their performance.

This fad warrants serious consideration. Times have changed over the last one and a half centuries, sometimes very swiftly. The new societal challenges that have made their way onto the public agenda in all sectors—public health, climate change, poverty, and population ageing, to mention but a few—constantly require public authorities to adopt suitable approaches. Yet these approaches cannot be reduced to formulating new public policies suited to each of these sectors. The challenge is also, if not more so than ever, to reform the way in which they are taken into account and tackled by the administrative services that are supposed to be responsible for addressing them. Additionally, the term "public management" has gained currency, to the extent that its meaning is sometimes not clear.

Do we really know where we are headed, and especially the effects and real impacts of the efforts made to get there? How can we assess the reforms decreed to change the public system? This book explores a somewhat original conceptual and analytical framework.

Our approach is not normative. However, it is based on the understanding that the facts should make it possible to formulate relevant prescriptions for both practitioners and academics. This framework and methodology are informed by an applied social science perspective: that of public management. They are developed and refined throughout the book, and their credibility is tested on a case study.

The purpose of this book is mainly ontological. It examines the ways in which organizations and their evolutions are managed and the activities that stem from them, from the perspective of the four pillars of management: goal setting, leading, organizing, and controlling (Thiétart, 1980).

Public management as we understand it here focuses on organizations with a public mandate or authority.

What happens when internal changes take place within a public administrative system, when new operational or efficiency principles are decreed by deliberate acts called reforms or in response to external circumstances? What about government acts that do not fall into the category of reforms named as such but nevertheless result in administrative change, whether innovative or regressive? Is the toolkit governing the modus operandi also changed, and if so, in which direction? Our book is not limited to the analysis of one or several reforms publicized as such. It also takes into account the changes induced or generated within a particular administrative system whenever its governance evolves.

This book is the fruit of a collaboration between its two authors.

The one is a management scientist, the other a political scientist. This collaboration dates back to the second half of the 1970s. It has unfolded on several fronts: the creation of a French-language journal on public policy and management, the training of managers for the State, large cities and regions in various European countries, the publication of academic articles and books, conversations with colleagues at international level, and the creation and running of study and research centres. We were aware that we were acting as pioneers in Europe in an academic field—public management—for which training and research have long been underdeveloped, and which tends to be confined to a particular disciplinary or sub-disciplinary genre. The present book draws heavily on a long series of research projects that we have conducted together or separately, and publications that we have authored.

Our perspective reflects one major aim: to provide a detailed exploration of the internal production function of the administrative system, that is, the relationship between the resources that the public authorities inject and the actual resulting achievements. In other words, this book is not concerned with ex post evaluation: its focus is not the societal impacts that the programmes of action entrusted to public authorities do or do not generate, whether those are the impacts sought or not. It merely opens the black box that are the actual outputs of the processes of change fuelled by major crosscutting reforms and by the use of new management instruments.

Chapter 2 expresses and justifies a sense of relative dissatisfaction with the contributions of different disciplines and sub-disciplines to the study of change in the public sector, mainly at central government level.

Chapter 3 proposes a framework of interpretation and analysis to allow academics and practitioners to better observe and understand current management developments in a particular public context. The term "assessment" is used metaphorically, as an approach to open the black box that a State administration system constitutes. It is therefore not to be confused with what in public management is presented as an ex ante evaluation approach, namely the study of the impacts that a policy generates in civil society. Nor is it an indirect form of control. Chapter 3 also presents the field chosen to test the validity of this perspective: contemporary France.

Chapter 4 reviews eight crosscutting central government modernization programmes successively launched since the late 1960s, considering their ambitions and their approaches. It details who undertook them, what their goals were, and what methods were advocated over the course of this unusual activism for a State reputedly reluctant to change.

Chapter 5 examines how these programmes were designed and constructed. While these major operations have followed one another in a discontinuous and even contradictory fashion, the detail of the way they were developed has remained largely the same even as heads of State have changed. Whether the left or the right is in power, policy makers entrust the development of their projects to a narrow circle of advisors and colleagues. The forms of action they favour reflect a specific professional culture.

Chapters 6 and 7 analyse the way in which three management toolkits have been appropriated by the administrative system: dashboards and indicators, cost-benefit analysis, and ex post evaluation. Their fate has differed:

dashboards were rapidly abandoned; cost-benefit analysis was gradually bogged down; and the use of ex post evaluation transformed its function.

The State often delegates the implementation of its policies to autonomous bodies. This agencification covers a wide range of functions. Some of these bodies are in charge of regulating an area or sector; others are entrusted with the production of goods and the delivery of services to the population within a given geographical area and within a predetermined domain. Chapter 8 examines the links between the development of agencification and the way in which central government proceeds to implement it.

Chapter 9 discusses acts that are endorsed by public services and are not explicitly focussed on public service modernization, or that are contrary to the theories espoused by such modernization. They can generate significant changes. The transformation of management does not necessarily or solely derive from government acts formally labelled as reform policy. Three examples illustrate this: the devolution of competences to local government; the quasi-statization of public health; and the territorialization of State services.

Chapter 10 demonstrates why and how the structure of human resources is crucial for initiating change processes. It significantly restricts or widens the scope of the organizational and financial structure governing the public sector.

Finally, two chapters draw general conclusions. Chapter 11 presents a summary of the French case. It reviews five key features highlighted in Parts III to V of the book that characterize the dynamics of the evolution of the country's administrative system over the last half century. Chapter 12 sums up the more general problem that our research explores, the hypotheses that it formulates, and the methodological approaches that it mobilizes. The case of France provides just one empirical field among other countries which could be studied in turn, despite their diverse institutional frameworks and path dependencies. Some lessons are drawn for public practitioners who wish to become managers of administrative change at their level.

What is often called the reform of the State and its administrative system reflects not only what those in power designate as State reform, but also everything that the public service does and how it does it. Beyond the proclaimed quest for greater efficiency and effectiveness, it is ultimately the relationship with citizens that is at stake.

We would like to thank Professor Catherine Paradeise for her patient and invaluable editorial work. We are grateful to Nonta Libbrecht-Carey for translating this book from French into English. Our colleagues Rod Rhodes, Johan Olsen, and Larry Lynn kindly gave us their encouragement.

References

Lynn, L. E., Jr. (2006). *Public Management. Old and New*. Routledge.
Thiétart, R. A. (1980). *Le management*. Presses Universitaires de France.

PART II

An Analytical Perspective

CHAPTER 2

A Conventional Assessment Agenda

A critical review of the academic literature reveals a series of empirical questions (Gibert, 2002). A distinction is often made between three components of public management: administrative structures, forms of organization, and staff. Yet the link between them has received little attention (Lynn, 1996). Moreover, the research agenda on the production of scientific knowledge on public sector reform has remained relatively conventional since the 1970s. This book proposes ways forward, by assessing these reforms.

It is worth noting that this relative continuity contrasts with the rapid succession of various normative approaches since the 1960s.

First, the management principle underpinning the "3 E" model advocated the best possible balance between economy, efficiency, and effectiveness. According to this approach, sound management secures the right inputs at the lowest cost (a good deal), gets the most out of the inputs (good value for effort), and gets the expected results from the outputs (the right outcomes) (Otrusinová & Pastuszková, 2013).

It was followed by the principle of best value. Value-based management involves a change in mindset from managing resources or output quantities to value creation. This approach advocates the use of reliable, transparent and simple information to mitigate risks (Martin & Petty, 2001).

A third approach, which is also the most well-known, is new public management (NPM). It prescribes systematically introducing principles and criteria inspired by the private sector within the bureaucratic structures and procedures of the public sector. For example, it advocates management by objectives and results, as well as performance audits.

A fourth theory, which some include under new public management, recommends lean management. This consists in implementing a system of organization of work that eliminates any waste hindering the efficiency and performance of a company or department. The lean school has exceeded its initial scope—the organization of car manufacturing—and is now perceived as a suitable method for combating all types of inefficiency. Hence, the interest in lean management extends from administrative services (lean office) to product development (lean development). Lean management is based on continuous improvement, also called *kaizen* in Japan; problem solving happens on the ground with the actors involved. Becoming a learning organization is one of the fundamental principles of lean management, which applies to all areas of a company (both productive and non-productive) (Womack & Jones, 1996).

A fifth approach, known as whole-of-government, claims to remedy the failure of new public management. It is designed to put an end to the dogmatic fascination with the sole model of the private company operating in the market. Two renowned academics, Christensen and Laegreid, explore how this concept might be interpreted analytically (Christensen and Laegreid 2007a). They contrast the structural approach with a cultural perspective and a myth-based perspective, and discuss results, experiments and lessons from the whole-of-government movement.

Two rather incompatible positions actually structure academic work on public management.

The first is managerial. It seeks to develop more effective tools and more efficient or effective methodologies than those previously available. This position is normative and instrumental. It puts forward proposals with a general scope, one-size-fits all solutions rooted in economic theory, experimental psychology, or business management. Contextual differences are erased, while ideological references are present. One of the most commonly invoked references asserts the superiority of the neoliberal model, both for the production of collective goods and to regulate modern society.

The other position is critical. It has been widely adopted and disseminated within the research communities associated with the social and economic sciences. Tracing the short-term effects or occasional punctuations caused by initiatives taken by public authorities (Jordan, 2003), it tends to focus on understanding how and why a particular public reform delivers (or not) on the promises it was intended to fulfil. In many cases, the values or goals that public authorities claim to serve hide a reality and practices that are not necessarily aligned with them. The academics who adopt this approach endeavour to fuel a process revealing how public affairs are actually conducted.

This book focuses on the second position. More specifically, a quick review of the literature sheds light on some common features characterizing academic publications and reveals a critical perspective that guides their ways of producing knowledge.

Academic production in the social and economic sciences tends to favour mono-disciplinary or even sub-disciplinary approaches.

Sociology offers several illustrations of this tendency.

The sociology of organizations is now one of its most recognized specializations in the field. Yet many of its researchers study public services as fields allowing them to formulate a more general theory of organizations or organized action.

Central to their agenda is the understanding of how members of a formal organization or of an informal social network of distinct organizations come to build and coordinate collective activities in a stable way, within these organizations or networks and with their environment. The intensification of the division of labour, the specialization of functions, and the race for productivity and innovation are a godsend for many authors still rooted in a corporate management perspective and for whom public management is not a core concern. While the sociology of organizations is a specialization, it is above all an approach that seeks to shed light on issues such as labour relations, labour movements, and social stratification. The evolution of public practices and the effects of managerial approaches are more marginal topics. From this perspective, there is little to no difference between a Taylorian private company and a public administration, including the trend towards bureaucratizing its functioning and the non-efficiency of its management (Crozier, 1964).

Two other specializations are even more macro-sociological or hyper-deterministic than the former, which studies the organization as a social entity. The question of public policy and its governance is not central to their scientific and ontological agenda either; instead, they adopt a more societal perspective based on discrete observations.

A first illustration of this approach is the way these specializations consider public policies as empirical evidence of how domination and social control operate within contemporary societies. This perspective originated in a publication investigating the structures of micro-power that developed in Western societies during the eighteenth century, with a particular focus on prisons (Foucault, 1977). The criminal justice system replaced the punishment of criminal acts with the creation of the figure of individuals dangerous to society, without regard for whether they have committed an actual crime.

The study of administrative elites offers a second illustration. This approach considers a specific public policy as particularly revealing of the inequalities at work in society. Policies produce and legitimize social and economic discrimination, thus reproducing cultural inequalities. In the case of France, a prevalent mechanism of social stratification is said to be at work through the systems of schooling, occupational training and higher education. The public and institutional frameworks decreed by the State reproduce and even reinforce the reproduction of social and economic inequalities. The senior civil service and the highly selective *grandes écoles* set a reference model based on the social and cultural capital accumulated by the elites (Bourdieu, 1989).

Such approaches are commonplace in political science.

As in the case of sociology, public management and governance have become a very active field of research, judging by the large number of research teams, training curriculums and publications on the subject. This development partly reflects trend and opportunity effects, which have been instrumental to this growing interest. More generous funding for research projects, heightened competition between universities, and new courses offered to students to access the labour market fuel this growth.

Political science research on public management is fragmented across multiple sub-disciplines or specializations, each with its own specific questions and approaches. For the most part, public management reform remains relatively distant from their research agendas.

Not all political science should be lumped together under the same critical banner; it has made some major contributions. Of course, not all of them are explicitly intended to build a theory of public management per se (Rainey, 1984), but they do contribute to developing conceptual and analytical material with sometimes decisive benefits for this theory. Five examples among many more exemplify this, even if their authors maintain a pronounced disciplinary grounding in a research area that is wider than or even different to management. In the examples that follow, their focus is the study of current political life in a State.

The countless existing public policies can be compared by means of typologies. One typology uses a common parameter to account for the social change structuring these policies, namely the degree of coercion that the State exerts on the subjects of a policy (Lowi, 1972). A creative line of work consists in generalizing the use of classification. In particular, it studies methods of political leadership (Offe, 1975), the instruments of influence employed by the State (Scharpf et al., 1976) (Mayntz, 1978), and the tools of government (Hood, 1983).

Another major contribution, initially largely owed to political science, relates to the implementation of public policies. From the early 1970s, implementation was identified as the missing link, on the grounds that the process of implementation is what truly determines the success or failure of a policy. Pioneering research on a US federal programme to combat poverty through economic development (Wildavsky and Pressman 1975) paved the way. On the ground, this programme came up against the ways of working of the local and federal authorities involved and the public it was supposed to benefit. This research was also somewhat of a first in terms of the quality of its analytical framework.

A third pioneering contribution examined the policy-making process itself. This was largely owed to the work of Charles Jones (1970), who split this process into five successive stages. To begin with, an existing issue becomes a public problem and is placed on a government authority's agenda. In the next stage, a decision is developed and formalized. This in turn leads to a stage of implementation of the decision, which then triggers evaluation and judgement processes. Finally, any policy will eventually end in one way or another. With this breakdown into five stages, the author sought to show that each phase corresponds to a different political arena, with different actors and political games involved. Moreover, this process may be iterative, with a later stage retroactively influencing an earlier one. Ultimately, Jones's contribution endeavours to move away from overly focusing on the decision-making stage alone, and shows that purely political activities take place in each of these five stages of the policy-making process.

A fourth seminal contribution relates to the nature of the content and ambitions of a reorganization. Informed by the incremental school exemplified by the successors of Charles Lindblom (1959), a study examined 12 so-called comprehensive reorganizations explicitly designed to change the administrative apparatus of government. It demonstrated the reasons for government organizations' failure to generate significant change

(March & Olson, 1983), and concluded with the following prescription: it is best to proceed incrementally, focusing on marginal change.

A fifth type of contribution is based on the finding that administrative reform policies are riddled with symbols which serve mainly to consolidate the legitimacy of political authorities. It shows how indispensable but difficult it is to translate these symbols into practices, especially since administrative reforms cannot be reduced to symbols, as Christensen and Laegreid (2007b) claim they do. The research by Roderick Arthur William Rhodes and his colleagues is worth mentioning with regard to political science. Drawing on fieldwork guided partly by a detailed ethnographic approach, they explored both the beliefs and the practices of public actors (Rhodes, 1999). The Anglo-Governance School (1997) was born from these researchers' demonstration that central government in Great Britain operates as a fragmented or differentiated polity (Rhodes & Dunleavy, 1995) and not as a coherent and integrated institutional whole.

Political science largely contributed to the development of a new specialization, policy analysis (Bardach, 1996; Thoenig, 1985), which was seen to offer a new way of understanding and theorizing the foundations of political life. This specialization set out to study the products of the activities of an authority invested with public power and governmental legitimacy. Policy analysis also offered a way to stand out from Marxist versions of State theory applied to the welfare State (Mény & Thoenig, 1989), particularly in European academia. However, it has not necessarily led to the constitution of a science of public management, even though it proposes managerial applications such as public policy evaluation (Wildavsky, 1989).

Some sub-disciplines' claims to enrich or even annex the field of public management and its reforms ought however to be challenged.

This is the case of public administration theory, also known as administrative science. This sub-discipline broke away from the strictly legal and normative anchorage it had maintained for almost a century, at the risk of neglecting the areas of law regulating organic public policies and the action theories they convey. It likewise distanced itself somewhat from a normative perspective such as the so-called scientific organization of work, the scientific foundations of which were being strongly challenged (Simon, 1946). It even went so far as to adopt approaches from other sub-disciplines, such as field observation and critical perspectives. Yet the temptation to remain purely descriptive and the lack of perspective on solely formal aspects have persisted. This sub-discipline has ultimately struggled to consider public management as an object of applied science in its own right.

It is worth noting, for example, that many of the authors concerned—be they British, such as Christopher Pollitt, Christopher Hood and Ewan Ferlie, Belgian, such as Geert Bouckaert, or American, such as Guy Peters, to name but a few—have an academic background in public administration per se. Although they remain affiliated to a department of public administration, they describe themselves as political scientists. We should note that leading figures in this field have openly regretted that too many of its members have little to no theoretical agenda (Pollitt, 2016). Their work adopts an essentially chronological perspective, and often takes the official discourses of public authorities at face value. At the same time, these authors have questioned whether it is really possible or even necessary to mobilize or construct a properly theoretically framed argument in research on public management and its reforms.

Other political science specializations have also studied public management and its modernization. This is the case, for example, of the general theory of the State, its nature and its prerogatives—a classic theme in philosophy and law. Some leading figures in France (Troper, 2015) and the United States (Rawls, 2009) have pursued this line of research.

More generally, in the social and economic sciences, references to what is often defined as public policy are commonplace, even though the bulk of contributions relate to different and specific topics. Thus, sectoral fields such as labour relations, labour law and even geopolitics can shed significant light on the governance of public affairs and provide a sample of promising entry points for explaining how public policy is conducted in a particular country or supranational public space. However, as Robert Dahl long since showed in his masterful study of the city of New Haven, a detailed study of three local policies in three different municipal areas—public education, urban renewal, political appointments—can at most explain the distribution of power in that city (Dahl, 1961).

This drifting of disciplinary continents and sub-disciplinary tribes has not been without consequences. It has created silo effects that are not conducive to the emergence of a public management science as such, a discipline with a specific agenda. At the same time, this science must remain open to the contributions of other disciplines or sub-disciplines. Anthropology, for example, explains the cultural roots of actors' preferences. This approach can be applied to the analysis of public policies, particularly when a public authority intervenes in areas considered risky because they generate apprehension and anxiety in the population (Douglas & Wildavsky, 1983).

Two other consequences are worth mentioning.

The first is a mischaracterization of a concrete situation, which is the case, for example, of the study of elites. This field developed through numerous earlier studies (Aberbach & Rockman, 2006 and Putman, 1976, among others). However, when applied to research on administrative elites, its sociographic approach produced conclusions about something else, namely how a country's administrative system is reformed (Bezès & Jeannot, 2006; Hammerschmid et al., 2016). Thus, the modernization of public management in France from the 1990s onwards has been described as instrumentally being an application of the principles conveyed by the new public management ideology, even though these principles have in no way been endorsed by the senior civil servants in charge of the State's central government. Such confusion sometimes results in a double misunderstanding. This is the case in the research project Coordinating for Cohesion in the Public Sector of the Future, funded by the European Union. On a methodological level, it uses an opinion survey in which respondents have to answer a written questionnaire. In other words, it gathers discursive material to measure attitudes and normative preferences. Inferring real behaviour and management practices from this would be premature.

The second shortcoming consists in diluting or even confusing the issue of public management in a sea of fashionable references that barely mask a lack of analytical rigour. Political science and sociology sometimes even import whole concepts directly from other disciplines or sub-disciplines. This is the case with the term "public policy," the use of which is shrouded in scholarly vagueness. It may reflect political scientists' and sociologists' interest in the study of political life or the governance of public affairs, but it can also be synonymous with public policy analysis. Articulating concepts used in other disciplines allows authors to differentiate themselves in their specialization. Such is the case of the term *"référentiel"* ("frame of reference") (Sabatier & Weible, 2014). Elaborating a public policy involves building a representation, an image of the reality on which public authorities act. Actors are said to be informed by this cognitive image as they structure their perception of the problem which they are responsible for solving, test their solutions, and formulate their proposals for action.

Few assessments allow us to qualify or even quantify the state of the research conducted in the social sciences. Yet even if few overarching data covering the whole field of academic writing are available, one characteristic prevails: heterogeneity.

An inventory of academic writings on change management in the public sector published between 2000 and 2010 (Kuipers et al., 2014) lists 133 articles published in the canonical journals of public administration, and examines the methods and theories these articles put forward. The results show that these are oriented in multiple directions, with just over 20 different frames of reference, of which institutional theory is the most frequently used. According to the authors, researchers actually study change management because it affords an opportunity to apply the theoretical approach that they already uphold. In some cases, the use of these methods and theories is largely just cosmetic. Very few in-depth empirical studies have tested middle-range theories, that is, an approach to theory construction aimed at integrating theory and empirical research. The fashionable "grand theory" is superficial. Moreover, change management is hardly explored, in just 14 of the 133 articles analysed. Worse still, most of these address the subject solely in terms of staff attitudes and behaviours in the face of change. Their analysis is limited to studying the surface of phenomena.

We should however not lose sight of the forest for the trees. The dynamics of disciplinary differentiation and its corollary, the heterogeneity of approaches, do not imply that the social sciences study public management reforms haphazardly. A large part of the literature focuses on three areas of research: the properties that characterize action by public authorities in a given field, the extent of the impacts observed, and the methodologies used.

First, the different approaches adopt and test the same causal hypothesis. They posit a reform as an independent variable and its impact on the management of public organizations as a dependent variable. The research question, which can be implicit or explicit, seeks to understand whether and how the way in which a public organization operates is affected by voluntarist reforms with the stated aim of improving its performance or modifying its functioning, and applies various types of instruments and tools to do so.

Such studies take the life cycle of a reform as their timeframe. Once upstream voluntarist decisions have been fully implemented or adopted, what imprints or consequences do they produce downstream (including in their implementation)? The prevailing assumption here is that a policy or programme designed to implement change has an end, and that this formalized or institutionalized end delimits the scope of the analysis: the curtain has dropped, the case is closed. Yet the effects of a programme are not limited to its formal term. The timeline to explore extends far beyond that timeframe. Short-term failures should not be overestimated: success may emerge in the long run, and vice versa. Moreover, reforms with a discernible lifespan remain the exception, and the administrative agencies in charge of change often exhibit a capacity to subsist that contrasts with the duration of the political authorities' interest in the reform they initiated. The completion of a public policy, far from being a normal or natural occurrence, can sometimes constitute a significant political event (Bardach, 1976). Finally, a reform ceases not only when it is interrupted, but also when it is affected by a significant change. Termination may also be partial. In this case, only one of its original facets is modified, be it the content, political sponsors, management, or definition of the problem it is supposed to address (DeLeon, 1982).

A second common feature of the social science literature relates to the magnitude of the impacts and changes that reforms bring about in public management. In many cases, such reforms do not appear to lead anywhere, irrespective of the ambitions announced and the methodologies initially applied. Authors who have conducted empirical studies of public organizations have offered various explanations for this.

A radical standpoint holds that the reforms carried out to transform public management are essentially incapable of changing the order of things (Crozier, 1995). It draws on the analysis of monographs on the public industry sector to assert and understand the limits encountered by attempts to reform the administration, positing organizational change as a vicious circle characteristic of bureaucracies. The dysfunctions and errors caused by bureaucratization can be combated in one way only: by reinforcing the variables that created the problem, in other words, through increased centralization, stronger proceduralization, and further internal social stratification. The State is both arrogant and powerless. Action dictated by ideology alone, simplistic solutions, or underestimating the issues surrounding the implementation of policies and reforms leads to dead ends, unless the profound cultural traits regulating the society governed by the State authority are first changed.

A more nuanced version of this pessimism argues that reforms are artefacts in the hands of decision makers who use them to demonstrate apparent rationality. The aim is to consolidate their own political legitimacy, both in their external environment and within their internal organization, even if it means adopting inconsistent standards. What matters is announcing a particular action for change, without more long-term commitment. The action is totally separated from its political effect. Once political gain is achieved, the action is no longer an issue. In short, what counts is not the changes brought about by the decision, but the announcement showing that one is taking action. The reform is an act or a product with a conspicuous function. There is therefore no point, neither for the public nor for the researcher, in placing hopes in reform. Such pessimism has been theorized by Nils Brunsson (1989, 2006), who highlights how leaders manage to satisfy seemingly conflicting interests through what he calls organizational hypocrisy. Both in companies and in public institutions, three fundamentally separate spaces coexist: the space where a principle is asserted, the space where the decision to adopt it is made, and the space where practices are supposed to change. Contact between these spaces must be carefully avoided. In the eyes of a public leader acting as a hypocritical reformer of organizational management, applying the principles he promotes is other people's responsibility.

The persistent scepticism that emerges from research thus manifests in various ways.

According to one version, public managers are not in control, for the reforms they seek to promote do not convey or articulate values that are tolerable or desirable in the eyes of society or that align with universal morality. This claim underlies many publications in which changes supposedly inspired by the NPM doctrine are studied and critiqued (Pollitt & Bouckaert, 2004). In fact, there is nothing original about the "discovery" of the public sector's inability to fully and independently set out and govern its own reforms. Contrary to Michel Crozier's position, these publications posit that change is possible but under certain conditions, provided the alternatives that may emerge at a more local level are not stifled by institutionalized and more overarching norms or values. This macrosociological theory was first developed at the Stanford Department of Sociology, based on studies of schools in the US. It stressed the decisive weight, within each school and each State, of the teaching profession compared to other stakeholders, with its own conception of the profession and of training. The neo-institutional theory was born (Meyer & Rowan, 1977).

Formal organizational structures reflect streamlined institutional rules. In modern States, they account for their expansion and growing complexity. They function as myths which public organizations incorporate, gaining legitimacy, resources, stability, and enhanced survival prospects. Organizations whose structures become isomorphic—in contrast with those primarily structured by the demands of technical production and exchange—sacrifice internal coordination and control capacities insofar as it enables them to maintain legitimacy. Structures are disconnected from one another. They may even become unable to have full control of ongoing activities. Instead of coordination, inspection and evaluation, they rely on confidence and good faith (Thoenig, 2012).

The third feature common to social science research on public management reforms is its methodology.

A significant proportion of these studies use the same techniques, which results in a repetitive research design and tends to overlook rigorous and complete knowledge of the interaction between a reform and its public management context. Facts and processes that are often major escape analytical and theoretical scrutiny (Thoenig, 2000).

The discursive is taken at face value, without perspective. It is assumed to provide a reliable indicator of observed realities. Practices, processes and behaviours are assumed to be known from data such as stated opinions, statements of intent, official flowcharts and documents, or now official ministry websites. As the social sciences have taught us for decades, this can be a fatal trap. In detective work, establishing the credibility and reliability of information is the analyst's responsibility (Gibert & Benzerafa, 2020). There is no shortage of techniques to do so: in-depth interviews, cross-checking sources, direct observations in the field, and so on. Special mention should also be made of the quantified data on allocated resources and outputs produced, which should not be taken at face value, as they too have a subtext (Pollitt, 2013).

Most research on reforms is monographic. It studies singular cases without interpreting them (Boswell et al., 2019). Even when comparisons are drawn, they consist of a simple ex post re-examination of these monographs, without scientifically building a theory of public management. Interest in comparative monographic approaches has grown under pressure from new public management academics (Christensen and Laegreid 2007a), although it has also fuelled strong criticism of these analyses' often acontextual nature.

Initially, publications on the subject were guided by a purely critical stance. NPM was denounced as an ideology of public governance imported from an exogenous source: economic and political neoliberalism. Faced with its failures and decline, many authors then turned to a more factual analysis. In fact, this trend coincided with the emergence of a new school of public administration seeking to set itself apart from classical sociology and political science. Evidently, this school's approach remains characterized by, if not trapped in, a somewhat traditional analytical stance. Implementation remains limited by a top-down vision. Very little empirical information is available about actual appropriation in everyday life and on the ground.

Some publications have nevertheless endeavoured to break away from the monographic straitjacket. For example, a comparison of six countries was carried out by Peters and Savoie (1998), with a largely institutionalist perspective. The study used a transformative theoretical approach, focusing on political design, cultural constitutional trajectories and external pressures to understand the processes and effects of reforms.

More generally, however, country-specific contributions remain repetitive and limited. They focus on studies on a clearly delineated type of reform. When a comparison is proposed, it is carried out in one of two ways.

The first approach to such comparisons is culturalist (Crozier, 1964). It categorizes the type of public management at play according to the dominant societal norms surrounding the renewal of public service in a country. The other approach focuses on the institutional and political regime in place in nation States (Peters & Pierre, 2016). It is characterized by an assumption adopted by authors from the most classical administrative science tradition (Peters & Savoie, 1998): if the dominant societal values change, administrative change becomes possible or even probable. This assumption has yet to be analytically demonstrated, which is no small scientific challenge.

Lawrence Lynn proposes a theoretical framework inspired by the new institutionalism school (Lynn, 2006). According to this framework, the characteristics of management can be posited as endogenous to the political economy of a country, which itself results from processes of path dependency subject to occasional punctuations causing discontinuous changes (True et al., 1999). Three dimensions affect these specific characteristics: their constitutional framework, the competence of public managers, and institutionalized values. Lynn presents this typology of State traditions as a tool to categorize countries.

Generally speaking, few comparisons in the field of public management are established ex ante according to an integrated research design mobilizing analytical parameters common to identical objects. Comparative approaches that focus not on different national regimes, but on a longitudinal axis over the long term and within the same State, are also rare. They study potential evolutions in public management, whether they are generated on a voluntarist basis or result from the collateral effects of measures that may not be presented as public sector reforms (Pollitt, 2016).

References

Aberbach, J. D., & Rockman, B. A. (2006). The Past and Future of Political-administrative Relations. *International Journal of Public Administration, 29*(12), 977–995.

Bardach, E. (1976). Policy Termination as a Political Process. *Policy Sciences, 7*(1), 23–131.

Bardach, E. (1996). *The Eight-Step Path of Policy Analysis: A Handbook for Practice*. Academic Press.

Bezès, P., & Jeannot, G. (2006). *Public Sector Reform in France: Views and Experiences from Senior Executives*. Country report as part of the COCOPS research project. www.cocops.eu.

Boswell, J., Corbett, J., & Rhodes, R. A. W. (2019). *The Art and Craft of Comparison*. Cambridge University Press.

Bourdieu, P. (1989). *La noblesse d'État : grandes écoles et esprit de corps*. Editions de Minuit.

Brunsson, N. (1989). *The Organization of Hypocrisy. Talk, Decisions and Actions in Organizations*. John Wiley & Sons.

Brunsson, N. (2006). *Mechanisms of Hope: Maintaining the Dream of the Rational Organization*. Copenhagen Business School Press.

Christensen, T., & Laegreid, P. (2003). Administrative Reform Policy: The Challenges of Turning Symbols into Practice. *Public Administration Review, 3*(1), 2–27.

Christensen, T., & Laegreid, P. (2007a). The Whole-of-government Approach to Public Sector Reform. *Public Administration Review, 67*(6), 1059–1066.

Christensen, T., & Laegreid, P. (Eds.). (2007b). *Transcending new Public Management: The Transformation of Public Sector Management Reforms*. Ashgate.

Crozier, M. (1964). *The Bureaucratic Phenomenon*. University of Chicago Press.

Crozier, M. (1995). *La crise de l'intelligence. Essai sur l'impuissance des élites à se réformer*. Interéditions.

Dahl, R. A. (1961). *Who Governs? Power and Democracy in an American City*. Yale University Press.

DeLeon, P. (1982). Public Policy Termination: An End and a Beginning. *Policy Analysis*, 4(3), 369–392.
Douglas, M., & Wildavsky, A. (1983). *Risk and Culture: An Essay on the Selection of Technological and Environmental Dangers*. University of California Press.
Foucault, M. (1977). *Discipline and Punish: The Birth of the Prison*. Penguin.
Gibert, P. (2002). L'analyse de politique à la rescousse du management public ? *Politiques et Management Public*, 20(1), 1–14.
Gibert, P., & Benzerafa, M. (2020). *The Claimed Goal and the Embarrassing Metric. Statistical Issues, MBO and Public Debate about French Police Performance*. University of Paris-Nanterre.
Hammerschmid, G., Van de Walle, S., Andrews, R., & Bezes, P. (Eds.). (2016). *Public Administration Reforms in Europe: The View from the Top*. Edward Elgar Publishing.
Hood, C. (1983). *The Tools of Government*. Macmillan.
Jones, C. (1970). *An Introduction to the Study of Public Policy*. Duxbury Press.
Jordan, M. M. (2003). Punctuations and Agendas: A New Look at Local Government Budget Expenditures. *Journal of Policy Analysis and Management*, 22(3), 345–360.
Kuipers, B. S., Higgs, M., Kickert, W., Tummers, L., Grandia, J., & Van der Voet, J. (2014). The Management of Change in Public Organizations: A Literature Review. *Public Administration*, 92(1), 1–20.
Lindblom, C. (1959). The Science of "muddling through". *Public Administration Review*, 19(1), 79–88.
Lowi, T. J. (1972). Four Systems of Policy, Politics, and Choice. *Public Administration Review*, 32(4), 298–310.
Lynn, L. E. (1996). *Public Management as Art, Science, and Profession*. Chatham House.
Lynn, L. E. (2006). *Public Management: Old and New*. Routledge.
March, J. G., & Olson, J. P. (1983). Organizing Political Life: What Administrative Reorganization Tells Us About Government. *The American Political Science Review*, 77(2), 281–296.
Martin, J. D., & Petty, J. W. (2001). Value Based Management. *Baylor Business Review*, 19(1), 2.
Mayntz, R. (1978). *Soziologie der öffentlichen Verwaltung*. Müller Juristischer Verlag.
Mény, Y., & Thoenig, J. C. (1989). *Politiques Publiques*. Presses Universitaires de France.
Meyer, J. W., & Rowan, B. (1977). Institutionalized Organizations: Formal Structure as Myth and Ceremony. *American Journal of Sociology*, 83(2), 340–363.
Offe, C. (1975). *Berufsbildungsreform: Eine Fallstudie über Reformpolitik*. Suhrkamp.
Otrusinová, M., & Pastuszková, E. (2013). Decision Making Model to Performance Management in the Public Sector Administration. *Finance and the Performance of Firms in Science, Education and Practice 2013*.

Peters, B. G., & Savoie, D. J. (Eds.). (1998). *Taking Stock: Assessing Public Sector Reforms* (Vol. 2). McGill-Queen's Press-MQUP.

Peters, B. G., & Pierre, J. (2016). *Comparative Governance: Rediscovering the Functional Dimension of Governing*. Cambridge University Press.

Pollitt, C., & Bouckaert, G. (2004). *Public Management Reform. A Comparative Analysis*. Oxford University Press.

Pollitt, C. (2013). 40 years of public management reform in UK central government—promises, promises.... *Policy and Politics, 41*(4), 465–480.

Pollitt, C. (2016). Managerialism Redux? *Financial Accountability and Management, 32*(4), 429–447.

Putman, R. D. (1976). *The Comparative Study of Political Elites*. Prentice Hall.

Rainey, H. G. (1984). Organization Theory and Political Science: Organizational Typologies, Political Variables, and Policy Studies. *Policy Studies Journal, 13*(1), 5–21.

Rawls, J. (2009). *A Theory of Justice*. Harvard University Press.

Rhodes, R. A. W., & Dunleavy, P. (1995). *Prime Minister, Cabinet, and Core Executive*. St. Martin's Press.

Rhodes, R. A. W. (1999). *Control and Power in Central-Local Government Relations*. Hans.

Sabatier, P. A., & Weible, C. M. (Eds.). (2014). *Theories of the Policy Process*. Westview Press.

Scharpf, F. W., Reissert, B., & Schnabel, F. (1976). *Politikverflechtung: Theorie und Empirie des kooperativen Föderalismus in der Bundesrepublik*. Scriptor Verlag.

Simon, H. H. (1946). The Proverbs of Administration. *Public Administration Review, 6*(3), 53–67.

Thoenig, J. C. (1985). Les politiques publiques. In M. Grawitz & J. Leca (Eds.), *Traité de science politique* (Vol. 4). Presses Universitaires de France.

Thoenig, J. C. (2000). Evaluation as usable knowledge for public management reforms. A) *Evaluation*, (4), 217–32; B) OECD (Ed.), *Government of the Future*. Paris: OECD, 197–210.

Thoenig, J. C. (2012). Institutional Theories and Public Institutions: New Agendas and Appropriateness. In B. G. Peters & J. Pierre (Eds.), *The Handbook of Public Administration* (pp. 169–179). Sage.

Troper, M. (2015). *Pour une théorie juridique de l'État*. Presses Universitaires de France.

True, J. L., Jones, B. J., & Baumgartner, F. R. (1999). Punctuated Equilibrium Theory. *Theories of the Policy Process*, 175–202.

Wildavsky, A. B. (1989). *Speaking Truth to Power*. Little, Brown & Transaction.

Womack, J. P., & Jones, D. T. (1996). Beyond Toyota: How to Root Out Waste and Pursue Perfection. *Harvard Business Review, 74*(5), 140–172.

CHAPTER 3

An Alternative Methodology

The modern instrument of so-called ex post evaluation is often presented as the perfect solution to rigorously assess a policy. However, it seems largely utopian, for at least two reasons.

The first is political. The managerial rationality underlying any reform clashes with the political rationality of the authorities that execute the content of this reform or are responsible for steering the implementation of a policy. This is a well-known public management issue.

The other reason relates to the timeframe of the reform programme itself. For example, over what timeline or timeframe should these effects be considered? Does a reform formally announced at a certain date generate outcomes at its official end date that are significant and can be clearly distinguished from those of other measures taken elsewhere, that gradually cause direct or indirect spill-over effects in the same area of reform?

The ideal of basing a judgement on an evaluation conducted by the book may seem out of reach in most cases, but that is not to say that we should forego the "second-best" solution that is assessment (Thoenig, 2001).

This book proposes an approach somewhat at odds with the way that the social sciences ordinarily proceed. Building on the critical review of the literature provided in the previous chapter, it is fundamentally pragmatic and modest, and does not claim to propose a methodology that will

© The Author(s), under exclusive license to Springer Nature Switzerland AG 2022
P. Gibert, J.-C. Thoenig, *Assessing Public Management Reforms, Understanding Governance*,
https://doi.org/10.1007/978-3-030-89799-4_3

entirely revolutionize the science of public management. It endeavours to provide a more suitable exploration of the interactions or causal relationships that form between established public management and associated reforms. This approach can be defined as a quasi-evaluation of public performance initiatives. It presupposes a clear conceptual understanding of the realities and actions studied (Thoenig, 2003).

3.1 The Foundations of an Assessment Framework

The concept of management refers here to the way in which public affairs as such are managed in practice. It relates to the administrative system that presumably serves a public authority. It is therefore not limited to the new instruments—management control, impact studies, and so on—that this authority uses and to the popular theories of the times—NPM, lean theory, and so on.

Administration is understood in a broad sense. It is not restricted to the management style adopted by the leaders or middle management of an organization. It also encompasses the functioning of street-level bureaucrats (Lipsky, 1980). This is a recurrent observation: the ranks invested with hierarchical authority are not ipso facto those with actual power. Establishing whether middle management is really the bureaucratic rank that determines outcomes is a matter for further inquiry.

As for the concept of public management, the term refers to what exists, and not just what is desirable. It relates to reality, actual practices, and observed behaviour and appropriation processes, as well as the cultural factors and cognitive references which inform them, in an obvious or latent way.

The concept of reform encompasses all the acts, decisions and intentions that influence or are supposed to contribute to the evolution of an administrative system.

Public authorities do not all label and promote initiatives with such an ambitious title in the same way. In one country, the term "reform" will refer solely to the application of a given theory, such as NPM. In another country, the label will more broadly refer to so-called State-modernization operations—with the term "State" being somewhat of an exaggeration in these cases, insofar as it is used to denote the administrative system only. Any operation involving change, such as the introduction of a new IT tool or a different way of receiving the public, may be described as a reform.

At face value, these wide-ranging reform initiatives do not all appear to be of the same kind. One could be tempted to overlook them when carrying out an assessment. However, these acts may prove not to be neutral, and may produce significant positive or negative side-effects impacting the administrative system in which they take place. The hypothesis that these initiatives contribute at least as much to generating impacts and changes as major reforms acknowledged as such needs to be tested. They may consist of acts such as the merger of two administrations, or measures concerning human resource management, or they could be seemingly purely budgetary arrangements—for example, amending part of a budget nomenclature—which, behind their apparent technicality, will affect important components of the existing public management framework.

The assessment of public management reforms spans widely diverse contexts of action. One distinction often made relates to the level at which administrative systems operate and the nature of the jurisdictions governing them.

Central government operates at the level of a State, whether unitary or federal. In addition to its regalian functions in the areas of justice, defence and foreign affairs, it plays an essential role in specific domains of competence and institutions. An example is public health, where despite appearing as distinct spheres, the competences and institutions involved fit within this level of government in both budgetary and legal terms.

The same is true at international level. The European Commission, its annexes and part of its competences, not to mention hundreds of international institutions such as the World Bank and the World Health Organization, face similar public management realities.

Moreover, the administrative systems in place are not the same everywhere. This begs the question: to what extent, both in time and in space, do pre-existing management capabilities determine the capacity of a central or municipal government to improve its performance? Hence the importance of rigorously analysing this management approach.

An analytical framework is essential if we are to open this black box. It formalizes these conditions. In what follows, three structures are defined to establish such an analytical framework.

The first is organizational. It relates to the distribution of roles, the division of labour and the distribution of competences.

The second is financial. It pertains to the allocation of the funds approved by the political executive and legislative bodies across the different strata and components of this administration.

The third relates to staff and human resource management. It encompasses elements such as the status of employees, the practices and procedures that govern access to certain functions, the profile of the selected skills, and so forth.

A key analytical question regards the prevalence of each of these three structures, and whether they each adapt when another one of the structures changes. Whenever this is the case, the capacity for change within a public-sector administration is significant and lasting. For instance, selecting a particular toolkit in order to generate managerial changes may not be enough. Evolution and change hinge on such systemic potential.

The purpose of asking this question is to help test two causal perspectives.

The first perspective is not really an original approach. It studies the content of reforms, the ambitions they claim to have, and the instruments with which they are equipped. All of these aspects may be causes that presumably generate changes in the way of responding to various exogenous challenges such as the demands of the public, the sudden emergence of electronic technology, or a fiscal crisis, to name but a few examples. Moreover, this approach assumes that macro-societal factors such as the dominant societal culture or the institutional tradition of a particular State determine receptiveness to a particular new doctrine.

This type of interpretation abounds in the literature on the life and death of NPM (Pollitt & Bouckaert, 2017). Pollitt and Bouckaert empirically demonstrate that new public management is first and foremost a symbolic operation, the outcomes of which remain difficult to identify. The instrumental reforms that can be observed in various countries are rarely replicas of the same model, even if the economic contingencies and exogenous challenges seem to be the same.

Sensitivity to the role of the State and its public service differs widely between countries governed by the Rechtsstaat doctrine—the rule of law—and those following the public interest model. The rule of law is a legal, philosophical and political concept; it implies the pre-eminence of law over political power in a State, and the obedience of all, rulers and ruled alike, to the law. In countries that apply the principle of public interest, the State ensures decisions' fairness and independence from private groups, and civil society expects neither vision nor meaning from these decisions (Pollitt et al., 2007). Changes have no macro-cause.

The second perspective to test inverts the causal relationship: the way public affairs are managed in practice is an independent variable. This perspective has received far less attention in the academic literature.

The scope of the research here encompasses all activities that take place around a reform process.

The dependent variable consists of the reforms that the pre-existing management style generates, structures and tolerates. It considers the way in which the context shapes the range of reforms, the instruments chosen, their appropriation, and their consequences on the management style. It also looks at the path dependency processes likely to affect all or part of the reforms underway or to come. In other words, whatever exists conditions its own reform. Pre-existing endogenous or contextual factors leave their mark on the reform agenda, define the need for change or not, control the selection of solutions, and determine the impact thresholds not to be crossed. Even more so than the public authorities, the administrative system sets the pace.

Moreover, the methodology limits the risk of remaining analytically trapped by formal appearances or stated discourses alone.

The reality is more complex than meets the eye. A normative theory considered most effective by academics will not necessarily be the one preferred by public managers. These two worlds each have their own rationality: scientific discourse for the one, the experience of context for the other. In a sense, this divide between scientific cosmopolitanism and the localism of action partly opposes the quest for the desirable to the art of the possible. But it also shows that there is a gap between supposedly modernizing experts and reputedly conservative managers. The former claim that things cannot carry on as they are, and while the latter admit that one could try to do things differently, they immediately imagine the ensuing complications for their own department. "Not in my backyard!" This interpretation would explain resistance to change, where consultants might serve as a scapegoat. More curiously, the tension between modernizers and conservatives may also arise between politicians and managers at State level. This is the case, for example, with regard to the scope of a reform programme. Its political promoters will favour a comprehensive approach, but once it has been announced they will be largely uninterested in what happens next. Wiser from experience, managers will let the storm pass and wait until the next reform is announced.

The methodology of this second perspective also cautiously draws on knowledge from other disciplines or sub-disciplines.

This includes knowledge from public and constitutional law, as well as organizational behaviour. Reducing resistance to change to quasi-pathological symptoms—fear, lack of self-confidence, risk aversion—that are supposedly peculiar to the personality of a bureaucrat makes for a hasty if not downright erroneous diagnosis. The problem relates not so much to individual traits as to the characteristics of the public organizations in which they work. These might include, inter alia, the training of managers, the standards and know-how that serve as references in the professional environment, employment contracts in relation to labour law, the issues that structure daily work, power plays between departments, possible competition with other institutions, accountability processes, the formal and informal information channels involved, the methods of internal control, the degree of effective centralization of decision-making, and so forth.

Contrary to the impression that organizational charts give, organizational worlds are not homogeneous; the truth at the top is not the truth at the bottom. Hence, discourse is not a reliable indicator of practices. Managerial roles in the public sector and the organizations within which they operate are not identical to those in the private sector (Rainey, 1989). Actors' rationalities vary, depending on the circumstances in which they find themselves at any given time. The cultural norms underpinning their action are not immediately explicit, yet it would be a mistake to imagine them devoid of cognitive capacities. Performance indicators should not be confused with activity indicators. Similarly, it is necessary to identify the allies on whom the various actors can rely. In short, the analyst cannot ignore the major phenomena that organizational behaviour as a discipline struggles to consider.

Furthermore, a longitudinal perspective better supports the plausibility of analyses.

It requires observations spanning a very wide range of situations, acts and sources, based on empirical fieldwork to enable short-term analyses of a particular reform in a particular organization, as well as medium-term monitoring of the administrative system in which that reform—and where relevant other reforms—has taken or is taking place. This requires considerable investment! Determining the state of the administrative system prior to and then following a reform goes far beyond its mere linear narration. The reform comes into existence as soon as reasons to add it to the government agenda are put forward, and continues all the way to its formal completion and the review of impacts more or less attributable to the instrumentalization it promotes, following the five stages that any public policy reportedly goes through (Jones, 1970). A longitudinal perspective offers conditions that facilitate the adoption of an assessment approach.

Medium- to long-term analysis affords a valuable before-and-after comparison. It sheds light on the way in which management or governance instruments are appropriated as they are disseminated. It helps to take into account the associated effects that may connect two or more areas of public policy, such as the legal rules governing road freight and those regulating the motor vehicle insurance code (Dupuy & Thoenig, 1979). Studying the implementation stage affords a better understanding of the work of managers, who produce and execute a policy according to action theories that may differ from those intended or advocated by policymakers. This was evidenced by the pioneering research of Jeffrey Pressman and Aaron Wildavsky (Wildavsky & Pressman, 1973) on the implementation of the fight against poverty, later generalized by Donald Moynihan (2005). Public policy analysis amply demonstrates that the actions initiated by the services in charge of the effective day-to-day implementation of reforms on the ground have far greater influence than governance theory suggests. The latter tends to overstate the importance of political rulers (Robichau & Lynn, 2009).

Finally, a longitudinal perspective facilitates the comparison of reforms within a same country, shedding light on the grey area of factors endogenous to the administrative system.

Analysis becomes far more difficult when comparing two or more countries. This obstacle is often too hastily sidestepped, as in the case of pioneering work on the adoption, by various countries, of new instruments such as the planning-programming-budgeting system (Caiden & Wildavsky, 1980) or NPM (Pollitt & Bouckaert, 2017). Differences and similarities are more or less expediently put down to the national culture, the Volksgeist, the historical roots of public law, or even the ideologies of the governing parties.

More robust answers ought to be explored. For example, if we look at the central government of a country where several reforms have been carried out over the years, to what extent are their effects cumulative? Which more precise criteria differentiate them from one another, and why? To what extent has the prevailing administrative system been changed or not? To what extent has this system let reforms develop de facto only when they allowed it to subsist the way it had been for a long time and to survive the various waves of the storm of modernization and globalization unscathed?

As there may be many empirical fields, no standard way of approaching and analysing them exists. Moreover, most of the required data are not readily accessible or pre-formatted to support a scientifically satisfactory analysis. Many sources of information have to be built up from scratch. They necessitate a wide range of techniques from different disciplines or sub-disciplines: consultancy archives, database analysis, in-depth interview techniques, participant observation, accounting analysis, and so forth.

In short, an assessment process is structured around answers to a series of basic questions to be empirically validated.

1. Do so-called reform policies contribute significantly to evolving management practices and if so, which ones are concerned?
2. Are there any significant observable changes that are not linked to reforms explicitly labelled as such? If so, why and how?
3. Are reform initiators also the managers of the reform process or not?
4. Are there identifiable processes of learning and capitalizing on know-how, and conversely recurrent impeding factors?
5. Are change trajectories continuous and linear or not?
6. Is any change necessarily in the direction of modernization?
7. How are injunctions to change made and appropriated?
8. Do the three basic structures of management—organization, finance, human relations—evolve independently of one another or not?
9. Do cultural factors slow down or accelerate the propensity for managerial change?
10. Does the increasing legislation on management enable spaces for change to emerge?
11. Are any isomorphic processes at work, and if so which ones?
12. Are changes in organizational management modifying the way in which the State builds its action in the service of society and democracy?

This assessment perspective will be applied throughout Chaps. 4, 5, 6, 7, 8, 9, 10, and 11.

3.2 A Test: Central Government Reforms in France

We will now explore the changes that not only the central government but also local government and social security management have undergone in France in recent decades. Two factors inform this choice.

The first is the wealth of information already available. We have produced and collected most of it over the last 40 years or so, as very little has been published on the subject in the English-language literature.

The second reason for our choice is the common representation of France within academic circles and among practitioners, both abroad and in France: that of a country where public management is paralysed by the weight of its past and therefore its bureaucracy, and which is struggling to modernize its administrative system.

Looking exclusively and superficially at its formal institutions, it is admittedly difficult to veer away from such a representation.

France presents itself as a republic; its democracy is grounded in people's sovereignty. Yet the authority that the central government exerts over the country's inhabitants, imposed directly onto them without any real intermediary, is a legacy of the Emperor Napoleon. The country is governed by a constitution known as that of the Fifth Republic, adopted by popular referendum on 28 September 1958. Its frame of reference is the declaration of human rights, which dates back to 1789.

France is comprised of 13 mainland *régions* (regions), divided into 96 *départements* (counties) and 34,800 *communes* (municipalities). The local government of these three types of territorial authority is elected by popular vote. These territories are simultaneously autonomous local government communities and areas of State action. The State closely controls the national territory through a network of local government units, as well as a network of governmental field agencies. The latter are not organically autonomous agencies: they are services that execute the policies and decisions made by the central administrations in Paris, which have authority over them. The regional field agencies of the central state ministries are headed by a prefect appointed by the central government. This major institution dates back to 1800, and Napoleon (Bonaparte at the time) claimed that France's good fortune was owing to its establishment.

At national level, France is a semi-presidential regime. Its head of State is elected for a five-year term, renewable once. He appoints the prime minister on a discretionary basis, and the latter formally chooses the ministers and other secretaries of State placed at the head of what are called the central administrations. The prime minister can dissolve the National Assembly. Yet the government is accountable to the National Assembly which has the right to veto its decisions. The prime minister presides over the council of ministers. Presidential power is often referred to as the Elysée, after the palace where the head of State officiates. The prime minister's main function is to coordinate the actions of his ministers. His office is often referred to as Matignon, after the building where his services are located. As for the numerous ministers and secretaries of State who make up his cabinet, the most influential are traditionally those heading the budget, economic affairs, and security and police services (Ministry of the Interior). It is also important to note the existence and influence of three public institutions: the *Conseil d'État* (council of State), the *Cour des Comptes* (court of audit), and the *Inspection des Finances* (inspectorate of finance). They act as control and compliance bodies for the application of financial, accounting and legal procedures.

Executive power is strong and parliament, comprised of two chambers—the National Assembly and the senate—exerts limited control, particularly on the executive's agenda and its ability to take decisions other than through laws. The majority of *députés* (elected representatives at the National Assembly) are generally from the same political faction as the head of State. An autonomous constitutional council rules on the constitutionality of laws. This kind of supreme court is comprised of nine members appointed for nine years. Three are appointed by the head of State, three by the president of the senate, and three by the president of the National Assembly.

France can be considered as a State governed by the rule of law, for the hierarchy of legal standards, which long remained rather theoretical, is now well controlled. It has the particularity of having two jurisdictional systems (not including the constitutional council). Alongside the courts of the judicial order, which are competent for disputes between private individuals and are traditionally considered the guarantors of public freedoms, exists an order of so-called administrative courts, which rule on disputes that private individuals may have with public authorities. The highest such court is the *Conseil d'Etat*, of which the autonomy from government was gradually secured over time. This duality has its roots in the French Revolution, which prohibited judges from interfering in the functioning of the State. While previously only the president could decide whether a public decision breached the legal standards of the State (the time of so-called "retained justice", *justice retenue*), the nineteenth-century republican State model marked a shift to delegated justice (whereby the administrative courts make decisions on behalf of the authorities). The situation has become normalized for some years now; the judges of the administrative courts have seen their status as magistrates recognized by the European Court of Human Rights. Nevertheless, the administrative courts have incorporated into their case law the idea that while it is their duty to ensure that the law is respected by the executive and the administrations, they should not obstruct the proper functioning of the latter. Significantly, the *Conseil d'État* is also an advisor to the government (for further reading, see Barzelay & Gallego, 2010; Chevallier, 1996; Hayward & Wright, 2002; Heady, 2001; Kickert, 2005; Knapp & Wright, 2006; and Suleiman, 2015. For a short formal description of the Council's public administration, see European Commission, 2018).

References

Barzelay, M., & Gallego, R. (2010). The Comparative Historical Analysis of Public Management Policy Cycles in France, Italy, and Spain: Symposium Introduction. *Governance, 23*(2), 209–223.

Caiden, N., & Wildavsky, A. B. (1980). *Planning and Budgeting in Poor Countries.* Transaction Publishers.

Chevallier, J. (1996). Public Administration in Statist France. *Public Administration Review,* 67–74.

Dupuy, F., & Thoenig, J. C. (1979). Public Transportation Policy Making in France as an Implementation Problem. *Policy Sciences, 11*(1), 1–18.

European Commission. (2018). Public Administration Characteristics and Performance in the European Union: France. In *The Public Administration in the European Union* (pp. 324–352). Publication Office of the European Union.

Hayward, J. E. S., & Wright, V. (2002). *Governing from the Centre: Core Executive Coordination in France.* Oxford University Press on Demand.

Heady, F. (2001). *Public Administration, A Comparative Perspective.* CRC Press.

Jones, C. (1970). *An Introduction to the Study of Public Policy.* Duxbury Press.

Kickert, W. J. (2005). Distinctiveness in the Study of Public Management in Europe: A Historical-Institutional Analysis of France, Germany and Italy. *Public Management Review, 7*(4), 537–563.

Knapp, A., & Wright, V. (2006). *The Government and Politics of France.* Routledge.

Lipsky, M. (1980). *Street-Level Bureaucracy: Dilemmas of the Individual in Public Service.* Russell Sage Foundation.

Moynihan, D. P. (2005). Managing for Results in an Impossible Job: Solution Or Symbol? *International Journal of Public Administration, 28*(3–4), 213–231.

Pollitt, C., & Bouckaert, G. (2017). *Public Management Reform. A Comparative Analysis into the Age of Austerity.* Oxford University Press.

Pollitt, C., Van Thiel, S., & Homburg, V. (Eds.). (2007). *New Public Management in Europe.* Palgrave Macmillan.

Rainey, H. G. (1989). Public Management: Recent Research on the Political Context and Managerial Roles, Structures, and Behaviors. *Journal of Management, 15*(2), 229–250.

Robichau, R. W., & Lynn, L. E., Jr. (2009). The Implementation of Public Policy. Still the Missing Link. *The Policy Studies Journal, 37*(1), 21–36.

Suleiman, E. N. (2015). *Politics, Power, and Bureaucracy in France: The Administrative Elite* (Vol. 1257). Princeton University Press.

Thoenig, J. C. (2001). Evaluating Public Sector Reforms. Learning from Practice. In H. Wollman (Ed.), *Evaluating Public Sector Reforms: An International and Comparative Perspective, Special issue of Revista Internacional de Estudios Publicos* (pp. 193–214). Universidad do Estado do Rio de Janeiro, Núcleo Superior de Estudos Governamentais.

Thoenig, J. C. (2003). Learning from Evaluation Practice. In H. Wollmann (Ed.), *Evaluation in Public Sector Reform. Concepts and Practice in International Perspective* (pp. 209–230). Edward Elgar.

Wildavsky, A., & Pressman, J. (1973). *Implementation: How Great Expectations in Washington are Dashed in Oakland*. University of California Press.

PART III

Comprehensive Policies

CHAPTER 4

Birth, Life and Termination of Comprehensive Approaches

Policy initiatives by a central government to change the modus operandi of its entire administrative management are understandably a classic topic of research and reflection among public administration managers and academics alike.

These major comprehensive operations cover part of the range of public reforms, which may be sectoral—limited to a ministry, for example—or specific to local government authorities. Comprehensive reforms are however the ones most visible to citizens and most publicized at the initiative of political rulers.

France provides fertile ground in this respect. Its central government seems to readily adopt and launch large-scale reforms of its administrative system (Pyun & Lallemand, 2014). An apparent frenzy contrasts with the (preconceived) idea that France is a conservative country engulfed in an omnipotent bureaucracy and that it would therefore be surprising for its reforms to warrant consideration. This is however not to suggest the country should make the Guinness World Record for public reform!

Between the late 1960s and the early 2020s, eight comprehensive programmes were launched. These were all major operations involving all or almost all administrative components of the central government. They each carried a specific name.

The Rationalization of Budgetary Choices programme (RBC) was launched in May 1968 and stopped in the early 1980s.

The Renewal of Public Service operation (RPS) was set up in February 1989 and ended in the second half of the 1990s.

The Reform of the State and Public Service (RSPS) was an operation launched in July 1995 and stopped in mid-1997.

The Organic Law Governing Budgetary Laws (OLGBL) was a reform voted in July 2001.

The Modernization Audits reform (MA) started in July 2005 and stopped in mid-2007.

The Public Policy General Review (PPGR) was launched in June 2007 and ended in mid-2012.

The Modernization of Public Action operation (MPA) started in October 2012 and ended in early 2017.

The Public Action 2022 programme (PA 2022) started in autumn 2017.

This chapter presents each of these eight successive operations in detail.

4.1 The Rationalization of Budgetary Choices

In May 1968, a first major operation was launched, called the Rationalization of Budgetary Choices (RBC). It actually replicated to a large degree the Planning Programming Budgeting System developed at US federal level in the 1960s.

A politically Gaullist government was seeking to impose a radical overhaul of the way the State prepared and voted on its budget (Thoenig, 1971). Whether to finance heavy investments over several years or to schedule more ordinary spending, the central government would have to prepare all expenditures with new procedures and instruments, to be approved through the vote on the annual State budget or through multiyear programming laws (Thoenig, 1974; Mazoyer, 2013–2014).

Michel Debré, then Minister of Finance, was appointed to flesh out the details of a comprehensive reform which he fervently supported. He was an influential politician and former prime minister under the presidency of Charles de Gaulle. In a previous position, as Minister of the Armed Forces, he had already introduced a budgetary innovation affecting his services only, in the form of a so-called programme law. Once he was appointed Minister of Finance, he assigned the RBC operation a broader purpose: to better spend public money in order to serve finely analysed objectives associated with programme budgets.

In his view, this offered a weapon to challenge the virtually automatic renewal of budgets year after year, which ministries' work practices routinized and on the basis of which they presented their financial proposals to parliament for approval. The RBC was also to prevent lobbies from successfully defending special interests. Thus, the quasi-automatic rollover of the services voted on, as prescribed by the organic ordinance governing the annual budget process, was dysfunctional. It created annual allowances. The allocations they proposed were not compared with alternative approaches to achieve the desired effects.

The RBC was therefore seen as the best way to fulfil two requirements at once. The first was to set the priorities that the State budget should serve, and the other was to compare the ways and means of achieving them. This would improve the way resources were used. It would afford both more adequate financial control and greater relevance in the allocation of budgetary resources. It would optimize the spending approved by decision makers.

Not only was Michel Debré politically hands-on as Minister of Finance, but the administrative departments of his ministry were also put in charge of overseeing the reform. They were thus responsible for detailing the procedures and instruments that other ministries would have to apply before submitting budgets to parliament. This undertaking involved two stakeholders: the executive branch that prepared the budget, and the legislative branch that voted on it. Yet the emphasis was initially on the upstream or methodological part of the process, postponing the revision of the organic ordinance governing the finance law, which was indispensable in order for parliament to consider the adoption of the budget presented in accordance with the RBC.

The services of the Ministry of Finance relied on systems analysis. Two complementary instruments were put forward: ex ante evaluation, and programme budgets (Huet & Bravo, 1973). A multi-year strategic planning system was set up. The preparation of programme budgets was entrusted to the executive, and all ministries were called upon to do their part. The credit forecasts prepared on the basis of expected impacts then had to be submitted to parliament, to complement its traditional decision-making approach based on the nature of expenditures.

This preparatory stage was entrusted to the administrative services and staff of the ministries and was closely overseen by the Ministry of Finance. It involved specialists trained in economic calculation and techniques such as cost-benefit, cost-effectiveness and multi-criteria analysis, and operational research. High-level contractors were recruited. However, leadership positions were still assigned to senior civil servants from the State's engineering corps, such as those from the famous École Polytechnique, and mainly to senior finance officials from the École Nationale d'Administration (ENA), who were presumed to hold great finance and budgetary expertise.

Finance officials, convinced that the central government was in a bad state, became the cornerstone of horizontal reform and the epicentre defining "best" practices. Considerable sums of money—the equivalent of tens of millions of euros—were spent on professional training seminars for civil servants in other ministries, skills building, and RBC studies. Just over 300 sectoral or focused analyses were conducted, covering all areas of State action. Over 100 analysts were put to work. Private-sector consultants were also recruited. The strictly econometric and financial reasoning of the Ministry of Finance and Budget became hegemonic. Completing inter-ministerial studies proved more difficult than successfully carrying out sectoral ones, as the former were both more cumbersome and more exposed to issues of compartmentalization between ministries and to rivalries between their potential leaders (Godard, 1970).

The hegemony of finance and budget was however to decline irreversibly subsequent to the social movements that shook France in the spring of 1968. Michel Debré left the government in the wake of President Charles de Gaulle's resignation. The new elections ushered in a less Gaullist right-wing president, and a change of direction from the programme announced in early 1968 began. In July 1968, François-Xavier Ortoli, the new Minister of the Economy and Finance, and then in June 1969 his successor, Valéry Giscard d'Estaing, both from the *Inspection des Finances*—the Ministry's senior civil servant elite—backtracked. It was agreed that the RBC would not be imposed on the other ministries. Furthermore, the State budget would continue to be prepared and discussed by parliament on an annual basis, without following a programme-based approach. The RBC would become just another voluntarist instrument internal to the administrative system.

Its take-up by the ministries differed more and more. In some ministries, it was used purely for management control purposes. In others, it served as a starting point for developing managerial accounting setting up staff training plans, or recognizing the legitimacy of economic knowledge. This was the case, for example, in the ministry in charge of public works and housing. Carrying out an inter-ministerial study was a lengthy process, for cooperation between the offices of the ministries was far from spontaneous. Just over 50 studies adopted a truly comprehensive perspective, for example on the fight for road safety, vaccination, perinatal care, or energy financing.

The RBC project was officially abandoned in 1984, 18 years after its launch. François Mitterrand was president and the left wing was in power. The political right hardly protested: the corpse inherited from Gaullism was already cold. No one on the political spectrum or in the administrative system expressed any regret at the idea that the State was depriving itself of a programme-based approach to spending.

4.2 The Renewal of Public Service Operation

On 23 February 1989, a second comprehensive reform was enacted: the Renewal of Public Service (RPS). It bore no resemblance to the reform launched by Michel Debré, for its stated ambition was to renew public service delivery, not to reform the budgetary process.

Michel Rocard, appointed prime minister of a socialist government, adopted a clear reformist approach. He wanted to improve the management of the entire administrative system, from the top to the bottom of the hierarchy and across all State administrations. The RPS reform was to cover two areas: the internal management of public organizations, where labour relations would be improved through more dynamic human resource management and greater social dialogue; and their external management, where public services were to improve the way users were received and the services provided to them (République française, 1990).

This undertaking employed concepts and methods inspired by business management, such as the quality circle, the service project, and the responsibility centre. Rather than imposing best practices imported from other countries or adopting sophisticated techniques, Rocard took the gamble of making sure his ministers felt even more responsible for their own actions regarding the efficiency of their departments' internal management. Until then, little thought had been given in the French administration to transposing the practice of responsibility centres from the private sector—with the exception of two initiatives. It had been attempted by the Ministry of Public Works with its own field agencies, which accounted for almost 90% of its total staff, and an official report on the concept of responsibility and decision-making centre had been produced by a member of the *Conseil d'État* (Demesteere, 2001).

Furthermore, and most importantly, in 1990 the RPS programme decreed the institutionalization of the ex post evaluation of public policies.

This initiative, announced through an intense media communication campaign, did not go unnoticed. Its intended purpose was to make the heads of ministries more accountable, in the eyes of the public, for the impacts of the public policies they led.

A new framework was created, which was surprisingly original. It consisted of two tiers. An inter-ministerial evaluation committee was chaired by the prime minister, with the main ministers concerned as its permanent members. It was responsible for launching evaluation initiatives and deliberating on how best to follow up on their results. The execution of the evaluations it commissioned was entrusted to another institutional tier, the scientific evaluation council comprised of academics and senior civil servants appointed solely on the basis of their professional competence in the field. This council oversaw the entire evaluation process, from the drafting of specifications to the certification of the reliability of the methods and techniques used and the validity of the conclusions. It also proposed the operator to whom the work should be entrusted. In short, the scientific evaluation council was independent. The institutionalized public policy evaluation framework aimed to break with practices that had until then remained sporadic and were not institutionally recognized (Deleau 1986).

Enhancing the efficiency of public policy management was one thing; improving democratic debate and expanding society's participation in public affairs was another. The RPS programme added a second dimension to the functional or managerial dimension of evaluation, which was ideological or driven by civic considerations. Democracy implied information sharing and therefore transparency, and to ensure transparency, Michel Rocard required that evaluation reports be made widely available to the citizens. Participation also implied that citizens be involved throughout an evaluation process, and have the right to demand an evaluation of a specific policy, or even to be co-opted as evaluators.

The launch of the RPS programme seemed promising, even if the part around service projects involved profound cultural changes across the services of a same organization. A self-representation, a collective identity and shared aspirations needed to emerge, particularly and especially between middle management and the field agencies. But not every service project gives rise to organizational change (Gibert & Caillé, 1993). To be perceived as legitimate, such a project must be linked to a shared strategic orientation, or this approach will struggle to be participatory and will become another hierarchical injunction with which to comply (Gibert & Pascaud, 1989).

As for the evaluation framework, its implementation was smooth. Parliament even acquired internal evaluation expertise, as did the *régions*, *départements* and cities. Sixteen evaluation projects concerning inter-ministerial policies, commissioned to the scientific council by the inter-ministerial committee and the prime minister, were completed in the first few years. The French experiment sparked curiosity and even became a reference for other countries such as Great Britain and Canada.

The situation however soon deteriorated. The ministries concerned by evaluations paid little attention to them. Rocard, who had fathered the programme, resigned as prime minister in May 1991. Between 1990 and 1993, the inter-ministerial committee met only three times, before ceasing all activity. There was no follow-up to its deliberations. The scientific council received no commissions for new evaluations from Rocard's three successors, the first two being socialists and the third centre-right. As for the Presidency of the Republic, it never considered the RPS operation as an initiative worthy of attention.

In late 1998, a new prime minister, Lionel Jospin, revived the framework which had ground to a halt (République francaise, 1998). However, he radically altered it. The scientific evaluation council became a national evaluation council. It was essentially comprised of representatives appointed by their home institutions, and no longer of independent members qualified solely on the basis of their expertise. The inter-ministerial evaluation committee was discreetly abolished, and the future evaluation programme was defined "in consultation" with the administrations concerned. In short, the autonomy with which Rocard had endowed the system was restricted; evaluation became a marginalized administrative procedure. Between 1999 and 2001, it still produced about ten evaluations. In May 2002, at the beginning of his second term as President of the Republic, Jacques Chirac let this framework fall into total disuse. Six years later, a decree formally abolished it.

4.3 The Reform of the State and Public Service

In July 1995, a third reform was launched, the reform of the State and the public service or RSPS (République française, 1995), which was also comprehensive.

Alain Juppé had just been appointed as prime minister of a centre-right government and wanted to distinguish his term from the legacy of the socialist left, both in form and in content. Policy evaluations were swept aside as Juppé exhibited an authoritarian style and made his impatience clear. He wanted results as fast as possible. He set out ambitious priority objectives: clarifying the missions of the State and the limits of the public services' scope. The central government should focus on strategy and regulatory functions only, and therefore relieve itself of operational functions. A large devolutionary process took place, relegating missions to the field agencies of the different ministries, which also had to be brought together and reorganized. Moreover, the RSPS had to reduce its staff numbers significantly. This approach involved the State being seen to spend less, in line with the trends observed in other countries in recent years (Thoenig, 1984).

This project was entrusted to a specially created central body, the State reform commission. An inter-ministerial committee for State reform was set up and chaired by the prime minister. It brought together all the ministers concerned in seminars and plenary sessions. Its mission was to draw up a three-year plan of concrete measures. Each minister was required to draft a strategy paper on the services and responsibilities under their remit as soon as possible. The commissioner, an inter-ministerial delegate, managed the reform. This role was assigned to a senior civil servant from the *Conseil d'État*. Here again, Alain Juppé distinguished himself from Michel Rocard, who had largely recruited members of the *Cour des Comptes*. The new inter-ministerial delegate enjoyed broad operational powers as the facilitator of reform measures, while the ministries saw their room to manoeuvre in this field considerably reduced. In short, the prime minister controlled almost everything, whereas Rocard had given the ministers extensive leeway to take concrete initiatives (Thoenig 2000).

Just 11 months after it was announced, the major comprehensive operation designed by the prime minister, named the RSPS, encountered an unexpected and insurmountable obstacle. President Chirac dissolved the National Assembly, and the elections that ensued produced a socialist and centre-left majority. Alain Juppé resigned. Lionel Jospin succeeded him at the head of a new left-wing government, with Jacques Chirac remaining President of the Republic.

Lionel Jospin also wanted to distinguish himself from his predecessor. Of course, he required his ministers to prepare multi-year programmes to increase the efficiency of their respective administrations, but he also made three changes. The first was semantic: the term "renewal of the State," that Michel Rocard had supported, was abolished by Alain Juppé who replaced it by the term "reform." When Juppé subsequently stepped down as prime minister, his successor replaced "reform" by "modernization of the State." Apparently the left-wing government and the right-wing government do not speak the same language. The second change was to reduce Matignon's authoritarian pressure on the ministers. The third involved institution building: the State reform commission was turned into an inter-ministerial delegation for State reform and placed under the direct authority of the prime minister. Its management was entrusted to a senior civil servant from the Ministry of National Education, who was also the director general of the civil service. The new delegation was made available to the minister in charge of the civil service and State reform. This delegation, comprised of 15 senior civil servants, was responsible for making proposals on State reform to the government, for coordinating the preparation of decisions to make in this area—mainly on internal management actions within the administration, for instance surrounding information technology and relations with users—and for ensuring their implementation. However, it did not have any decision-making powers.

In 2002 a new prime minister, Jean-Pierre Raffarin, was appointed to head the government following a change of majority in parliament. Raffarin, a centre-right politician, repealed the decree signed by his predecessor and decreed a purely organic change. The inter-ministerial delegation for State reform was replaced by a delegation for the modernization of public management and State organizations, as well as two other entities: a delegation in charge of users and administrative simplifications (DUAS); and an agency for the development of electronic administration. The new delegation was established in 2003 and two and a half years later, it was also abolished.

4.4 The Revision of the Organic Law Governing Budgetary Laws

On 1 August 2001, under Prime Minister Jospin, a fourth major operation was completed: the Organic Law Governing Budgetary Laws (OLGBL), to revise existing procedures governing the making of budgetary laws. It enacted a new financial "constitution" for the State (République française, 2012a; Giberrt & Thoenig, 1993).

The announcement of the OLGBL caused quite a stir. This law was noteworthy for at least three reasons. First, it revived a project that had been axed about 15 years earlier, with the end of the RBC programme. Second, on a political level, it was prepared and endorsed by both the parliamentary opposition and the majority. It was put on the agenda and formulated by two members of parliament, not senior civil servants and ministers in office. Finally, it marked the entry of the legislative branch, and therefore popular representation, into the field of major administrative reform operations, which had until then been governed almost exclusively by the executive.

In the French hierarchy of standards, an organic law sits between the constitution and ordinary laws. It specifies the organization and functioning of public authorities. In the case of budgetary affairs, it relates to the work of parliament and the government in this area. Given the complexity of the issues at hand and the details to be addressed on a legal and technical level, an initial period of four years was planned to carry out full-scale experiments. The reform introduced by the OLGBL was an instrument of legitimization. It forced the government to make the objectives of its budgetary requests explicit, while also requiring the different ministers to account for the results obtained with the resources granted to them by parliament, in pursuit of the objectives they had announced. It paved the way for a shift from the management by means of public finances to their management by objectives. It also reduced the information asymmetry characterizing the division of power between the executive and the legislative, to the benefit of the latter. It thus appeared to satisfy an essential prerequisite for any State modernization project, one that was slow to be fulfilled even though it had underpinned RBC operations since the late 1960s.

The new organic law introduced greater flexibility in programme management. For example, programme managers were given considerable latitude for transferring funds from one category of expenditure type—operations, staff, investment—to another. The only exception to this was staff funding: ministries could not supplement such budgets with other resources. The concept of asymmetrical fungibility of funding was thus coined.

The OLGBL, however, offered no definition of spending optimization, not even in relation to the impacts of the actions funded. Regarding the methodological and technical requirements for studying and defining these impacts, the law referred to implementation legislation to be drafted at a later stage by the executive and the ministries. As for evaluation, it was mentioned in passing only, without really being distinguished from management control (Benzerafa et al., 2011), (Benzerafa & Gibert, 2015), (Benzerafa et al., 2016).

In June 2003, Prime Minister Jean-Pierre Raffarin required each ministerial department to draw up a document called a ministry strategy reform, with a view to identifying the internal reforms needed within public services in order to implement the new budgetary procedure. The ministries were asked to define them through a systematic review of their own missions and the State administration organizations servicing them. Three principles were adopted to develop the new ministry strategies: a systematic re-examination of the missions and the organizations servicing them; a quality-based approach; and a change in staff management methods through devolution, reduction in the number of civil servants, recognition of merit, and staff planning. The government's stated aim was to bring these ministerial strategies under the remit of the legislative branch. In total, 230 detailed measures were implemented, through which the government expected to save one and a half billion euros and cut almost 10,000 jobs. The OLGBL received very close and detailed attention, particularly within the Ministry of Finance, where a specialized temporary directorate was set up to draft all the implementation legislation for the organic law.

4.5 The Modernization Audits Reform

In July 2006, a fifth wave of comprehensive operations was launched by Dominique de Villepin's government. It recommended generalizing a method called modernization audits (MA).

Two official texts successively defined the programme and methodology. The new centre-right government put Jean-François Copé, an ENA alumni and Minister Delegate for the Budget, in charge of managing the operation. He was also intent on forging ahead.

In the meantime, a directorate general for State modernization was created at central government level under the remit of the Ministry of the Economy, Finance and Industry, merging four administrative structures that were previously independent of one another. The one was in charge of management and State organization reform. Another was dedicated to user relations and administrative simplification. A third was the temporary directorate for budgetary reform, and the fourth one was in charge of the development of e-government. Its leadership was entrusted to an engineer from the Ecole Polytechnique who had worked for an international consultancy firm before being recruited by Jean-François Copé, then Minister of State Reform, in 2004. His service had a staff of about 160 public servants. This organizational jigsaw, already observed under the RESP programme, baffled many ministries, which no longer knew where to turn when it came to reform implementation.

The term "modernization" replaced that of "reform." In reality, and despite this label, the audit operation was presented first and foremost as a tool to streamline services or procedures. Its stated purpose was to make internal management more efficient, and to increase the productivity of administrative services and lower their cost. The explicit quest for more effective public policies, with outcomes that better matched societal needs, remained very timid. This stance allowed the services of the Ministry of Budget and State Reform to encroach a little more on the jurisdiction of the *Cour des Comptes* in the area of public cost control.

The purpose of the audit was to identify opportunities for budget savings. The Minister of Budget spoke of developing the production of such modernization audits on an industrial scale. This system would track the failures of a service, procedure or mission, with the understanding that the minister concerned would propose operational solutions, and that each audit would come with a concrete action plan. The auditors would mainly be members of the various State inspectorates, most of which were largely accustomed to carrying out compliance checks and not audits. They would have two to three months to carry out an audit and to draw conclusions for operational use.

Between October 2005 and April 2007, seven waves of audits were launched. Nearly 170 audits were effectively launched, covering almost 150 billion euros of State expenditure. A wide range of domains were audited: the processing of staff pay; the cost, for external services, of resorting to local subcontracting; the management of the employment allowance; public school hours; business aid; and so forth.

In practice, these documents were not so much audits, in the primary and narrow sense of account auditing, as what could be called diagnoses of intra-administrative functioning, which culminated in recommendations for action. However, only a small minority quantified the savings that such recommendations would produce. The outcomes covered in these documents largely related to more qualitative considerations, such as the quality of relations with users. As for the ministries audited, they did not appear to play the game imposed on them with great enthusiasm. The Minister of Budget wanted to launch no fewer than 100 new audits within three months, all of them sector-specific. Only one audit was comprehensive; it concerned the State's purchasing policy.

The Ministry of Finance wanted to forge ahead at full speed. In 2007, the Minister presented a progress report to parliament and the council of ministers, with a resolutely positive tone. One month later, paradoxically, the MA operation was dropped outright. This abrupt end coincided with the end of Jacques Chirac's term as President of the Republic and the election of a new incumbent, Nicolas Sarkozy.

4.6 THE PUBLIC POLICY GENERAL REVIEW

On 10 July 2007, a sixth reform was officially launched, named the Public Policy General Review (PPGR).

New government, new comprehensive reform. It was explicitly called a modernization policy. Nicolas Sarkozy was its proclaimed advocate. Similar reforms had been carried out in many countries, particularly in Canada from 1994 to 1998, where it was labelled a programmes review. In France, its sponsors claimed that it would be different from all previous policies of the kind.

The reform was designed to span several domains which, with the exception of the improvement of human resource management, included measures extending beyond the scope of the administrative management of central government alone. These areas covered broader issues, such as the reduction of legal constraints, the reduction of administrative controls, and the reform of relations between the State and local authorities. The main areas of focus included merging services, merging tax and government accounting administrations, e-payment, pooling the support functions of the police and the gendarmerie, and reducing the number of civil servants. In addition to sector-specific audits, four so-called interministerial projects were launched, one of which involved reviewing the recruitment examinations for entry to the civil service.

The goal formally assigned to human resource management was to foster support for and confidence in the idea of administrative modernization among civil servants. According to the political sponsors of the PPGR, this area needed to be given particular attention, as the review would inevitably fail without the support of civil servants. Their buy-in was seen as a decisive prerequisite for "less State" in France.

In fact, the main purpose of the PPGR was to control State expenditure. It sought to restore a balanced budget by the end of the president's five-year term, by reducing the growth of public spending by 1% each year, in other words twice as fast as in previous years. With the new organic law, no ministry would be able to escape this objective. More efficient management of public organizations was therefore required. This would have to be coupled with more effective public policies. Ultimately, the quest for added value took second place and largely remained a talking point. The PPGR set clear-cut priority imperatives for financial rationalization. Seven billion euros in savings would be made over five years. One in three retiring civil servants would not be replaced. An annual 4% to 5% productivity gain would be achieved.

This programme was openly geared towards trimming down the State. Operational spending cuts were to be made, with a ten-billion-euro target to be reached within three years through the use of inter-ministerial procurement contracts, performance-based pay for senior managers, and drastic cuts to operating expenditures. The same effort was required of State operators. Thus, the PPGR did not challenge the missions pursued by the administrations.

This programme was managed through a new framework called the council for the modernization of public policies. It brought the ministers together under the leadership of the President of the Republic. The general rapporteur was Éric Woerth, who in the meantime had been promoted to Minister for the Budget, Public Accounts and the Civil Service, replacing Jean-François Copé. He was not an ENA alumnus like Copé, but had graduated from a major Paris business school and had worked as a business consultant.

The approaches of the PPGR programme were identical to those of so-called modernization audits, but with a wider scope and more human resources (Chevallier, 2010). A systematic audit of State spending was entrusted to *ad hoc* teams which, as well as including members of various ministerial and inter-ministerial inspectorates who generally had little auditing training because they specialized in control of legality and procedural compliance, massively involved large private business consultancies.

A deadline was set for this programme: April 2008. This date corresponded to the beginning of the process required to build the three-year budgetary programme for 2009 to 2011, in application of the new OLGBL. Six successive reports were presented by the government to review the progress of the measures undertaken as part of the PPGR. Reform packages were launched, which primarily involved reorganizing the administration's organizational charts. Measures relating to government intervention policies per se were deferred to a later date. In June 2008, a review of 374 decisions taken was made public. While it evidenced remarkable ambition, most of these decisions had yet to be implemented. The PPGR operation had to be accelerated. A quarter of the measures were behind schedule or had not yet been implemented, especially those affecting civil servants, which required parliamentary approval. Officially, 665 audits were to be carried out—a truly Herculean undertaking. President Sarkozy announced that the decisions and measures taken would have to be included in the 2009-2011 financial planning law.

The PPGR sparked much stronger reactions than the modernization audits, including fierce mobilization by State employees and their unions. They denounced the system's authoritarian nature, the lack of consultation, and the disenfranchisement of public services that they claimed was associated with the programme. The non-replacement of retiring civil servants was a source of great concern.

Ultimately, the results of the PPGR proved to be rather poor. None of its stated objectives were achieved: the modernization of public services; the improvement of the quality of service to users; and significant budgetary savings. The savings that the executive hoped for would clearly fall short of the expected 7.1 billion euros over three years (Henry & Pierru, 2012).

4.7 THE MODERNIZATION OF PUBLIC ACTION OPERATION

In late October 2012, a seventh comprehensive programme was set in motion after François Hollande was elected to succeed Nicolas Sarkozy as head of State. Hollande decreed outright that the PPGR programme was dead and buried. He replaced it with the Modernization of Public Action or MPA (French Republic, 2012b).

The left in power proclaimed that it would do better and more than the right did under Chirac and Sarkozy. It would modernize the State differently. Yet while the label changed, the MPA demonstrated the same ambition as the preceding programmes: to make public policy and the entire administration more efficient, with a view to achieving budget savings, in other words, by limiting public spending. This financial efficiency was justified on the grounds that the MPA would make public policies better suited to societal needs. The language used by the socialist left was identical to that used by the political right.

The highest State authorities spent a lot of time distributing roles to determine who would be in charge of the reform. They also merged two pre-existing administrative organizations to create a new entity. This general secretariat of the MPA was entrusted with the inter-ministerial coordination of the reform of devolved government services—not an insignificant portfolio, given the ongoing reorganization of the map of local authorities, particularly by merging *communes* and creating inter-municipal organizations in both rural and urban areas. The general secretariat reported directly to the prime minister. As for the ministry responsible for the State budget, it theoretically no longer had any authority over missions relating to modernization and the administrative organizations mandated to execute them, except for those directly linked to the organic law, such as programme management control.

The institutional jigsaw was extended with provisions for the structural reform of central administrations. The general secretariat was given inter-ministerial powers, to coordinate, facilitate and support the work carried out by the multiple ministerial administrations. Additionally, an inter-ministerial committee for the modernization of public policy was set up for all the ministers to meet on a regular basis, including the minister in charge of the State budget. Its general rapporteur was the minister responsible for the civil service and decentralization, who became Minister of State Reform. The prime minister's powers thus grew in both the political and the administrative spheres.

As the months went by, it seemed as though the operation launched in 2012 focused primarily on intra-administrative reforms. The general secretariat had nearly 200 agents, just under half of whom were civil servants, and a budget of over 40 million euros. This budget was to encourage and support specific operations ranging from ongoing training to consultancy and addressing internal management problems such as the quality of service provided, the digitization of operations, the use of data, the use of scoreboards, and securing IT systems.

The stated end goal was rationalization, and therefore containing public expenditure. Efficiency rationales still prevailed. This was evidenced by the launch of some 60 new policy evaluations. On the one hand, the leaders of the general secretariat instructed the inspection services to better distinguish between their evaluation mission and their regular control, auditing or even performance auditing responsibilities. On the other hand, the stated aim of the projects in areas ranging from housing to household waste and from business aid to outpatient surgery was to continue or even increase budget savings. Detecting the effects or impacts of public policies in order to better manage the objectives assigned to the choices made by policymakers was not an explicit priority.

This reform also revealed a change in what was included in the relationship with citizens and users. Until then, with the exception of the DUAS era, the central administration in charge of the reform process had in no way benefited from its own inter-ministerial organization. Instead, it essentially operated as a specialized State reform body, translating and legitimizing a reform with the ultimate purpose of increasing the efficiency of its administrative components. Moving forward, the government leadership would steer this specialized reform body towards an autonomous and more political mission: observing and taking into account the quality of relations as perceived by public opinion. New instruments would gradually be adopted, from opinion polls to the monthly publication of open data indicators monitoring a large number of services provided.

The MPA programme was in turn put on hold as well, following the presidential and parliamentary elections in the spring of 2017. The tipping point was the same as for previous programmes: the arrival in power of a new President of the Republic and a new government. The socialists gave way to Emmanuel Macron, who claimed to be "neither left-wing nor right-wing." He appointed Edouard Philippe as prime minister, also an ENA alumnus from the political right.

4.8 The Public Action 2022 Programme

In September 2017, an eighth comprehensive reform was solemnly announced in a circular sent by the prime minister to the members of his government: the programme titled Public Action 2022 (PA 2022), 2022 referring to the year in which Emmanuel Macron's term of office would end (French Republic, 2017).

The MPA programme that had been developed under the socialist presidency was described as a failure and was discontinued. A purely administrative comprehensive reform limited to central government would be a mistake. On the contrary, to be successful, the programme had to adopt a broader perspective. Its scope would therefore also include social security institutions and local authorities. PA 2022 set its sights far and wide, encompassing all or almost all sectors producing public policy, not just the central government and its operators. Promises and precise deadlines were announced, with the systemic transformation of public policy established as a priority objective. An official barometer of public policy results was thus launched in January 2021. However, the indicators used by the ministry in charge of the civil service were not the same as those used by the Ministry of Budget, which governed the OLGBL programmes. This detail was far from insignificant, as it reflected the desire to make public policy performance easier to understand for the general public.

The term "systemic" suggested that the government would not simply juxtapose a series of sectoral reforms and disparate measures. Its ambition was to enact profound and coordinated change in the way the State was governed. The political sponsors of the new programme also announced a so-called participatory dimension that was to contrast with the authoritarian and centralized approach of previous programmes. Regional and national forums were launched involving users, public servants and young people of all ideological leanings.

This however did not prevent PA 2022 from announcing that it intended to proceed in a way and with a tone that differed little from previous major reforms. The priority was to cut State spending and deficits as a share of gross domestic product by three points by 2022. Political leadership of the programme would be in the hands of the President of the Republic and the prime minister. Each of the ministers would be made first-in-command in the area covered by their services.

The first stage focused on establishing a diagnosis and priorities for action. It was entrusted to a committee presented as acting independently. In addition to this, five inter-ministerial projects were launched to explore the toolkits to employ for human resources, the territorial organization of public services, and budgetary and accounting management. In parallel, 13 regional forums were set up. An operation was also launched to involve users and public servants. In the second stage of the programme, the President of the Republic and the prime minister would have to decide on the next steps. A third stage, scheduled to start in March 2018 and end in 2021, would see the development and operational implementation of ministerial and comprehensive transformation plans.

The supervision of this central leadership framework was entrusted to the Ministry of Public Action and Accounts, the new name of the Ministry of Finance and then Budget. Its services were put in charge of preparing the roadmap for and monitoring the work carried out by each of the government officials in their respective areas of competence. The supervision of the PA 2022 programme relied on two dedicated resources: money, and a specialized functional service. A special 700-million-euro fund was set up, to be spent over five years. A return on investment was expected within three years in the form of sustainable operational savings, with one euro of annual savings for every euro invested. The projects proposed would be selected by the services of the Ministry of Finance, that is, by a circle of public budget officials, even though the public transformation project covered a much broader spectrum.

A small circle of people who were politically, socially and administratively very close to the President of the Republic made a significant mark on the whole PA 2022 operation. The composition of the committee that was to inform the programme illustrates this clearly. Fifteen out of 34 French members, in other words almost half, were ENA alumni. Half of them had previously worked in a minister's office. Ten of the committee members had even worked in the prime minister's office and/or in the office of the President of the Republic at some point in their career as civil servants, with three having held both positions. Quite plainly, this committee resembled a club, with similar people at its core, comprised of members of parliament, business leaders, elected local officials and senior civil servants.

Was this setup any different from previous ones? No. Comitology was already involved in most of the previous comprehensive policies and was structured in the same way. The President of the Republic chose and appointed the committee members, and set its working agenda. This committee had to produce a report identifying significant and lasting reforms on 21 public policies considered as priorities. The scope to cover was extensive, ranging from guaranteed minimum income to sports. Within less than six months, the committee was to review all the missions and public expenditures of the State's whole range of public administrations, local authorities and public agencies. It also had to decide on the most suitable way to maintain and execute each public policy, including whether to end them or transfer them to other sectors than the State. Each member of the government was strongly encouraged to submit a proposal for structural reform by 2022 as part of the PA 2022 operation. These proposals would identify the scope of policies to reform, the portfolios to change or transfer to third parties, and the lasting financial savings that could be made in their respective jurisdictions (Gibert & Thoenig, 2019).

The committee was entrusted with open reflection about public-sector missions and expenditure in France. It had to think about transformation "differently." As this pertained to public policy, and not a simple transposition of approaches used in business, it required going beyond both the references and reasoning taught in training courses where procedural or institutional language prevailed, and the normative language of economic science. While three economists represented the research world on the committee, specialists in social science applied to the management of public affairs, change in public organizations, and the management of public policies were totally absent, with the exception of a Swedish citizen who had experience as a practitioner and was a consultant in this field. None of the committee members had recognized expertise in the field of evaluation.

The PA 2022 programme's position remained ambiguous. It constantly mixed requirements or targets for public spending cuts with requirements or targets for a desirable model of society. The two were not compatible, especially with the committee only being granted six months to submit a substantiated report that offered more than general information or wishful thinking, and also had more of a financial and budgetary focus. It was encouraged to adopt the narrow position of a management controller and, if needed, was free to propose drastic cost reductions.

Committee meetings were marked by high rates of absenteeism. Tensions, if not friction, surrounded the work from start to finish. For example, there was a sharp divide between advocates of local authorities' autonomy and supporters of recentralization under the remit of the State. Everyone's preconceptions resurfaced. For example, local authorities' spending was claimed to be excessive and extravagant, while the State was presented as more virtuous by nature. There were strong differences of opinion around prioritizing budget-saving measures only. The task force favoured budget-saving measures, which would save around 30 billion euros. It prioritized comprehensive approaches by suggesting, for instance, that middle managers in the public services no longer be recruited as statutory civil servants but on a contract basis, a measure that would affect nearly 120,000 positions. It insisted on the objective of reducing the public deficit during President Macron's term in office as part of France's commitment to the European Union's budgetary criteria. The report for example proposed removing the Ministry of Sports, giving greater autonomy to public school principals, transferring building permits—a measure prized by mayors—to inter-municipalities, and so forth. The more detailed proposals on particular public policies, as well as the more managerial ambitions around governance and managerial changes in public services, remained far more timid.

Between late 2017 and mid-2018, the national context surrounding the PA 2022 programme changed from being a resource to being a constraint for the government. Its recommendations could potentially entail major political and social risks. Even tighter government control was established to ensure that the executive branch retained the quasi monopoly it enjoyed on State modernization affairs, without feeling committed to initiatives it did not control. In 2019, public sector strikes, social demonstrations in the streets, a dramatic rise in unemployment, and looming elections all caused the executive to tread cautiously. In the summer of 2019, the minister in charge of the civil service and the budget dropped the plan to cut 50,000 civil service jobs. By early 2020, only about 10,000 jobs had been cut. For the year 2021, the prime minister instead assigned the PA 2022 programme the mission of strengthening State services by creating new jobs. As for the public deficit, it promises to shatter all imaginable ceilings. The government's ambitious goals of 2019 have since been shelved.

A revolution in public management through comprehensive measures is clearly not underway. With the onset of the COVID-19 pandemic, priorities changed dramatically. Work on the major operation has slowed down, if not stopped. More than ever, issues such as the chronic lack of horizontal coordination between the dozens of administrative silos operating at central government level remain a major problem in the eyes of the public, and the Achilles heel of the national authorities in charge of the executive, as the management of the pandemic in 2020 amply demonstrates.

References

Benzerafa, M., Garcin, L., Gibert, P., & Gueugnon, J. F. (2011). Le management par objectifs met-il fin à l'ambiguïté dans la gestion publique ? *Politiques et Management Public*, 28(3), 353–389.

Benzerafa, M., & Gibert, P. (2015). Dynamique des indicateurs de reporting externe : le cas des indicateurs des projets et rapport annuels de performance annexés aux lois de finances. *Revue Française d'Administration Publique*, 3(155), 763–778.

Benzerafa, M., Garcin, L., & Gibert, P. (2016). Le volet performance de la LOLF. Standardisation et résilience d'un genre entre rationalité politique et rationalité de gestion. *Revue Française de Gestion*, 7(260), 11–31.

Chevallier, J. (2010). Révision générale des politiques publiques et gestion des ressources humaines. *Revue Française d'Administration Publique, 136*, 907–918.
Demesteere, R. (2001). L'ambiguité de la notion de responsabilité en contrôle de gestion. *Politiques et Management Public, 19*(3), 79–100.
Gibert, P., & Pascaud, G. (1989). Des projets d'entreprise et les organisations publiques. *Politiques et Management Public, 7*(2), 119–162.
Gibert, P., & Caillé, N. (1993). Projet de service et innovation. *Revue Française des Affaires Sociales, 3*, 219–226.
Gibert, P., & Thoenig, J. C. (1993). La gestion publique : entre l'apprentissage et l'amnésie. *Politiques et Management Public, 11*(1), 1–18.
Gibert, P., & Thoenig, J. C. (2019). *La modernisation de l'Etat. Une promesse trahie ?* Classiques Garnier.
Godard, J.C. (1970). *La rationalisation de choix budgétaires. La méthode R.C.B.* Paris: Services du Premier ministre, Comité central d'enquête sur le coût et le rendement des services publics.
Henry, O., & Pierru, F. (2012). Les consultants et la réforme des services publics. *Actes de la Recherche en Sciences Sociales, 193*(3), 112–123.
Huet, P., & Bravo, J. (1973). *L'expérience française de rationalisation des choix budgétaires.* Presses Universitaires de France.
Mazoyer, H. (2013-2014). Réformer l'administration par le savoir économique. La rationalisation des choix budgétaires aux ministères de l'équipement et des transports. *Genèses, 93*, 29–52.
Pyun, H., & Lallemand, A. (2014). To Reform the Public Administration, Is It An Impossible Mission? Case Study of French Public Administration Reforms Since 1980s. *Gestion et Management Public, 3*(3), 75–88. https://doi.org/10.3917/gmp.031.0075
République française. (1990). *Décret n° 90-82 du 22 janvier 1990 relatif à l'évaluation des politiques publiques.* Journal Officiel, Imprimerie Nationale.
République française. (1995). *Décret n° 95-1007 du 13 septembre 1995 relatif au Comité interministériel pour la réforme de l'État et à la Délégation interministérielle à la réforme de l'État.* Journal Officiel, Imprimerie Nationale.
République française. (1998). *Décret n° 98-1048 du 18 novembre 1998 relatif à l'évaluation des politiques publiques.* Journal Officiel, Imprimerie Nationale.
République française. (2012a). *N° 2001-692 du 31 octobre 2012. Promulgation de la loi organique relative aux lois de finances (LOLF).* Journal Officiel, Imprimerie Nationale.
République française. (2012b). *N° 0254 du 31 octobre 2012. Décret n° 1198 portant création du Secrétariat général pour la modernisation de l'action publique et décret n° 1199 portant création du Comité interministériel pour la modernisation de l'action publique.* Journal Officiel Imprimerie Nationale.

République française. (2017). *N° 5968/SG. Circulaire du Premier ministre du 26 septembre 2017.* Journal Officiel, Imprimerie Nationale.

Thoenig, J. C. (1971). *Le PPBS et l'administration publique. Au-delà du changement technique. Annuaire International de la Fonction Publique* (pp. 97–114). Institut International d'Administration Publique.

Thoenig, J. C. (1974). La rationalité. In M. Crozier et al. (Eds.), *Où va l'Administration Française ?* (pp. 141–162). Editions d'Organisation.

Thoenig, J. C. (1984). Serviteur de l'Etat ou manager public : le débat en France. *Politiques et Management Public, 6*(2), 81–93.

CHAPTER 5

A Recurrent Process of Fabrication

What is often referred to as State modernization in France does not neatly fit within the categories generally used for international comparisons. The presentation of each of the major operations in the previous chapter does not seem to yield clear conclusions.

It would therefore be highly tempting to consider France as a special case, and there is no shortage of explanations to back that up: a backward civic culture, the cynicism of its political elites, and the conservatism of the civil servant unions, to name but a few.

To avoid the limitations of a monographic approach, assessment has the advantage of steering clear of an overly descriptive history of events, exploring instead the measures set out beyond the repertoire of good reasons and discourses. It is worth comparing these measures in terms of two criteria: the main public management methods that they promote; and the actor(s) behind a particular major operation, along with the roles they play when a policy is added to the agenda.

The relative proportion of continuity and discontinuity in this regard is decisive. A detailed inventory of the reforms concerned is essential if we are to assess comprehensive reorganization of administrative frameworks. However, this is no easy task.

From a public management perspective, a preliminary question must be asked. How should the administrative changes advocated by their promoters be characterized?

5.1 Apparent Discontinuity

The past half-century of initiatives suggests that the train of reform is made up of a succession of discrete elements. It seems that any attempt to reform the central government's administrative system is destined to be stillborn. Fifty years of government initiatives have made the course of events unintelligible. The labelling of comprehensive programmes conceals a virtual absence of achievements, while the constant stopping and starting is a source of despair for reformers. The steps forward are very limited, with somewhat of an exception around the amendment of the framework law governing budgetary laws, which are set in stone by the organic laws governing the State.

This Table 5.1 thus suggests strong discontinuity. When a new government team comes into office, the previous operation underway is highly likely to be repealed or stifled, and a new comprehensive programme prepared in its place. It would be very tempting to attribute this solely to the successive governments' temporary whims. This is an easy step to take, but one that leads populist observers to invoke the irresponsibility of the governing elites. Clearly, the ambitions of the eight programmes reviewed do not follow one another in a linear or cumulative way. Half a century of comprehensive reforms has resulted in a heterogeneous, even chaotic assemblage of numerous measures covering diverse fields.

The timeframe and duration set for a wide-ranging organizational reform are however decisive. Designing a framework to last can make the difference in terms of its effects. Setting an end-date from the outset does not have the same impact as leaving it open-ended. Likewise, a very short timeframe, one year for example, has consequences identical to those induced by the absence of a timeframe, especially as the electoral cycle is short. A reform is thus rendered all the less credible in the eyes of the administrative services expected to comply with it. All they have to do is lay low and wait for the incumbent government's next whim or reform. This is a low-risk form of resistance to change.

In the case of the major comprehensive operations affecting the administrative management of France's central government, strong discontinuity is evidenced. New programmes do not necessarily follow in the footsteps of those that preceded them. They take a radically different direction, removing any trace of the orientations set by the measures that preceded them even if, in some cases, this means following the same path

Table 5.1 Major operations launched in France since 1968

Major operations	Main methods	Initiators of the operation mobilized
Rationalization of budgetary choices	Cost benefit Cost analysis Cost accounting Control systems Programme budgeting	The newly appointed minister of finance
Renewal of public service	Public policy evaluation Service projects Responsibility centres	The newly appointed prime minister
Renewal of the State and public service	No specific approach or methodology selected (lack of time)	The newly appointed prime minister
Review of the organic law governing budgetary laws	Programme budgeting Annual performance projects Annual performance reports Fungibility	The prime minister and parliament
Modernization audits	Control of efficiency, capabilities and capacities	The newly appointed minister of finance
Public policy general review	Organizational mergers Strengthening the functional capacity of central staff units	The President of the Republic at the start of his term and the new minister of finance
Modernization of public action	Organizational coordination between field agencies Organizational change experimentation Policy evaluation	The newly elected President of the Republic
Public Action 2022	Institutional redesign of central government agencies	The President of the Republic at the start of his term and the newly appointed prime minister

Source: Authors' own.

but putting a new label on it. As a result, new measures do not always have time to get off the ground.

This discontinuity is also due to the areas covered by these major operations. They combine five dimensions in different ways:

- the management and steering of public organizations,
- the modes of action of the State,
- the definition of the central government's fields of action,
- the organization of public authorities,
- the State's relations with citizen-subjects and society.

The scope of the operations can include several of these dimensions. The eight successive programmes from 1968 to 2022 have all related to the field of management and the steering of administrative organizations. However, some have also varied in time and can be associated with other domains.

In 1968, following the adoption of the new planning-budgeting-system approaches, the RBC introduced ex ante economic policy evaluation in France. In 1989, the RPS programme supplemented the use of ex post policy evaluation with the introduction of quality circles and citizen consultation. In 1995, the RSPS also expanded to the organization of public authorities, in other words macrostructures. The OLGBL review followed suit in 2001: it changed another macrostructure, namely the relationship between the executive and the legislative. In 2005, the MA programme focused on the use of financial and accounting management audits. Ambitions were broadened again in 2007, as the comprehensive operation called PPGR sought to cover three areas at once. In addition to the management and steering of public organizations, it set out to reform the State's scope of action and the ways in which it engaged with fellow citizens. In 2012, the MPA programme, like its predecessor, also aimed to cover three areas. In fact, it focused on the State's mode of action but did not address its scope. In 2017, the PA 2022 initiative set its sights far and wide. Its promoters wished to cover four areas, while a fifth area—the State's scope of action—did not appear to be publicized as an ambition.

Some major comprehensive operations directly concerning the central government have also covered intergovernmental relations. For example, the reform of the territorial administration of the State, a comprehensive operation resulting from the major programme known as PPGR, which came into force in January 2010, affected both macro and microstructures. First, it redefined the roles of the *région* and *département* directorates of the central government, establishing the regional level as the locus of sub-national public policies and the *département* level as that of local services. Second, it grouped together, at *département* level, numerous previously distinct devolved State services, merging them into two or three inter-ministerial directorates.

All in all, this more-or-less chaotic discontinuity hardly attests to the central government's ability to learn from the successes and failures of its measures, and more generally to capitalize on learning processes. The more it attempts to change, the more it stays the same.

This has significant implications for conducting an assessment. To build on solid foundations, a reasonably long-term outlook is needed, even if it means looking beyond the cycle of a single reform. The devil is also in the detail of the processes involved in making these reforms, which may prove far removed from the ambitions announced by the politicians who design them.

5.2 The Same Tune

The political players at the head of the government may change often, the scope of the measures may vary with the programmes, and the approaches chosen may sometimes differ radically from one reform to another, but the tunes played for over half a century have hardly shifted at all.

Relative continuity in the approaches and methods adopted has become increasingly apparent. This succession of comprehensive central government reforms is a testament to the national authorities' persistence. An unexpected obstinance seems to transcend political currents. Four of these reforms were launched by governments from the centre-right. Two were initiated by left-wing majorities. One was launched by a president claiming to be neither right- nor left-wing. The eighth, the OLGBL amendment, was supported and approved by both the majority and the opposition of the time.

The reasons for investing in a reform offer and the way of doing so have fundamentally remained the same over the years. Their recurrence across party lines suggests that whether left-wing or right-wing, government officials who gain leadership of the executive are not mere illusionists acting out of political cynicism to fool the citizens. Nor do they naïvely underestimate the weight of the administrative reality under their control and for which they are responsible. The context in which these programmes emerge, take shape and are decided upon has an impact on their way of tackling problems—with the exception of the process to develop organic law, which is co-constructed by the executive and parliament.

Recurrent features structure the development of a comprehensive policy, with successive players adding a more personal and distinctive touch here and there. We have just provided a detailed outline of a form of continuity at play. The geometry of the domains addressed varies from one major operation to another. Revolving around the constant theme of reform of the central government's administrative system, the areas covered change according to the ambitions of the State governance. The project is tailored by its designers. Although its scope has fluctuated over the course of the eight programmes, the tune played by the various orchestras that have succeeded one another at the head of the State has remained the same. It presents seven common features.

The first recurrent feature is the way in which executive leaders proceed to launching a comprehensive reform. Most of the detailed design work is carried out at the highest level of the central government. Top-ranking political leaders assign or subcontract this task to senior civil servants who are often either members of their cabinet—the Presidency of the Republic, the prime minister's office—or from the major corps recruited by the ENA—the *Inspection Générale des Finances*, the *Cour des Comptes*, and the *Conseil d'Etat*. If necessary, a high-level statutory administrative structure is created for this purpose, headed by a person with such a professional profile. This has been the case in all major operations since the launch of the RBC in 1968.

A second dimension of this contextual continuity is the political and media publicization of these reform initiatives. To begin with, the incumbent rulers seek to make their mark on their term in office. As soon as a new President of the Republic or prime minister comes to power, their unprecedented comprehensive programme is publicized. This programme, a demonstration of the leader's supposed serious and proactive attitude, consolidated by their newfound legitimacy, is solemnly announced in repeated speeches broadcast throughout the country by the government's press services. It is designed to make headlines. The full message is twofold. The first part is bold and proactive: "I mean business, and it's for your own good"; the other, more implicit part seeks to reassure certain stakeholders, who will vary, depending on the circumstances: "I will nevertheless remain politically cautious."

The first few days really matter. It is as though it were important not to wait too long to satisfy what very much resembles a ritual conferring a credible and respectable identity that allows a president to be taken seriously, particularly by detailing the commitments and specific operations to be launched. Marketing takes priority for a while. What happens after the actual launch of a major operation is another story in the eyes of its political backers. Once the communication campaign is over, they will move on to something else. However, the aim of a programme is to achieve presentable results in the short term, that is, before the end of parliament's electoral term and/or that of the President of the Republic. Why should successors reap the benefits? It is therefore necessary to promptly undertake projects which, crucially, do not immediately give rise to too much resistance, strikes or demonstrations, or alienate supporters and electoral allies.

A third recurring feature, often explicitly formulated, is the drive to stand apart from previous government teams, whether they were from the parliamentary opposition or belonged to the same political majority as the new team.

Advertising the new programme's clear discontinuity from previous ones matters. In various ways, the underlying and often explicit message of new executive leaders is that they will do better than their predecessor. If need be, they blatantly discredit the previous team's record, claiming that their modernization goals and choices were a failure. They accuse them of having taken the wrong path and of therefore being unable to bring about acceptable change, irrespective of the brief timeframe of its implementation. For example, the comprehensive programme PA 2022, announced in September 2017, depicted the French administrative landscape of the mid-2010s as a dead star. The new government described the programme carried out under the presidency of François Hollande as declinist, whereas their programme carried a vision for a new age.

Another way of disqualifying predecessors' programmes is simply not to follow up on the measures they had launched, or not to use the associated frameworks. One obvious case was public policy evaluation. The framework developed by Prime Minister Rocard was simply ignored by his successors as an inter-ministerial steering instrument. It was revived a few years later by Lionel Jospin when he in turn became prime minister, but in a heavily amended and marginalized form, and was officially shelved a few months later.

France's central government is a graveyard of comprehensive reformist impulses. With a few rare exceptions, forgetting the past serves a demarcating function. The most noteworthy exception was the review of the budgetary process as part of the OLGBL. As explained above, this had major and lasting consequences on the management of the administrative system in and of itself. Unsurprisingly, the system was put in place for an indefinite period of time and, what is more, actively involved parliament.

A fourth constant over this half-century of comprehensive administrative reform initiatives is that they all came from the top.

These major comprehensive operations were designed following a predominantly top-down and non-participatory approach. They were governed by authoritarian means on the impetus of the ministerial authorities in Paris, their offices, or the personal networks of political decision makers. The style was discretionary, lacking any real consultation or prior substantive debate with other stakeholders, even if participatory consultations with representative organizations such as civil servant unions, employers' associations and associations of local political leaders were envisaged. This was the case in the PA 2022 programme. But consultation does not mean negotiation. The same goes for parliamentarians' consultation with their parties, including those belonging to the majority in charge of the executive. Decisions were taken in the form of decrees and circulars drafted at the highest level of the State apparatus, by the Minister of Finance, the minister in charge of State reform or the prime minister. The measures detailing them were entrusted to a very small circle of senior officials and advisers. The supervision of the monitoring, if not the control, of their execution was entrusted to services that were directly under the remit of the prime minister or even the President of the Republic and the political leaders of the Ministry of Finance. By comparison, ministries and State secretariats such as those in principle responsible for the operational oversight of projects regarding the management of civil service staff were marginalized. The highest level of the executive had the final say. The definition of the content of a programme and its mode of governance escaped the operational levels; it landed from above and they were required to execute it in accordance with the principle of hierarchical compliance. Internal consultation as a driver of management was at best limited, even if the RPS policy launched by Prime Minister Rocard was somewhat of an exception in terms of the management approach it advocated. Reform remained the preserve of a very small, closed and elitist inner circle.

The competence mobilized by the public authorities is in fact that of a State technocracy (Thoenig, 1987). In the present case, it stems mainly from a form of training that emphasizes legal procedures and approaches. It is neither technical nor managerial. Senior civil servants belonging to three major State bodies—the *Conseil d'Etat*, the *Inspection des Finances* and the *Cour des Comptes*—play a leading role. They inspire the programmes and orchestrate the laws and other decrees, fleshing out the details. In principle, they oversee the way in which procedures are implemented by the State services.

This circle is socially closed and cognitively homogeneous. Three frames of reference for action prevail: law, finance and, secondarily, economics. These languages are conveyed by professional cultures such as public law and budget management. Professionals and experts from other backgrounds are still very largely marginalized, if not virtually absent. Admittedly, the use of independent consulting firms has been common since the late 1960s and the RBC programme, but it remains essentially confined to methodological subcontracting functions. The same applies to academics, particularly specialists in the social sciences, public management sciences and public policy analysis. While they sometimes sit on committees, their impact ultimately remains very modest, irrespective of the quality of their contribution.

Unlike other leading countries in the field of State reform and modernization, French senior civil servants and government officials have steadfast confidence in their ability to integrate the public management innovations developed in particular in the United States or advocated by the OECD, without the advice or assistance of professional intermediaries. Neoliberal ideologies such as NPM seem exotic and even dangerous to them. Scientific research is not considered useful, except in the exceptional case of a few rare academic economists. All in all, the major comprehensive operations are thought out and designed in autarky. Few members of this elite have any real knowledge of the modernization policies carried out or underway in other countries. To this day, there is still the occasional member who, though considered an expert in the field by their peers, does not even know how to read the fundamental texts of public management published in English, the lingua franca of the discipline. The cognitive capital mobilized for comprehensive programmes singularly lacks international openness, at a time when it could be considered indispensable.

A fifth feature characterizes the common tune performed by the rulers.

Their comprehensive programmes clearly prioritize budgetary considerations. They exhibit financial rationalization objectives. Before the COVID-19 crisis, reducing the expenditures and operating costs of public services was considered an absolute must. In the programme they announced in September 2017, Emmanuel Macron and Prime Minister Édouard Philippe followed in their predecessors' footsteps: modernizing the State meant drastically reducing its spending. The figure announced was 25 billion euros per year, based on massive cuts in civil servant positions, the digitization of administrative procedures, and the redefinition of public missions. This stated ambition differed from that of previous programmes in just one respect: the way it was to be implemented.

The so-called PPGR programme launched in 2007 under Nicolas Sarkozy's presidency was designed with the intention to replace every second or third retiring civil servant across the board, in all central government administrations. When François Hollande became president, he deemed this approach too brutal if not reckless. In 2012, to distance himself from it and to appease the civil servant unions, he assigned the task of reducing public expenditures to the so-called MPA programme. Surprisingly, there were no quantified targets for detailed budget cuts, including the non-renewal of civil service roles, and no deadlines were set. Similarly, while in 2017 Emmanuel Macron spoke of the major benefit of significant cost containment, he was slow to specify how the cuts and gains should be distributed across early retirements, job cuts and pay.

A sixth feature of the French avalanche of comprehensive reforms is striking to the observer: they afford inhabitants of the country multiple benefits of various kinds.

The theme is a classic of anti-bureaucratic discourse, not only in France but also in other countries. Modernization is justified on the grounds of reducing financial costs by paying fewer staff and increasing productivity. However, at the same time, it is also claimed to guarantee a much better quality of public service, easier service provider access and processing of administrative formalities, a more attentive service, and better tailored handling of citizens' needs. Citizens are promised tools for expression that are no longer limited to universal suffrage and mediation by intermediaries such as local and national elected representatives.

As early as the 1980s, the RPS programme invoked the active participation of citizens as both an ideological and a functional requirement. Some 30 years later, Emmanuel Macron's discourse on the PA 2022 operation has rekindled this idea by presenting State modernization as a field of social innovation. His collaborators claim that the new age of public policy is first and foremost that of citizens' assemblies. Public marketing is extending through new and more interactive forms of participation. They address the new issues emerging—sustainability, environmentalism, the desertification of rural areas, and so on—through new consultation bodies such as local referenda and citizens' assemblies. The central government must be devolved. The governance of public affairs must be decentralized to public regional or local government authorities. The map of municipalities must be reformed by creating inter-municipalities that are better able to handle local affairs.

A seventh common feature of these comprehensive programmes is that they rely heavily on two methods: the creation of *ad hoc* institutional arrangements, and methodological modernization.

Comprehensive policies extensively resort to institution building. They advocate reforming the organizational charts of the services and competences of the central government's senior administration. They are exceptionally creative in setting up dedicated bodies in Paris and at the top of the ministerial pyramids to oversee the implementation of new measures. These bodies sometimes report to the prime minister's office, sometimes to the Ministry of Finance, and sometimes to a third minister. Existing services, on the other hand, are stripped of some of their responsibilities overnight or abolished altogether. These manipulations can even occasionally lead to overlapping competences between central services, when the creation of a new entity has not yet led to the closure of the one set up by the previous government's team. This situation was evident, for example, in the major MPA operation launched in 2012. Who does what and how becomes a real enigma. Deciphering the exact remits and drawing the precise limits of the services' respective competences is a matter of intellectual prowess for the observer.

The 1990s and 2000s are highly representative of this phenomenon, as the previous chapter suggests. While the name and status of these administrative bodies varied—delegation, general secretariat, directorate general, and so on—their missions were vague and their real activities not immediately identifiable, and they often rapidly came to an end. Powerful ministers coveted control of these bodies, and less powerful ones were suspicious. A few rare lucid voices, such as Jean-Marc Sauvé, former vice-president of the *Conseil d'Etat*, even dared to speak of Potemkin villages to describe this inflation of institution building. To them, the State's handling of administrative modernization amounted to a propaganda-driven façade. The fact is that it often seems to have run out of steam, with the redesign of formal structures guided by the aim of symbolic display rather than actual change to the incumbent services' practices and the motivation of staff. In the meantime, their short-lived existence causes civil servants, particularly those in the ministries that are accused of overspending, to react with incredulity and caution. The dogs of modernization may bark, but the caravan of management services will continue to go by as usual.

Most of the major comprehensive operations, moreover, offer their own miracle methodology as a key tool for administrative reform. The RBC programme, for instance, focused on economic calculations applied to the selection of investments through upstream evaluations. The RPS programme measured the societal effectiveness of any given State action through the ex post evaluation of a particular sectoral policy. The RSPS set up an inter-ministerial framework which, through a new State Reform Commission, would be devoted to establishing a both overarching and detailed modernization plan, setting the priority areas of central government missions and clarifying ministry officials' agenda for the next three years. Since the late 1990s, comprehensive policies have been playing the same tune. Methodologies partially based on new information techniques are considered essential levers of modernization.

Substantial funds have been allocated to bring the day-to-day running of public services into the computer and then digital age. The stated ambitions have been clamorous. For example, the RSPS programme provided that the State, working in "start-up mode," would build a new kind of public policy, augmented by digital tools. In short, technology is supposed to provide the universal key to progress. Yet there is reason to doubt public administrations' command of technology, at least judging by the difficulties and even the complete failures that have been observed in many of their most ambitious undertakings. Three major failures, among many others, provide ample evidence of this. The fiasco of the so-called Louvois software program designed to manage the remuneration of military personnel forced the Ministry of Defence to replace it with a new system from 2021. The project named the "national payroll operator," intended to manage the payslips of all State employees, was abandoned because it was totally defective. Finally, serious issues were encountered in the implementation of the Chorus application for budgetary management.

Focusing on organizational charts and techniques tends to mean neglecting the use of modern management approaches that make it possible to mobilize people in their everyday work context, to encourage and negotiate their participation in the development of their organization, to enhance the quality of listening between levels of the hierarchy, and to decompartmentalize sectors. Thus, to date and as far as major comprehensive operations go, the opening of human relations management to the social sciences in 1989 under the Renewal of Public Service programme has remained an exception.

The toolkit used to develop comprehensive programmes denies the singularity of the contexts in which the dynamics of change and the appropriation of their modalities by operational services are supposed to take place. It faithfully serves the political rationality of the executive leaders. At the same time, they work in autarky, beyond the reach of the other ministries and their administrative leaders. Their way of operating essentially mobilizes the approaches with which they are familiar: public law, the primacy of procedures, management through formal structures, top-down management by hierarchical authority, the primacy of compliance and cost control, and the conflation between efficiency and effectiveness of public acts. The advances made by the organizational management sciences are still largely absent. Stakeholder involvement remains virtually non-existent.

The rise of consulting firms is a relatively recent development in administrative modernization.

Until the mid-2000s, consultants were kept out of general government. Senior civil servants, particularly those in the budget services, had until then never decreed anything worthwhile in analytical accounting. They remained focused on expenditures as major concepts of budgetary accounting. A key concept of analytical accounting, such as costs, was foreign to them; it was often perceived as being of no value or relevance to the public sector. The organic law governing budgetary laws introduced in 2002 tempered their disdain somewhat. A clear breakthrough occurred in 2005 with the arrival of a finance minister who came from McKinsey, a large international consulting firm. The Modernization Audits and then Public Policy General Review programmes doubled their spending on consulting agencies, excluding IT services. This volume subsequently dropped somewhat from 2011 onwards, once the PPGR programme was ended. The large international firms were entering the scene. In 2005, the minister created a new department by merging four services and agencies. This apparently key department was called the general directorate for State modernization. It acted as a mediator between management consultants and the central administrations. Audits were the favourite product. This directorate general was allocated almost all of the modernization funds that had until then been scattered across each ministry. From 2007 to 2012, 115 million euros went towards consulting services provided by the leading international consulting firms, often at prices that were more advantageous or even lower than what they charged companies and banks.

The tenders, carried out in batches, associated a strategy firm and a more operational firm, with the former outsourcing to the latter.

Is this to say that private management is a Trojan horse making its way into the fortress of the senior administration? The reality is that the entry product is audits: either a product used by ultra-centralized management which serves to bolster its control and constraint functions, or an approach which is compatible with or even reinforces the steering by the Ministry of Finance. The ministry values audits of this kind because they enable it to identify opportunities for future spending cuts, the priority mission assigned to modernization programmes. In this sense, the situation is far from a sudden conversion to NPM. The hope of the consulting firms is that they will gradually be able to extend their offer to other projects, such as service projects and strategy.

This type of arrangement was taken up under the Public Action 2022 programme launched in 2017-2018. It was funded far more generously by the State. While reliable official figures are lacking, we can estimate that its purchasing budget was easily double of that allocated between 2007 and 2012, if not more.

Reference

Thoenig, J. C. (1987). *L'Ere des Technocrates.* Editions d'Organisation.

PART IV

The Appropriation of Toolkits

CHAPTER 6

Dashboards and Cost-Benefit Analysis

In order to conduct an assessment of a management instrument, an analytical framework is crucial. Our framework is organized into three main parts.

The first part concerns the genesis of the instrument. It considers the circumstances of its introduction into a given public administration system. It also examines its goals, which will have been made more or less explicit by those who developed it, or may have been highlighted by academics, or may even correspond to a theory espoused by the public authorities. It situates the instrument as it is commonly perceived, in terms of the two main purposes it serves: supporting decision-making; and reinforcing this administrative system's accountability.

The second part of the framework focuses on the major factors shaping the evolution of the forms, uses and status of the instrument. It highlights the punctuations, that is, the points at which the instrument analysed makes a comeback after first having been taken up significantly, and then having on the contrary remained somewhat sidelined or having essentially fallen into oblivion. This reappearance may be triggered by an intellectual innovation, an isomorphism informed by foreign influences or international doxa, a simple blip in its history, more appealing repackaging, or just a new use. This part of the framework also serves to capture the institutionalization of the instrument, understood here as its embeddedness in the field of positive law, particularly public law, and the consequent

© The Author(s), under exclusive license to Springer Nature
Switzerland AG 2022
P. Gibert, J.-C. Thoenig, *Assessing Public Management Reforms,*
Understanding Governance,
https://doi.org/10.1007/978-3-030-89799-4_6

creation of more or less general obligations to use it. If we consider judges as co-producers of the reality of reforms, it is also necessary to briefly describe their position on failures to observe the provisions enshrined in positive law.

The third part of the framework establishes a summary assessment of the current situation of this instrument. First, it identifies the wide range of uses and forms of appropriation of the instrument observable today. Second, it considers the balance between the different roles it is given around decision-making and accountability, as well as other possible forms of appropriation.

6.1 Tools That Reign but Do Not Govern: Dashboards and Indicators

The dashboard as a management tool has been known since the 1930s in France. For a very long time, it was developed within French companies without receiving any particular attention from academia. Books on the subject were written by consultants or practitioners in business. The dashboard was seen more as a practice than as a concept. It was not until the emergence of the management control paradigm, which replaced the old budgetary management paradigm and the shorter-lived controlled budgetary management paradigm, that the dashboard became of interest to academics. They categorized it as an instrument for implementing the new paradigm.

A dashboard is a document that brings together a limited number of indicators to help steer an organization or one of its departments (Gibert, 2009). This very basic definition excludes the compilation of collections of figures, such as social dashboards or economic dashboards. It also makes it possible to differentiate the dashboard from a service's reporting, a form of internal reporting which is also presented as a collection of indicators.

One of the reasons why academics long considered the dashboard of little interest may relate to an imbalance within the academic literature. This imbalance lay in the attention granted to the three dimensions that must be activated for a dashboard to make an effective contribution to the management of an organization or one of its departments: the teleological, metrological, and semiological dimensions.

Teleologically, the dashboard is supposed to relate to the objectives targeted and must therefore be linked to the functions of the organization or service in question, or to its strategy, to be more precise. It must also provide synthesized information and integrate a small number of indicators. This imperative is generally stressed by academics more than it is implemented in practice, for the dashboards used often tend to be voluminous, due to the fear of forgetting information that might prove essential at a later stage.

Metrologically, indicators are quantified representations of monitored phenomena; they should not be confused with the phenomena themselves. This is not too much of a problem for indicators relating to financial phenomena such as sales, profits or profitability, which are most often drawn from a company's accounts, and are therefore informed by standardized information. However, it is more problematic for so-called physical or volume indicators. Their elaboration requires meticulous definitions within templates that set out the method to calculate the indicators, the variables used in this calculation, and the data source that makes them operational. This work is necessary to avoid overly simplistic or biased representations of the phenomenon monitored, or the risk of their significance being misunderstood. Since the non-market nature of most public organizations precludes the use of financial indicators that could capture their outputs and outcomes, this requires physical indicators and considerable preparatory work.

Semiologically, and irrespective of their actual use, dashboards are designed to provide a meaningful—albeit simplified—picture of the functioning of the organization or service to which they apply. They express results better than long reports, which they can be considered, somewhat facilely, to complement or substitute. Smiley or traffic light notification graphics support this signalling function.

For a dashboard to be launched and used, its author must focus on these three dimensions. They must ensure that the measures displayed are as relevant and accurate as possible. Yet books on the dashboard long gave considerable attention to the semiotic function, in other words the formatting of the dashboard, instead of considering it only as a way of capitalizing on the groundwork carried out as part of the first two functions, which present far more challenging problems.

For a long time, French administrations granted little importance to dashboards. Their management concerns focused more on the means than on the results of public action. They thus made do with the largely predominant use of budget control documents closely linked to public accounting. In the most innovative approaches at the time, which were used by a central committee of inquiry into the cost and efficiency of public services, the nodal factor was the search for cost price. The indicators revolved around the activity measurement necessary to calculate unit costs (Descamps, 2007).

The turning point occurred with the first major comprehensive operation called the Rationalization of Budgetary Choices, launched in 1968. Its impact on the development of indicators and dashboards was twofold.

First, it informed reflection on the nature of public action indicators and the problems they raised. The second part of the RBC introduced programme budgets, distant precursors of the OLGLB programmes, thus requiring the dual task of clarifying objectives and monitoring their completion. Indicators were to track the performance of programmes against targeted objectives. It was during the preparation of these programme budgets that the distinction between means, output and impact indicators was first made explicit. This distinction was inspired by the American trilogy of inputs, outputs and outcomes, that is, the basic element of what is now referred to as the public policy chain.

Second, as part of its so-called management modernization component, the RBC involved operations to launch dashboards. These accounted for a significant part of the RBC actions reported by the different ministries—13% over the whole 1971–1982 period—even if the reality of what actually constituted a dashboard at the time can raise some doubts: "we can also question the relationship between the reality of the actions undertaken and the description provided. There is not always a real difference in degree between an action geared towards the search for a few indicators, one that seeks to create a dashboard, and reflection on a comprehensive management system extended to a full network of services. Chance, the whim of an operation's proponents, or even the trend of the moment, can influence the choice of the label characterizing an action" (Poinsard, 1987, pp. 40–41). Even in a ministry at the forefront of management modernization initiatives, such as the ministry responsible for regional infrastructure at the time, the results overall remained grim. Most of the time, dashboards recorded achievements without attempting to define targets or forecasts that could be used for variance analysis. Dashboards were not used as an everyday management tool. They did not articulate the different levels of responsibility, thus leading to the relative disappointment of the departments required to provide information which they did not see being used.

Some actions, however, stand out and are telling of the culture shock that management by objectives can trigger, especially when these objectives are translated into indicators that must reach target values.

In 1972, at a time when the RBC was still active, the Ministry of Transport wanted to introduce management by objectives. But the main civil servants' union in France denounced the fact that, under cover of enabling every public servant to be fully fulfilled in their work, the State was seeking to commit them to the objectives of government policy when civil servants had never been required to adhere to all government orientations (Gibert, 2008). In other words, the definition, negotiation and quantification of objectives emphasized the link between government policies and the daily work of civil servants, who saw this as detrimental to themselves. They stressed that civil servants had to remain answerable and faithful to public service.

Another significant action involved the national employment agency. A method of participative management by objectives was introduced in a clearly top-down manner, with a view to stimulating organizations more effectively than with the usual qualitative instructions and guidelines. It was intended to redirect staff efforts towards job placement rather than just receiving jobseekers, which the general management suspected its services of doing all too often. This shock was also experienced as brutal. The presidential elections of May 1981 led to a return to a more qualitative management system.

In the early days of this left-wing government, indicators and dashboards tended to be neglected somewhat. Programme budgets were soon put aside and then abolished. The government showed a preference for soft management rather than the combination of management by objectives and management control. While a balance was gradually restored, it was not until the late 1990s that the first punctuation occurred, with the appearance of the balanced scorecard (Kaplan & Norton, 2001).

The balanced scorecard soon caught the attention of the academic community, which investigated its relationship with the dashboard. It concluded that unlike the conventional dashboard, the balanced scorecard was based on a strategic model. This scorecard structured four categories of indicators, interconnected through relationships assumed to be causal: finance, customer, process and learning.

Fierce academic debate ensued regarding the degree of innovation that the balanced scorecard really offered, the more or less centralizing nature of its top-down construction, and the potentially more participative nature of the "French-style" dashboard (Bessire & Richard Baker, 2005; Bourguignon et al., 2004; Epstein & Manzoni, 1998). All in all, the plasticity of the two instruments, together with the difficulty of comparing the already long-standing application of a tool lacking a solid and widely shared doctrine, with a new tool for which its inventors had gone to great lengths to specify an academically legitimate doctrine, resulted in widely diverse conclusions regarding the positioning of the two tools. Still, many analysts agreed that the balanced scorecard was a particular way of setting up dashboards or dashboard systems (Gibert, 2009).

Meanwhile, some French public organizations were setting up a few balanced scorecard-type dashboards, generally under the influence of consulting firms. The most noteworthy scorecards were those of the Ministry of Defence and the national family allowances fund (the *Caisse Nationale d'Allocations Familiale*). In other cases, the application of balanced scorecards was limited to the use of the four categories highlighted by Robert Kaplan and David Norton (2001), without applying the rest of their method (Benzerafa, 2007). At the same time, alternative dashboard methods were elaborated, based on the development of more or less sophisticated portfolios of indicators. These models sought to cover the entire chain of public policy: resources, activities, achievements and impacts. They also reflected some administrative managers' desire to monitor the objectives pursued, along with the key success factors and the main constraints applied to them.

A second punctuation was the major operation to pass the organic law governing budgetary laws in 2001.

The dashboard and the associated indicators made a comeback with the OLGBL and the obligations it placed on government to set targets and be accountable for performance, through appendices to the budget review acts. Officially, these obligations were limited to providing parliament with a range of objectives, indicators and target values—budget—or observed values—budget review act—for each indicator at national level. In reality, the executive branch extended it to all State public administrations through the obligation to fund the operational programme budgets across which these programmes were distributed. When these budgets were broken down by local constituency—inter-*régions*, *régions*, *départements*—the national target levels were in turn broken down into target levels for each corresponding constituency.

Closer scrutiny however reveals the formation of a dual system of indicators in the most advanced administrations in this field. On the one hand, there were the indicators linked to the OLGBL; on the other, indicators were included in the dashboards that administrations had set up to encourage their own devolved services to implement tools to assist them in their management and/or to organize internal accountability to their central administration. This was the case for the Ministry of Agriculture and the Ministry of the Interior. In addition to this duality, the managers of the State's local services showed greater interest in tools designed for their internal use than in those required by the organic law.

The OLGBL was presented as a vector for management change—a pitch sometimes poorly received—primarily in areas where indicators were still rather unfamiliar. Ministries also designed new indicators to set narrower limits to contractualization processes. They expected that the operators involved would have less autonomy in expressing their own wills, and that the central government would benefit from a greater capacity to control them. This was the case for universities. In areas with more of a numbers culture, the OLGBL indicators were adopted following a distinctly bottom-up approach.

At organizational level, there was a formal management control network linked to the requirements of the OLGBL. It fell under the remit of the budget directorate of the Ministry of Finance, which was virtually directly responsible for controlling OLGBL programmes and had a network of management controllers for these programmes in each ministry.

A third punctuation was triggered by what was known as the Compstat (computer statistics) system.

President of the Republic and former Minister of the Interior, Nicolas Sarkozy, was strongly drawn to the Compstat system set up by the city of New York in 1994 to fight the urban violence prevailing in the city at the time. This system put pressure on police stations. Biweekly meetings were held to report on their actions, based on the analysis of large quantities of information gathered through a sophisticated information system consisting of a combination of technology, information and a form of organization intended to be extremely reactive (Willis et al., 2007).

Nicolas Sarkozy wanted the transposition of such a system in Paris. A few meetings on the New York model were held, with extensive media coverage. The system was never generalized or maintained in the long term. However, a convergence occurred through an OLGBL-type finance law, between this inspiration and Programme 176 of the so-called "security" mission of the national police. Among other things, this programme included an indicator called the number of deportations of illegal aliens.

This indicator had not been the subject of any particular debate in parliament, neither in plenary session nor in committees, where more rigorous examinations of budget documents submitted by the government to parliamentary assemblies traditionally took place. Neither the relevance of the indicator nor the level of the target set—28,000 deportations—had been debated. In fact, a figure of 25,000 and not 28,000 deportations of illegal aliens to be carried out was divvied up between the different police services.

The situation took a turn when the news spread that the Ministry of the Interior had summoned some 20 prefects. These prefects came from *départements* that were behind on the target that had been discretionarily imposed on them. According to the press, this meeting promised to be a difficult moment for them. According to Minister Brice Hortefeux, a conservative politician and close supporter of President Sarkozy, the meeting afforded an opportunity for debate, dialogue and territorial analysis. This summoning set off a firestorm. A public debate raged in the autumn of 2007 (Mauzac, 2007). This was an opportunity for the media to strongly challenge the relevance, validity and legitimacy of the indicator. Media coverage of an action announced and quantified in budgetary documents thus occurred only when the prefects of the *départements* that were behind target were summoned to Paris, in other words, when quantification appeared to demand action. This response lag is very telling of the appropriation, by the political class, of the performance figures presented in budgets.

The actual development of the use of indicators and dashboards was punctuated by a number of events that periodically drew attention back to these two management instruments, but which provide little information on their long-term evolution.

The first was technical. As the work to create indicators and dashboards spread across the administration, many civil servants discovered the invisible part of the iceberg (Gibert, 2009): unpleasant surprises abounded. Monitoring an objective could create the need to set up several indicators for an objective, to avoid a monolithic and most often reductive or even caricatured representation. The result was an inflation of indicators in the performance projects or annual performance report and recurring complaints by members of parliament who found themselves faced with too many indicators.

A second surprise was that the translation of an objective into an indicator could be seen as a betrayal if it was not led or closely controlled by the author of the objective.

A third drawback was the fact that the process of translation constantly entailed the interpretation of anything vague and abstract, and the need to clear up the vagueness and ambiguity that words and expressions could contain. This vagueness was sometimes unintentional, but more often than not it was deliberate, to avoid criticism by anyone who might be disappointed and by opponents. In other words, objectification through an indicator could prove politically inopportune, for it ran counter to the widespread idea that vagueness and ambiguity could be functional for the governance of organizations or public policies.

The fourth piece of bad news pertained to illusions regarding the importance of pre-existing information in information systems and the computer applications that could be used to feed the indicators being developed. Pre-existing information had been calibrated based on the uses for which it was originally intended. There was no reason why this calibration should fit the information's new use in a particular indicator. If the differences in definitions between the information sought for the indicator and the existing information were minimal, an imperfect adjustment without too much bias was feasible. If this was not the case, however, new information would have to be entered, thus losing the benefit of the hoped-for synergy. This is a reminder that information makes sense only within the context of its use—an adage that governments and the media alike have difficulty accepting.

The fifth unpleasant surprise was the corollary of the above-mentioned translation work. The long-term existence of a scoreboard or reporting instrument depended on the continuity of the objectives chosen and their translation. A positivist understanding of performance at least had the advantage of offering robust measurement standards. A constructivist perspective, on the other hand, meant that the scoreboard developed by a head of department could be considered irrelevant by their successor, who would redo the work or give up because they were not comfortable with the exercise.

The sixth problem was the need to audit the information based on which the indicators were calculated. This applied particularly when the information was declarative. Unintentional errors could abound where the information was entered too quickly. False information resulting from cheating was also to be feared, as shown by a striking review of data provided by the national gendarmerie (Mattely & Mouhanna, 2007).

The seventh and final difficulty was that the development of dashboards and indicators was not the end point of the work. On the contrary, it had to be the starting point for the operational phase. Once the information production phase was complete, the management phase could begin. The question that needed to guide reflection was thus about the way in which the information provided by a dashboard led to changes in the minor or major choices made within an organization or service, and to additional investigations into the pain points that might appear in the documents examined.

All these considerations tempered the difference in representations between cost accounting or management accounting, frequently seen by administration managers and local authority leaders as real labyrinths, and the dashboard, often defined by its supporters as a non-bureaucratic instrument. The high cost-benefit ratio waned with use. Another consequence was that there was little common ground between indicators set up following a methodical approach and hasty compilations of figures scraped from various sources, put forward without mention of the calculation methods applied to them or their sources.

The critique of management by results or management by numbers seemed to lump these heterogeneous elements together.

Transfer of learning was limited. The institutionalization of management control outside of the OLGBL was still rather feeble. Although there were management controllers in the ministries said to be spendthrift, or in the directorates of these ministries, there was no real management controller for the whole State administration. The budget directorate of the Ministry of Finance considered itself responsible solely for coordinating and facilitating the more or less informal network of so-called ministerial management controllers, who dealt with the tools specific to a particular ministry.

The State's doctrine was limited to a manifestation of soft law. This was illustrated by the practical guide to management control in government departments, a document published in 2002 by the inter-ministerial delegation for State reform and sporadically updated. It was intended solely for training and learning purposes and was therefore not to be used to set standards. Its purpose was to create an inter-ministerial frame of reference, and to foster the development of a shared language and the pooling of knowledge on management control in government departments. This meant that beyond the work required by the OLGBL, each public entity did what it wanted or what it could.

In the field of the OLGBL, however, a real learning process developed surrounding projects and annual performance reports.

Indicators made it possible to open black boxes in order to provide an adequate level of transparency by incorporating into the documents real templates that were initially missing. This was significant: instead of presenting a set of labelled figures, which the reader could interpret according to their knowledge and preferences, the methodological transparency that was gradually established allowed everyone to know the real content of the indicator.

The latter was characterized by a precise method of calculation, with full visibility of the variables comprising it, the way in which it was informed, and the data sources feeding it. This meant that readers with some knowledge of the matter could get an idea of the indicator's metric limitations: data input that did not align exactly with its raison d'être, the reliability of the basic data, the discrepancy between the name of the indicator and what precisely it measured, and so forth. The introduction of this relatively strong transparency, which was not often noted, was totally disregarded by the critics of management by numbers or management by results.

A second, more general observation relates to the purposes these instruments served, which varied widely.

The proliferation of indicators and dashboards was a reality. It was largely due to the fact that they provided a substrate for other instruments, the use of which was made compulsory in many public entities, or which was largely adopted through example. This was the case with contractualization internal to the State. While budgetary experts wanted to remove the State's financial commitments from most of these contracts, they systematically demanded indicators. Not a single contract escaped their introduction and the obligation for the co-contractor to use them for reporting, be it a university, a social security organization, a hospital or a State operator. In ex post policy evaluation, even where the evaluation was not limited to impact, providing relatively serious figures was mandatory. No cost accounting in a government administration was possible without counting the objects for which costs were accumulated. However, the nature of these objects was in no way straightforward if they were not material products (Gibert & Thoenig, 2019).

A plethora of figures thus existed, many of which cannot be described as management or performance indicators since they were simply data, without any possibility or real desire to act on them. Unfortunately, this plethora was a source of confusion. The State's flimsy doctrine offered no clear categorization of the different possible purposes of quantifying public action, nor any way of differentiating between the characteristics of the performance measurements associated with these purposes. For example, there was no typology distinguishing between six different acts: evaluating, controlling, budgeting, motivating, promoting, celebrating, learning and improving (Behn, 2003).

Without getting down to this level of precision, it is possible today to distinguish three very different uses of management or performance indicators in the practice of the French administrative system, which a cavalier approach tends to mix up.

First, these indicators are used to set up scales designed to objectify the distribution of resources between local and regional services or establishments of the same kind across the country.

Their ancestor was a points system known as 539 at La Poste, the postal service, when it was part of the former Ministry of Post Offices and Telecommunications. All operations carried out in post offices were measured in centi-minutes, a unit of time equivalent to one hundredth of an hour, used to time tasks. For many years the postal service also had its statistics department count the volume of its activities exhaustively one week a year, before resorting to surveys for this purpose. This very Taylorian system was used to distribute staff resources across the *département*-level directorates.

The Ministry of Infrastructure adopted a somewhat similar approach, which it called mission-means matching, to allocate resources among its field agencies. It thus took into account the fact that these agencies could have a very different portfolio of missions, depending on their geographical location: for example, clearing winter snow from roads in one *département*, and works surrounding the seafront in another.

The innovation in this type of practice relates not to the objective pursued but to its extension to fields increasingly removed from the industrial domain. This is the case with the distribution of resources to hospitals according to their activity, assessed using the number of patients treated across homogeneous groups, that is, the so-called activity-based payment system. This distribution method was also applied to universities, through a specific system. It was essentially based on the number of students belonging to homogeneous groups of students. This system, called San Remo, was later replaced by the system called SYMPA (*SYstème de répartition des Moyens à la Performance et à l'Activité*—performance and activity-based resource allocation system). Unlike its predecessor, it aimed to allocate a share of resources based on the quality of the work done both in teaching and research—under the category of performance! This was largely put on hold in 2015. A parliamentary report noted that four years later, the share of performance remained marginal in the public funding of universities (Adnot, 2019).

The stakes associated with these types of indicators are considerable, insofar as they act as a substitute for the market for services that are barely commodified, if at all, such as universities. They are so high that this logic cannot be followed through, for example by removing funding from those that are least successful according to the criteria adopted, in order to significantly increase the funding of the most successful institutions.

Such an approach would trigger a vicious cycle, with no way out. The sanction of the market causes the companies with the poorest performance to disappear or to be bought out by better performing companies. But this adjustment mechanism is very difficult to transpose to the distribution of funding between services or institutions with a monopoly on a given territory, or between one-of-a-kind institutions, since the sanction would primarily affect the population served by those services or establishments. This leads to the system being tweaked with a multitude of exceptions or simply being abandoned, as in the case of universities. The reference to the market in the doctrine of new public management then becomes more allegorical than real.

The second type of use of management or performance indicators encompasses all the indicators prescribed by the OLGBL law of 2001 or required by the various contracts entered into by the State with some of its operators or components. It is significantly different from the first.

The allocation of budgetary funding is here clearly disconnected from the targeted or actual performance of a programme. The same goes for contracts. The requirement to present targeted or actual performance is just a way to legitimize the distribution of resources to programmes or operators. This search for a new form of legitimization reflects the perception that the old legal legitimacy that traditionally underpinned administrations is no longer sufficient to justify them alone, and that the concept of performance, however vague, ought to be imposed on public organizations in the same way as private ones.

A third type of indicators are those used in the dashboards set up by directorates or ministerial departments.

They are the only ones that truly constitute steering tools and therefore the only ones actually integrated into the management of departments. They roughly follow the logic of French-style dashboards, a tailor-made tool for the head of a crucial responsibility centre. Their main drawback is that because they are customized, these tools risk lasting—in other words maintaining their effectiveness—only as long as the innovative manager who commissioned the dashboard remains in that position.

All in all, everything points to the fact that the situation of dashboards and indicators after the three punctuations mentioned earlier seems somewhat paradoxical.

Dashboards and indicators are omnipresent and are supposed to play multiple roles, yet they have never been institutionalized as such. They were mentioned only very briefly in texts such as the OLGBL in 2001 and the organic law of 2009 on the obligation to carry out an impact study to draft a bill. They featured in just a few passages that bore greater resemblance to user guides than to a clear State doctrine, in documents prepared by civil servants belonging to the administration's network of management controllers.

This dashboard and indicator pair, a giant with feet of clay, suffers excessive disregard due to its disproportionate notoriety. The saying "what you measure you get" clearly underscores the ambiguity of management by numbers. In a positive sense, it means that the establishment of an indicator makes it possible to direct and mobilize efforts towards a desired outcome (Paradeise, 2012). In a negative sense, it means that you get only what you measure and nothing else. Get the right indicator wrong, build an indicator that is reductive or biased towards the phenomenon you want to observe or tackle, and you will get a good result in terms of the indicator but not in terms of the underlying issues.

The stakes of quantification may not be as high as a cavalier perspective suggests, but that is not to say that fearing the counter-productiveness of careless quantification is unfounded. Is this really different from traditional qualitative approaches? The remarkable ability of any service or administration made up of somewhat seasoned civil servants to conform to the moulds prescribed by the instrumental policies of the day has been observed time and again. Practising civil servants have offered "projects," "quality circles" and "evaluations" when asked. Academics offer "professionalization" and even "multidisciplinarity" when required. Fortunately, the content may fit the bill, but it may also deviate significantly.

Ultimately the true adage should not be "what you measure you get," but "what you want you get." In a disciplined State, hierarchies formally get what they ask for, in whatever form they ask for it. However, the reality of what they get ought to be analysed carefully, in terms of both numbers and rhetoric.

6.2 Cost-Benefit Analysis and Friends

The use of cost-benefit analysis essentially dates back to the RBC period in France in the late 1960s (Thoenig, 1971). Considered the best decision-making tool at the time, it was sidelined even before the decline of the RBC, but never disappeared.

From the 1990s, with the rise of environmental concerns, governments' overt drive to fight the inflation of standards, and the French State's adherence in principle to regulatory impact assessment, this type of analysis made a comeback. However, the use of simpler methods of ex ante evaluation reduced its actual use, while the way in which the constitutional and administrative courts appropriated it transformed its role by making it an auxiliary of manifest error of assessment, a principle of jurisprudence designed to limit the anomalies of discretionary power.

Ex ante evaluation is part of the policy-making sequence, where it is used to determine whether the solution that policymakers are envisaging to solve a problem creates value for society (Bridgman & Davis, 2003). Within this framework, it can be seen as the equivalent of accept-reject decision-making for business investment choices. It can also be used to rank different options for a same problem, such as the best route for a motorway, or for different problems, such as the best programmes to combat various diseases. In the latter cases, it amounts to the transposition of investment project ranking methods for companies. In both cases, it can be considered a decision-making tool.

Ex ante evaluation had its moment of glory in France while the RBC programme launched in 1968 was underway. This programme consisted of three different elements: analytical studies, programme budgets, and modern management methods. Analytical studies were presented as the main tool for rationalization. In the doctrine disseminated by the government, they were equated with the use of ex ante evaluation methods. These methods were grouped into three categories: cost-benefit, cost effectiveness, and multi-criteria choice methods.

This original doctrine was appropriated in various ways. For example, a book, which became a reference, was devoted entirely to ex ante evaluation methods, giving no attention to the other two components of the RBC (Cazes et al., 1973). In the practices reported by each ministry, the term "analytical study" encompassed any method for the more or less rational preparation of decision-making. There were also debates at the time between the advocates or users of cost-benefit analysis, such as the ministry in charge of building and maintaining highways, airports and major national harbours, those of the cost effectiveness method, such as the Ministry of Defence, and those of multi-criteria methods, such as the Ministry of Agriculture (Gibert & Gagey, 1976). This was an important issue, as it pertained to the appropriateness, practicability and implications of the different methods for estimating the value of alternative solutions designed to solve a public problem. It referred, at least implicitly, to the issue of public value (Behn, 2003). The choice was between three significantly different conceptions of how to highlight a decision's effects a priori.

With the cost effectiveness method, calculations were structured around a desired effect considered essential: losses inflicted on the enemy in the military sector, for example, or the preservation of human life in the fields of health and road safety. This approach avoided the difficult issue of aggregating heterogeneous effects. However, it concealed neglected effects such as injuries and disabilities in the two abovementioned examples, or the destruction of property inflicted on the enemy in the military field, for example. The cost effectiveness method thus reflected an extreme focus on the concept of value in public decision-making.

Cost-benefit analysis involved the identification—as part of a system analysis—and inclusion of the various direct and indirect effects, both monetary and non-monetary (time, noise, life) that could be expected from the decision to implement each option. To calculate the overall outcome of a solution, these heterogeneous effects had to be aggregated. This aggregation involved monetizing non-market effects, in other words, using fictitious prices, valuating human life, time saved or lost, noise, and so on. These fictitious prices and values have delighted economists ever since, but they are a source of complexity and disagreement. Their calculation can fluctuate between a quasi-positivist perspective that posits the value of human life as the sum of the discounted cash flows of an individual's income up to their life expectancy, and normative perspectives. Such normative premises could state that all human life is equal by definition and therefore not differentiated by income cash flows. Even when economic factors are considered, for instance to price carbon missions so as to influence stakeholders' behaviour, normative perspectives supply the reference to legitimize policies.

In the multi-criteria methods, the expected effects associated with desirable objectives as well as the various effects considered undesirable by the public authorities and/or stakeholders were used as criteria to rank conceivable alternative solutions for a decision. This removed the need for a shared unit of measurement of effects, which could only be monetary, and could even spare the need to quantify each effect, since subjective ratings of each of the solutions compared could be used to assess effects criteria. System analysis and the exhaustiveness it required in principle to identify and process effects were very much present in the cost-benefit and multi-criteria methods, but less so with the cost-efficiency approach. The possibility of ranking the alternative solutions examined was a given in cost-benefit and cost-effectiveness analysis, but was more problematic with the multi-criteria method and in particular in its sophisticated variants. With these, the analysis resulted in the identification of core solutions involving a more or less extensive number of elements, which prevailed over the others but could not be classified amongst themselves (Roy, 1968). The reasoning exogenous to the decision makers, in other words the value of the non-market effects determined by cost-benefit experts, conflicted with the reasoning that could be endogenous to multi-criteria methods, since the effects criteria used were determined by the decision makers.

Thus, unlike in the case of the PPBS in the United States, where cost-benefit analysis was generally the gold standard, the concept of rationalization common to the three methods involved widely diverse variants, even if the aura of cost-benefit analysis gave it primacy, particularly among engineers from the major technical corps of the State, the great planners of the time. Senior civil servants from the ENA were far less sensitive to the appeal of these ex ante evaluation methods, and to the RBC as a whole.

Cost-benefit analysis was and remains the archetype of ambitious economic reasoning to overcome the tension between desired effects and externalities, and between the market effects and non-monetary effects of a decision, and thus to provide a single figure supposedly capturing the value of a societal project. It is the very type of instrument that offers a fairly clear overview of public management practices compared to similar practices in private management. It can be seen as a kind of extrapolation of capital budgeting based on discounting and especially the net present value method. Like the latter, it factors in the positive or negative effects occurring at different moments in time, sometimes over periods of 20 years or more, and therefore helps in making an intemporal choice. It differs from the net present value method of a classical investment choice in two respects.

In traditional investment choices, the viewpoint adopted is in principle that of the organization or company considering the investment, even if it is being considered by only one branch of the company in question. With cost-benefit analysis, the perspective is that of society as a whole—the nationwide society in the case of the State or one of its agencies—and not that of the State, let alone one of its ministries or other subdivisions. Public value is used as a standard of measurement in the case of cost-benefit analysis, whereas a private value is adopted in the case of the net present value method of capital budgeting.

A second major difference relates to the nature of the effects taken into account: cash flows, positive or negative and anticipated in the case of the classic net present value method; and all types of monetizable effects—value of time, noise, human life, carbon emissions, and so on—as well as monetized effects for cost-benefit analysis.

A third difference pertains to setting the discount rate, which is in principle defined as the weighted average cost of capital for the risk class of the investment concerned, in the case of net present value, and based on macroeconomic considerations for cost-benefit analysis.

In other words, there is both a shared source of inspiration and a fundamental difference between public and private decision-making tools. Their common rationality is understood as the normal preference for the prevalence of the positive effects of an investment—understood as any action which has intertemporal effects—over all its negative effects, taking into account the value of time and therefore the moments at which the different effects are supposed to occur. This shared source of inspiration can be considered as one of the fundamental vectors of the concept of management. The core difference relates to the effects taken into account, and is grounded in the differentiation of purpose: profit or, more precisely, the remuneration of the capital involved, in the case of private investment, versus the creation of public value in the case of public investment.

When the first high-speed train line was launched, the SNCF (*Société Nationale des Chemins de Fer français*) carried out a classic investment choice study showing that the solution it had chosen for a high-speed connection between Paris and Lyon and beyond, to the south-east of France, was forecast to be highly profitable for the company—which was not insignificant for a public company with a structural deficit. Based on the grounds that what was good for the railway company was not necessarily good for French society, the State asked it to carry out a cost-benefit analysis, which also proved highly favourable.

In their heyday, cost-benefit analyses were talked about more than they were practised. The same trend was noted in the United States with the PPBS (Wildavsky, 1969). The decline of the RBC and a left-wing government that formally put an end to a dying operation in 1984 contributed to the withdrawal of cost-benefit analysis. The arrival of ex post evaluation also played a role. Analysts who supported the latter emphasized its intellectual value compared to the excessively analytical focus required by an a priori quantification of the foreseeable effects of a decision in cost-benefit analysis and cost effectiveness. They also pointed out that it circumvented the regrettably corollary implementation problems associated with these methods.

Cost-benefit analysis did not disappear. More modestly, it focused mainly on questions of choice of infrastructure. The development of a high-speed rail network involved cost-benefit calculations, as had the launch of the first track. A similar process also took place for the development of major road infrastructure, particularly motorways. Limiting cost-benefit analysis to the most modest uses served as a test before gradually extending it. The public finance programming law of 31 December 2012 and its application decree of 23 December 2013 require a socio-economic evaluation of investments financed by the State. This cost-benefit analysis became mandatory for large investments exceeding 20 million euros. Among other things, it must be supported by a detailed description of the investment project, as well as the variants and alternatives to the project. The opinions to be submitted must be substantiated by relevant socio-economic indicators and public policy performance indicators. All of the work required exceeds the scope of a standard assessment and leaves considerable room for ambiguity as to what constitutes relevant socio-economic indicators and policy performance indicators. However, practice and the guides drawn up by government bodies show that this aligns with the tradition of cost-benefit studies (Quinet, 2013).

A general secretariat for investment has been appointed by the government to be the guardian of the temple or, if you will, the regulator of this evaluation framework. It is responsible for organizing an inventory of projects subject to evaluation and for preparing a general annex to the finance bill annually, called an evaluation of major public investment projects. It also commissions a second expert opinion for very large projects, appoints the relevant experts, and ensures their independence.

There is thus a real institutionalization of ex ante evaluation in this area.

A more ambiguous dimension of the revival of the cost-benefit instrument is France's publicized affiliation with the regulatory impact analysis movement that has been largely promoted by the OECD. The major French version of this instrument was called the *Etude d'impact des projets de loi*. Several iterations existed before it was fully institutionalized by an organic law of 15 April 2009. The law makes it mandatory for government to support the bills it submits to parliament—with a few exceptions, involving classified information for instance—with an impact study (Table 6.1). The expected content of the said study resembles a rigorous justification of all bills, judging by Article 8 of the organic law reproduced below (Gibert, 2018).

It is worth noting the importance, in this article of the law, of the requirements set out in the paragraph on the assessment of economic consequences. The wording suggests that a genuine cost-benefit analysis or a similar method is expected, at least for the option chosen by the government. This very much aligns with the international doxa. In the United States, for example, the term "cost-benefit State" has been coined to refer to the use of regulatory impact analysis (Sunstein, 1996).

Close scrutiny of French parliamentary life reveals a considerable discrepancy between the requirements set out in this law and the actual

Table 6.1 How bills should be justified. Organic Law, April 15 2019, art. 8

Article 8: Bills shall be subject to an impact assessment. The documents reporting on this impact study shall be attached to the bills as soon as they are sent to the *Conseil d'État*. They shall be deposited on the desk of the first assembly to which they are referred at the same time as the bills to which they relate.

These documents set out the objectives of the bill, list options for action other than new legislation, and set out the reasons to adopt the new legislation. They set out in detail:
- how the bill will be articulated to European law, whether enacted or still in the draft stage, and its impact on the domestic legal order;
- the state of application of the law on the national territory in the field(s) covered by the bill;
- the arrangements for implementing the provisions envisaged over time, the laws and regulations to be repealed and the proposed transitional measures;
- an assessment of the economic, financial, social and environmental consequences, as well as the expected financial costs and benefits of the proposed measures for each category of public administration and natural and legal persons concerned, indicating the method of calculation used;
- an assessment of the consequences of the provisions envisaged on public employment;
- the consultations that were carried out before submission to the *Conseil d'État*;
- the provisional list of necessary implementing legislation.

content of the impact studies presented by the government. While the provisions of French and European law regarding the legal framework of proposed bills are well respected, the presentation of the options rejected is botched or even omitted when it comes to the assessment of economic consequences. It is most often treated rhetorically, and the application of the various analytical methods diverges from what would be expected. Where the text of the organic law might lead one to expect a socio-economic assessment of a bill, one finds developments that resemble an explanatory memorandum far more, when an impact assessment is supposed to be clearly different (Gibert & Benzerafa-Alilat, 2016).

The wish to have major investment projects assessed a priori has led to a revival of cost-benefit analysis. The obligation to present an impact study for draft legislation would also have caused such a resurgence. Cost-benefit analysis was resituated in a broader context where it appeared as only one of a number of instruments, which pre-emptively relativized its importance. Yet it should integrate all types of effects, both costs and benefits. With environmental concerns comes a demand for targeted studies. The same type of requirement also applies to the costs that the central government is likely to generate for local authorities through its regulations.

Environmental assessment applies to projects involving construction or installation work, or other interventions in the natural environment or landscape, as well as plans or programmes by both the central government and local authorities or the public institutions they fund.

It is defined in the law as a process comprised of three elements: a report assessing the impact of the project on the environment, drawn up by the project owner or contracting authority and known as the impact study; a number of consultations; and the examination, by the authority competent to authorize the project, of all the information presented in the impact study, received as part of the consultations carried out and from the project owner or contracting authority. The assessment carried out by the project owner or contracting authority is a self-assessment. Its focus is certainly specialized, but the range of issues to be examined is wide. It includes effects on the population and public health, biodiversity, land, soil, air and the climate, material assets, cultural heritage, and landscape, as well as their interactions, as set out in the public environmental code.

The government wished to limit the proliferation of standards imposed on local authorities—one manifestation among others of the consequences of the standards inflation lamented by the political class. It is worth noting, in this respect, that close investigation shows that this class is itself behind a significant share of this inflation.

Significantly, a law enacted in October 2013 established a national council for the evaluation of standards, responsible for the ex ante evaluation of standards applicable to local authorities and their public institutions. It is made up of members of parliament and elected members of the different types of local authorities, as well as central government representatives. The government must consult it on the technical and financial impact on local authorities and their public institutions, of draft laws and regulations creating or modifying standards applicable to them. It can also be asked to assess existing regulatory standards, and may at its own initiative examine draft technical standards resulting from standardization or certification activities outside of a law or regulation, if the proposed standards are expected to have a technical or financial impact on local authorities. The draft texts submitted to the council must be supported by a presentation report as well as a technical and financial impact statement. This document is to be drawn up by the ministry proposing the text or by the general secretariat of the government. In the case of bills, the provision of an impact study removes this requirement.

The scope of the mechanism is therefore quite broad, since it includes an ex ante evaluation—the obligatory consultation for projects—as well as the possibility of an ex post assessment at the council's initiative. However, the assessment documents are left to the project leaders, in other words the executive and its administration. The texts do not impose a method. The template for the impact statement to present was established by the central administration. It is therefore not surprising that the court of audit and the national council for the evaluation of standards have both complained about the deteriorating quality of the information provided in these statements, particularly regarding the quantification of effects on local authorities. It is not however possible to determine whether the incompleteness noted is due to the absence of a database or to a lack of rigour in the work required to fulfil the purpose of the law. Despite these weaknesses, the national council for the evaluation of standards appears to be generally satisfied with the system, since it issues on average only about ten unfavourable final opinions per year.

To conclude and in summary, the take up of ex ante evaluation reveals a culture that is far more extensive than intensive. At first impression, the institutionalization of ex ante evaluations through several mechanisms currently suggests a far more established situation than 30 years ago, especially if we factor in the various practices and soft law supplementing institutionalized mechanisms. Thus, among the range of specialized evaluations, it is worth mentioning the health impact assessment promoted in France by the regional health agencies since the early 2000s, which evaluates the health consequences of public interventions in other fields (Jabot & Massot, 2021). Similarly, circulars have increased the ex ante evaluation work required for legislative and regulatory standards by making it compulsory, in principle, to analyse their impacts in terms of the fundamental issues of equality between all young people, intergenerational justice, and non-discrimination in access to rights and public services.

However, a more cautious analysis relativizes this sense of development of ex ante evaluation. The reason for this is twofold.

First, rigorous evaluation methods such as those presented at the beginning of this section are seldom used.

The legislative impact studies and the statements of impact on local and regional authorities offer a poor assessment of effects. Not only is the quantification of these effects largely lacking, but the methodology for their assessment is even more limited as a result. When cost-benefit studies are carried out, they are sometimes coupled with multi-criteria analyses which bear little resemblance to the sophisticated method used in the RBC era. These multi-criteria analyses allow each stakeholder to formulate the assessment of its pleasing for the project; the multi-criteria dimension then merely reflects a procedural rationality.

The second factor relativizing the impact of the institutionalization of evaluation is the change in the nature of ex ante evaluations caused by the practice of evaluative obligations.

Ex ante evaluation was initially seen above all as a decision-making tool. Somewhat idealistically, it was supposed to constitute a resource for decision makers without forcing them to choose the option with the best cost/benefit ratio or to refuse an action if its ratio was lower than 1. However, the obligation to evaluate changes the nature of the tool. It generally also means that the result is made public, which does not formally affect decision-making power but makes it more difficult for governments to adopt decisions that fared poorly in their assessment. Above all, this obligation has proven to be an instrument of control. This is clearly the case for environmental assessment, which can lead to a declaration of public utility not being made or being cancelled, thus making a project's implementation impossible. The same risk exists with socio-economic assessments. It is less present in the case of legislative impact assessments, given the leniency of the judge competent in this area, the Constitutional Council (Benzerafa-Alilat & Gibert, 2016).

This de facto transformation of a decision-making tool into a tool for control reinforces the confusion witnessed between management and control, which has long been denounced (Landau & Stout, Landau & Stout, 1979). It also legitimizes the predominance of internal control systems over management control systems (Gibert & Thoenig, 2019). It appears all the more questionable given that the control in question can ideally be productive when the stakeholders are involved as early as possible in the ex ante evaluation process, in accordance with the doctrine advocated by the European Commission in Brussels, for example. However, this is usually not the case in France, where most evaluations are highly endogamous.

References

Adnot, P. (2019). *Rapport d'information fait au nom de la commission des finances sur la prise en compte de la performance dans le financement des universités.* Sénat.

Behn, R. D. (2003). Why Measure Performance? Different Purposes Require Different Measures. *Public Administration Review,* 63(5), 587–606.

Benzerafa, M. (2007). L'introduction de la Balanced Scorecard dans les administrations de l'Etat en France. Premières conclusions d'une recherche empirique. *Politiques et Management Public,* 25(4), 81–97.

Benzerafa-Alilat, M., & Gibert, P. (2016). De quoi l'Etat rend-il compte dans ses rapports annuels de performance? *Revue Française d'Administration Publique,* 160(4), 1041–1064.

Bessire, D., & Richard Baker, C. R. (2005). The French tableau de bord and the American Balanced Scorecard: A Critical Analysis. *Critical Perspectives on Accounting,* 16(6), 645–664.

Bourguignon, A., Malleret, V., & Nørreklit, H. (2004). The American Balanced Scorecard Versus the French tableau de bord: The Ideological Dimension. *Management Accounting Research,* 15(2), 107–134.

Bridgman, P., & Davis, G. (2003). What Use Is a Policy Cycle? Plenty, If the Aim Is Clear. *Australian Journal of Public Administration,* 62(3), 98–102.

Cazes, B., Levy-Lambert, H., & Guillaume, H. (1973). La rationalisation des choix budgétaires. *Revue Economique,* 24(3), 519–519.

Descamps, F. (2007). La création du Comité central d'enquête sur le coût et le rendement des services publics: 1946–1950. *Revue Française d'Administration Publique,* 5, 27–43.

Epstein, M., & Manzoni, J. F. (1998). Implementing Corporate Strategy: From tableaux de bord to Balanced Scorecards. *European Management Journal,* 16(2), 190–203.

Gibert, P. (2008). Un ou quatre managements publics? *Politiques et Management Public, 26*(3), 7–23.
Gibert, P. (2009). *Tableaux de bord pour les organisations publiques*. Dunod.
Gibert, P. (2018). Réflexions sur l'appropriation française de l'analyse d'impact de la réglementation (A.I.R) dans le cas de la mise en œuvre des études d'impact des projets de loi. *Politiques et Management Public, 36*(3–4), 243–272.
Gibert, P., & Benzerafa-Alilat, M. (2016). De quoi l'État rend-il compte dans ses rapports annuels de performance? *Revue Française d'Administration Publique, 4*, 1041–1064.
Gibert, P., & Thoenig, J. C. (2019). *La modernisation de l'Etat*. Classiques Garnier.
Gibert, R., & Gagey, D. (1976). Une méthode de réduction progressive de l'incomparabilité. Conservation des forêts suburbaines et passage des autoroutes. *Bulletin de la Rationalisation des Choix Budgétaires, 24*, 34–45.
Jabot, F., & Massot, C. (2021). Similitudes et différences entre l'évaluation d'impact sur la santé et l'évaluation de politiques publiques. *Santé Publique*, 1–10.
Kaplan, R. S., & Norton, D. P. (2001). Transforming the Balanced Scorecard from Performance Measurement to Strategic Management: Part 1. *Accounting Horizons, 15*(1), 87–104.
Landau, M., & Stout, R., Jr. (1979). To Manage Is Not to Control: Or the Folly of Type II Errors. *Public Administration Review*, 148–156.
Mattely, J. H., & Mouhanna, C. (2007). *Police. Des chiffres et des doutes*. Michalon.
Mauzac, E. (2007). Les vingt cinq mille. *La lettre du Management Public, 69*(3), 1–2.
Paradeise, C. (2012). How Much Is Enough? Does Indicators-Based Management Guarantee Effectiveness? *Revue d'Economie du Développement, 20*(4), 67–94.
Poinsard, R. (1987). La modernisation de la gestion administrative: un bilan. *Politiques et Management Public, 5*(2), 21–63.
Quinet, E. (2013). *Evaluation socio-économique des investissements publics. Rapport de la mission présidée par Émile Quinet*. Commissariat Général à la Prospective et à la Stratégie.
Roy, B. (1968). Classement et choix en présence de points de vue multiples. *Revue française d'automatique, d'informatique et de recherche opérationnelle. Recherche opérationnelle, 2*(1), 57–75.
Sunstein, C. R. (1996). Congress, Constitutional Moments, and the Cost-Benefit State. *Stanford Law Review, 48*, 247–309.
Thoenig, J. C. (1971). Le PPBS et l'administration publique. Au-delà du changement technique". *Annuaire International de la Fonction Publique*, Institut international d'administration publique, 97–114.
Wildavsky, A. (1969). Rescuing Public Policy from PPBS. *Public Administration Review, 29*, 189–192.
Willis, J. J., Mastrofski, S. D., & Weisburd, D. (2007). Making Sense of COMPSTAT: A Theory-Based Analysis of Organizational Change in Three Police Departments. *Law & Society Review, 41*(1), 147–188.

CHAPTER 7

Evaluation and a Comparison

This chapter is a direct continuation of the previous one, which discussed the use of dashboards and cost-benefit analysis. The first section analyses the fate of a third management or public policy instrument: ex post evaluation. The second section then provides a comparison of the three instruments reviewed—dashboards, cost-benefit analysis, and evaluation—and their development and appropriation.

7.1 A Chaotic Journey: Ex Post Evaluation

The many different forms of ex post appropriation of public policies make it difficult to provide a definition that would definitively cover all these variants. At the risk of seeming reductive in our assessment, we adopt the definition put forward by Evert Vedung (2010): evaluation is a rigorous retrospective assessment of public sector interventions, their organization, content, implementation, and achievements or impacts, which is designed to play a role in future practical situations.

This definition has the advantage of highlighting three characteristic elements of the instrument. First, its object is public interventions. Second, its aim is utilitarian: evaluation is not a gratuitous act, for it aims to draw lessons for future public policy, even if the scientific rigour it strives for may seem excessive. Third, its field of inquiry takes into account multiple dimensions encompassing the nature and methods of the implementation and publicizing of results at the different conceivable levels. It does not judge the methods of evaluations, be they participative or not, and centred around the theory of action or not, nor the person of the evaluators, all of which create variants and are interconnected with the abovementioned uses and appropriations (Gibert, 2010).

How did evaluation originate in France? While the ex post evaluation of public policies became standard practice in the 1970s, particularly in the United States, it took longer for interest in it to grow in France, where it spread a little later than ex ante evaluation.

A few young academics studied it after spending time in North America (Thoenig, 2000). Some rare evaluations were carried out as part of initiatives that received no media coverage, were independent from one another, addressed issues that were not particularly politically sensitive, and were led by practitioners who did not necessarily belong to the administrative elite. They relied on ad hoc funding by a few researchers using study and research budgets allocated by ministerial services with little influence in the field of public management. From 1971 to 1978, 36 evaluations more or less worthy of that name were conducted. The fields covered related to national policies, particularly agricultural, environmental, public health, employment, and innovation aid policies. An evaluation of the national youth employment pact carried out in 1977 was the first to consider social assistance to the unemployed.

From the early 1980s onwards, references to evaluation became increasingly fashionable. There were nearly 300 studies on the topic, covering a wide range of methodological levels (Nioche & Poinsard, 1984). The inspectorates general of various ministries, while initially indifferent, began to show curiosity, hoping to add a policy evaluation competence to their traditional functions—particularly procedural compliance control and organizational audit—or at least to display it. A reform think tank close to the *Cour des Comptes* attempted to define a doctrine and know-how in this area. At the time, virtually anything could be expected of evaluation, which some saw as the key to administrative reform and others perceived as a way for central bureaus to control the activities of devolved services and agencies.

The institutionalization of evaluation in the decree of 22 January 1990, as part of the major comprehensive programme known as RPS (Journal officiel, 1990), appears as a significant step. Evaluation was presented as a reference instrument for conducting public policies (Thoenig, 2000). In a circular sent to his ministers on 23 February 1989, the new Prime Minister

Michel Rocard stated that there could be no autonomy without accountability, no accountability without evaluation, and no evaluation without consequences.

The system put in place at the time concerned only inter-ministerial evaluations. It made the prime minister the epicentre of comprehensive projects in this area, and comprised three key elements: a political leadership body, the inter-ministerial evaluation committee, which brought together the ministers under the chairmanship of the prime minister; a national fund for the development of evaluation, which financed the work; and a scientific council for evaluation, which guaranteed the quality and independence of the work.

For some zealots, this initiative was a source of great hope, even utopian ideas, for democratization. They believed it would allow for central government to be reformed, while the political intelligence of the nation was improved. Evaluation should not remain managerial—the preserve of the State administration system's leadership. If it was applied to themes involving the competences of several ministries, it should also be co-produced by stakeholders, and become pluralist and emancipatory (Viveret, 1989).

Comprehensive evaluation was off to a strong start. Some 20 commissions were taken on, relating to policies spanning a wide range of issues, from the protection of wetlands to the social integration of troubled teenagers. However, difficulties soon arose.

The hyper-centralization of the mechanism instituted by Michel Rocard did not encourage a lasting commitment by potential sponsors. From the outset, the comprehensive dimension of evaluation was handled by the highest members of the executive and them alone. The inter-ministerial committee ceased to meet after just three sessions. This halted the institutionalization of the link between the identification of policies to evaluate and the results of evaluations, on the one hand, and government action on the other. It soon became apparent that the better funded ministries, namely those of the budget and the economy, did not resort to inter-ministerial evaluations. They preferred having full control over what they commissioned, rather than taking up the free services provided by the national evaluation development fund. Commissions for evaluations dried up, and the system ran out of steam. This trend actually started at the end of Michel Rocard's term of office. The system was even put on hold by one of his successors, Alain Juppé.

Another development was even more significant in the long term: a head-on clash between the usual working practices of the senior administration and the practices of the scientific council for evaluation—the regulatory body set up to guarantee the quality of evaluations. In 1993, this council issued an opinion on the evaluation of the social integration of teenagers in difficulty. It stated that the claims made in this evaluation were not substantiated by the report and the studies on which the evaluators based them. The opinion was published at the same time as the evaluation report, in accordance with the principle of transparency that prevailed at the time. The members of the body responsible for this evaluation, unaccustomed to being publicly criticized, reacted strongly. This incident put the left-wing government in a politically uncomfortable spot.

This affair would be of anecdotal interest only were it not for the fact that it revealed a culture clash which left a mark for nearly 30 years. For this controversy highlights a general problem, regarding the cost of institutionalizing evaluation. One explanation, often provided at the time, pointed to a misunderstanding due to the undiplomatic behaviour of those in charge of the scientific council for evaluation. Its members were said to be unaware of the muffled ways in which intra-administrative rivalries were expressed, and therefore to underestimate them. This version of the story is just the tip of the iceberg, as subsequent evaluation practice in France showed.

In 1998, the new prime minister, Lionel Jospin, revived the comprehensive evaluation framework but abolished the inter-ministerial committee, on the grounds of its inefficiency and representativeness, and turned the scientific council into a national council. This change was more than symbolic: experts' role was restricted, while the major administrative bodies gained more importance.

The legislative branch, which had been absent from Rocard's mechanism, in turn made its own move. An experiment to create a parliamentary office for the evaluation of public policies fell flat. The National Assembly then created an evaluation and control taskforce, and the senate established a committee for the evaluation of public policies. Specialized evaluation bodies were also created. The National Assembly set up a taskforce for the evaluation and control of social security and a parliamentary office for the evaluation of health policies. Although these bodies' activities remained somewhat limited compared to standard practice in many other countries, French MPs hoped to also be able to boast an evaluation competence and to show that the executive should not have a monopoly in this area. In reality, they used it very little.

In 2008, a short-lived State secretariat was created under the remit of the prime minister, in charge of three functions: forecasting; the evaluation of public policies; and the development of the digital economy. It disappeared two years later without leaving any trace of its contribution to evaluation practice.

Also in 2008, an amendment of the constitution enshrined public policy experimentation at the highest legal level. Article 24 now states that parliament, which votes laws and controls government action, also evaluates public policies. Article 47 stipulates that the *Cour des Comptes* is to assist parliament in the monitoring of government action, the execution of finance laws, and the application of social security financing laws, including the evaluation of public policies. It is also to carry out evaluations at the request of the National Assembly's evaluation and control taskforce. This activity has actually remained very modest, since it is quantitatively limited to two or three reports per year. The *Cour des Comptes* is also to carry out a small number of evaluations each year, on topics of its own choosing.

In 2012, as part of the programme known as the MPA, the government planned to have all public policies evaluated before the end of François Hollande's presidential term. This would require an ambitious methodology. It would involve nothing short of building a collective vision of the issues, objectives, results and implementation methods of each policy. It was important to arrive at a "shared" conclusion and to ensure that the stakeholders of the policy under evaluation were involved in the work. Although evaluation was to be informed by a shared conclusion, its stated purpose was nevertheless managerial and had to relate to the efficiency of the policy. The aim was both to make the actions of the different actors more coherent and to significantly improve the efficiency of public policy. A requirement was set to respond to new needs while meeting the government's budgetary commitments.

From 2017 and the start of Emmanuel Macron's five-year term, the policy of comprehensive evaluation of all public policies disappeared, meaning that there was no longer an institutionalized mechanism at executive level. The National Assembly, on the other hand, showed interest in evaluation by establishing an "evaluation spring" through the vote on the law on regulations, with the aim of reasserting its appropriation of the constitutional competence granted to parliament since 2008.

All that for this? Overly stringent meta-evaluators or a truly disappointing reality? More than 20 years after taking off in France, in practice policy evaluation remains a tool of limited use. False hopes abound. So do failures.

Admittedly, a count by the French Evaluation Society showed that between 2007 and 2017 a total of around 500 ex post evaluations were launched. This figure should be interpreted with caution, however, almost as a way of promoting the instrument commercially, even if it meant stretching far afield. The numbers hide widely diverse understandings of evaluation. Each institutional player has its own. In its broadest sense, it could refer to any analysis of data using qualitative methods resembling the monitoring or even control of a policy.

Existing meta-evaluations arrive at harsh conclusions. Given the repeated absence of interpenetration between sociology and evaluation practice, one of these is very negative regarding the evaluations carried out, at least at local level (Ould Ferhat, 2013). It denounces their simplistic interpretation of causal relations, the lack of deconstruction of representations, the practical imperatives hindering in-depth understanding, their normativity, their utilitarianism and political instrumentalization, and their sanitized critique.

Another evaluation commissioned from private consultants by the general secretariat for the modernization of public action offers a rare example of risk taking by government, which was willing to have the possible shortcomings of its operation exposed (KPMG and Quadrant Conseil, 2017). It shows both the type of appropriation of evaluation observed for this operation and the methodological weaknesses that the panel of evaluations audited revealed. The choice of subjects, left to the relevant ministry's initiative, involved a set of themes that varied widely in scope and in the issues at stake, such as the licences of live performance entrepreneurs at one end and housing policy at the other. This choice was made without coordination with other evaluation frameworks, which may have created more or less desirable overlaps. The evaluation teams, which were mainly comprised of civil servants from control departments or bodies, rarely had access to evaluation expertise and even more rarely turned to external experts. The lack of definition of policy objectives made it very difficult to assess their effectiveness. In half of the cases, it was difficult for the auditors to distinguish between conclusions that were based on factual findings and those that were based on the evaluators' opinions. Very few of the evaluations reported the action theories underlying the policies evaluated.

In all cases, the diagnostic stage was very brief, so as to devote the maximum amount of available time to recommendations. All in all, the desire to prepare future decision-making clearly prevailed over the identification of the knowledge to be drawn from the analysis of the past.

An evaluation of the policy pertaining to legal aid provides an example bordering on caricature: specifications defining the recommendations to be made; an extremely short two-month timeframe for carrying out the diagnosis; completely fragmented questions; a partnership limited to the participation of lawyers' representatives on a steering committee and the failure to distribute a questionnaire to users; a methodology based on interviews as well as discussions within the steering committee; and a systematic bias towards minimizing financial costs.

Many of the evaluations conducted as part of the MPA operation can be classified as politically controlled. This type of control can be inferred from the mandate given to the evaluators, particularly when it sets detailed or even compulsory limits on the scope of the study, the recommendations to be made, or the timeframe for their implementation.

These examples however cannot be used to assess the overall state of evaluation practice, for it involves numerous sectoral mechanisms, particularly in the field of health, which last longer than major comprehensive operations and have greater resources than do studies commissioned by smaller local or regional authorities.

What causes, then, explain the somewhat immature situation of ex post evaluation in France until the 1980s (Thoenig, 2000)? Why do some observers speak of the poor institutionalization of ex post evaluation in France, while others consider France as a positive example in this respect?

The answer lies in the fact that the term "institution" is used in two different ways. Optimists implicitly refer to the permanence that seems to be bestowed upon evaluation through its inclusion in relatively high-ranking legal standards, namely at least a decree, a law, an organic law or even the constitution. Sceptics, on the other hand, associate institutionalization with the existence of a community of more-or-less recognized experts, methodologies that are to some extent shared, and professional rules that are strictly observed. This is where the shortcomings of the situation in France lie, due to the country's administrative culture, on the one hand, and on the other, to the behaviour of the professionals that usually perform evaluations.

The situation in France actually reveals a game involving four groups of actors, the outcome of which is hardly positive.

The first group is comprised of the political sponsors and the administrators who directly assist them, particularly in the ministerial cabinets.

Admittedly, almost all governments nowadays claim to support ex post evaluation. Yet sponsors' stated appetite for evaluation ought to be examined with great caution. To the political world, a properly conducted evaluation, in other words one that is entrusted to a third party, is a threat and a source of criticism more than a source of useful insight into the consequences of its policies. Their attitude is: evaluate, sure, but on one condition, we must control the process from start to finish. Subcontractors can be in charge of collecting and processing data, but we will handle the analysis, the conclusions and the implications.

The first ruse that governments use is to commission evaluations of objects for which they cannot be held responsible. This was the case a few years ago with the evaluation-reviews of the policies of predecessors in power. A typical example at national level is the evaluation-review of the GRPP carried out under Nicolas Sarkozy and evaluated under François Hollande (Inspection générale de l'administration et al., 2012). This evaluation-review enabled Hollande to state in a press release of 25 September 2012 that, based on the recommendations of the taskforce, the government was embarking on a new policy of public action modernization, which resolutely departed from the short-term strategy and "blind" (sic) method of his predecessor's GRPP. Another manifestation of this tactic is to evaluate objects that can be called policies only in the broadest sense of the term, namely everything that the State does in a given field. The object to evaluate is then comprised of measures taken over time, in pursuit of widely diverse or even contradictory objectives, guided by heterogeneous theories of action. Negative assessments of this object by the evaluator cannot then be attributed to those in power and in the vast majority of cases the main recommendation will be to draw up a real policy, that is, a more coherent whole, an appeal to rationality that cannot overshadow the powers of the moment.

In addition to shifting the object to evaluate in this way, there is no shortage of avenues available to a government wishing to demonstrate virtue by having its own policies evaluated while limiting the risks of the evaluation turning against it. The vague nature of many policy objectives makes it possible to challenge the impact indicators that evaluators use, for in order to develop these indicators they will have had to perform inherently contestable translations of the objectives. The publication of the evaluation may be limited to a summary that smooths over rough edges or to an *ad usum delphini* version, while the first version remains known only to the evaluation sponsor. The evaluation protocol structuring the evaluators' work may constrict them in a way that excludes the most threatening problems to raise. The timeframe granted to the evaluator due to the policy requirements may preclude any in-depth investigation (Gibert & Saussois, 2014).

The second player in the game consists of the major administrative bodies.

The administrative elites consider themselves qualified to carry out evaluations because in their eyes their members master a skill that outsiders do not. They are administrative generalists, which is not the case of consultants, let alone academics. Their ability to manage a new instrument is what they claim to be their seal of excellence. The journey of evaluation has essentially been defined and delimited by the leaders of central government. Although it has become a major point of reference for comprehensive modernization policies, it is kept on a tight leash by State officials who have not received in-depth analytical training, and it is developing without close and continuous links with the academic research community. As a result, it does not meet one of the two primary requirements of ex post evaluation as an instrument of modernization: being entrusted to independent professionals.

The third player in the game is consulting firms.

The rise of ex post evaluation has led to the growth of the evaluation industry, with the creation of evaluation firms specialized in general or sectoral evaluation, most of which are small and work mainly for local authorities. Large firms carry out little evaluation per se, which contrasts with their growing use for major comprehensive reforms. These firms have come to see evaluation as a very low-profit activity.

The fourth player in the game is the academic community.

This actor is a heterogeneous group split up along disciplinary lines. Evaluation appears to be of interest primarily to social scientists, particularly sociologists and political scientists, as well as management experts and economists. But these different disciplines' participation in the evaluation movement is no foregone conclusion. This is reflected by the composition of the professional society of evaluators, where most members are local government officials and evaluation consultants. There are very few representatives of the academic world.

Policy analysis, conceived as a sub-discipline of political science, initially claimed to be a science of action that embraced prescription. However, this position was short-lived. Academicism prevailed. These prescriptions needed to be hidden, for working with practising managers was like sleeping with the devil (Bézes and Pierru, 2012). Evaluation was accused of spreading a managerial ideology through NPM (Lacouette-Fougère & Lascoumes, 2013). Added to this was the rise of a constructivism advertised as such or latent, with a so-called cognitive approach to public policy (Muller, 2000), where reflection on meaning took precedence over work on factual precision and detailed analysis of implementation and costing problems.

The few management experts found in public management long studied mainly the management of public organizations rather than the management of public policies. Most of them have lost interest in evaluation.

French economists were slow to take an interest in ex post evaluation. Rightly or wrongly, the latter fell under applied economics, cost-benefit analysis or econometrics, whereas the mainstream focused more on theoretical economics with a predominantly deductive approach. Some of those who were drawn to evaluation made statements bordering on arrogance, pointing to the small number of individuals—including themselves—capable of doing ex post evaluation in France. Moreover, faced with the existence of a mass of evaluations in which they were not involved, they resorted to differentiating between—not to say opposing—evaluations centred on implementation and performance analysis, on the one hand, and impact analysis on the other (Bono et al., 2021). They called for restoring the balance to better include impact assessment, despite the small number of economics laboratories capable of doing so. This position reflects a poor understanding of the logic of evaluation and a reductive view of the concept of performance.

The logic of evaluation calls for a feedback loop between the characteristics of implementation and the results—whether expressed in terms of public policy outputs or in terms of impact—and not for the separate study of the process of implementation of a public policy and its provisional or final results. As for performance, its implicit reduction to monitoring the outputs of a public policy is bewildering and reminiscent of the most regrettable excesses of NPM sycophants. In short, this position reflects a lack of understanding of the solid link between the logic of evaluation and public management.

A host of factors thus hinders or at least slows down the transition from the legal institutionalization of evaluation to more in-depth institutionalization, which would involve bringing closer together the different actors who request and offer evaluation around more or less compatible methodologies, deontologies and conceptions of evaluation. An evaluation policy consisting of something other than an untenable agenda, with a distribution of roles to institutions that does not fail to take into account their expertise or overlook the fact that the prevailing administrative culture is hardly compatible with that of evaluation, could help to alleviate this situation.

7.2 A Comparative Assessment of Three Toolkits

At first, things seem quite clear as regards each of the three instruments.

Indicators and dashboards are informed by a cybernetic approach to management control. The monitoring of objectives and their key success factors is supported by targets. The observation of discrepancies between actual results and these targets must be the starting point for reflection on the relevance of a strategy and its execution, irrespective of whether this is formalized by complementary tools such as planning and programming, as in the case of the RBS operation in 1968. The dominant paradigm is indeed retroaction on the choices made in the prospective stages of a management cycle, through the analysis of the results presented in a dashboard published periodically.

As regards ex ante evaluation using the cost-benefit method, even though it is always presented as a decision-making tool and in no way as a constraint on decision makers, the fact that every study is made public is seen as an attack on discretionary power. When experts and those who "know" say that Solution X is better than Solution Y, the decision maker's choice is somewhat limited. In practice, rigorous cost-benefit analysis is a constraint for decision makers because they are strongly encouraged to choose the solution to a problem with the best cost/benefit ratio.

Although the term "cost-benefit State" emerged only later with the regulation of this instrument's use, some saw it from the outset as a frontal attack on political rhetoric in the field of public choices and on decision makers' verbose argumentation. As for ex post evaluation—that the utilitarian variant of policy analysis made fashionable—it is underpinned by the idea that while all public policies are explicitly or implicitly based on a theory of action, only the implementation of a policy and a proper evaluation of both its results and its implementation can improve its chances of it being effective. Learning by doing is therefore the dominant paradigm of ex post evaluation and of its close relative, experimentation.

In theory, the three instruments are decision-making tools that work on different time scales.

The dashboard is meant to help with responsiveness. In the reality of the French administration, it performs poorly on this front, given the length of the time periods it covers. At best, these periods are quarterly; more often than not, they are biannual or annual. Admittedly, in ordinary times the guarantee of resources afforded by an annual budget means that responsiveness is not a matter of financial survival in the public administration in the way it may be in a private company.

Ex ante evaluation mostly supports major decision-making. These are the decisions for which the cost/benefit ratio is probably most useful. With ex post evaluation, the decision-making support dimension theoretically consists in highlighting desirable changes to a policy or replacing it with an alternative policy. In practice, exercising this role is problematic, insofar as such an evaluation can only be carried out after a certain amount of time has lapsed since the implementation of a programme, the evaluation is itself time-consuming, and the programme being evaluated may no longer be at the top of the government's agenda by the time a serious evaluation can be carried out.

In theory, therefore, the three instruments play very different and complementary roles in the quest for public policy effectiveness and efficiency.

If we posit that in both the public and the private sectors, cost is largely determined by formative decisions such as the degree of complexity of a policy, the choice of greater or lesser degrees of capital-intensive modes of production, and the choice of processes, then the focus must first be on ex ante evaluation. Trying to improve efficiency at a given degree of legal complexity and with a given production method can only lead to modest results. The contribution of dashboards, like that of cost accounting, can but be disappointing. However, the quality of ex ante evaluations, like that of any forecast, is always problematic and improving it would theoretically require the use of ex post evaluation results.

In terms of accountability, the dashboard's close relative, reporting, best exemplifies the conjunction of the old accountability obligation and quantitative modernity. The limit to the reality of this function lies in the difficulties that hierarchies have in clarifying their expectations of the services under their remit and, more generally, in the difficulties of operationalizing the notion of performance in the public sector (Benzerafa-Alilat & Gibert, 2016). As for cost-benefit analysis, it can be an accountability tool if the decision maker communicates the solution they have chosen based on a cost-benefit analysis. An ex post evaluation made public is an accountability tool. It must therefore be made public without any underhand tricks such as adopting a publication style consisting solely of an evaluation summary, a protocol or specifications that prevents the evaluator from addressing potentially thorny problems. Obviously, it is only an accountability tool if it relates to a programme initiated and owned by those in power at the time of its publication.

The life of the three instruments cannot be equated with a long, quiet or stagnant river. It has been interspersed with many punctuations that differ widely in kind and origin.

Some of these punctuations stemmed from the implementation of major comprehensive reforms. Indicators and dashboards were initially boosted by two of the three components of the RBC, namely the programme budget and modern management methods, and again by the performance component of the OLGBL. Cost-benefit analysis and the other ex ante evaluation methods were much the same as the first component of this RBC. Ex post evaluation, on the other hand, came to the fore in the SPR era. It was in principle generalized to all public policies by the comprehensive MPA operation in 2012.

Other punctuations occurred where French governments embraced international doxa with a greater or lesser degree of conviction. This was the case in particular with the introduction of the legislative impact study, the main French version of the regulatory impact assessment, which breathed new life into ex ante evaluations.

Sometimes punctuations arose from academic debates combined with the activism of consulting firms. This was the case of the indicators and dashboards attending the revival that was triggered by the balanced scorecard's emergence. These debates and consultants' offerings may themselves have been the indirect cause of a punctuation when they influenced decision makers in the adoption of major reforms, for instance in the case of ex post evaluation, with the comprehensive public service renewal programme. Other punctuations can be linked to sectoral concerns, as in the case of environmental concerns, with the introduction of compulsory environmental impact assessments or health impact assessments, both involving ex ante evaluation methods.

The institutionalization of these three instruments can be characterized by the level at which the instrument sits within the hierarchy of standards, as well as the degree of precision of the duties it creates within the political-administrative sphere for the authorities or officials who are subject to it.

Overall, the most striking feature of the last half-century is the rise of institutionalization. In the late 1960s, at the time of the RBC, it was minimal; an order and a decree established the RBC, which meant that it was the preserve of regulatory power and that its permanence or rapid disappearance was at the sole discretion of the government in place. By the early twenty-first century, this was no longer the case. The use of management instruments was enshrined in laws, namely for socio-economic assessment and environmental assessment in the case of ex ante evaluation. Sometimes these instruments were even enshrined in organic laws, such as the OLGBL in the case of performance indicators and the organic law of 2009 in the case of legislative impact studies and therefore ex ante evaluation. This incorporation into the law took place at various levels, through decrees, ordinances, laws and even constitutional law. Since 2008, Article 24 of the Constitution stipulates that parliament shall evaluate public policies, which involves ex post evaluation even if this is not explicitly stated in the text.

This rising trend may serve as supporting evidence for observers who see a managerialization of the law at play. However, it cannot be assessed without also taking into account three other elements.

First, this institutionalization, endorsed if not intended by the legislative and constitutional powers, coexists with more flexible law governing diverse uses of the three instruments in many circumstances.

These are simple circulars which, in the framework of the comprehensive operation known as PA 2022, organize the new accountability system set up by Emmanuel Macron. The president wanted to set up a kind of barometer to measure the performance of many public policies. It would make it easier to attract the attention of public opinion than the annual performance reports defined in 2001 within the framework of the OLGBL, which were more institutionalized but had become outdated. The ex post evaluation policy carried out under the presidency of Francois Hollande, Emmanuel Macron's predecessor, was not even governed by a decree, unlike the first inter-ministerial evaluation policy launched by Michel Rocard within the comprehensive operation called RPS.

The second element is the widely diverse level of precision of institutionalized rules.

Some texts provide extensive detail on the work to be carried out. This is the case of the organic law introducing impact studies, and of the laws on ex ante socio-economic or environmental assessments. Others are very concise on this point. This is the case of the OLGBL, which stipulates only that precise objectives and indicators must be appended to the annual budget. However, the rest of the performance framework that emerged from this operation was defined by the government and not by parliament. This was also the case with the inclusion of evaluation—most likely ex post—in the French constitution. This inclusion was symbolically highly significant, as policy evaluation acquired the status of a third parliamentary function, alongside voting on the law and monitoring government action. However, its implementation in the form of a scientifically oriented evaluation proved difficult.

The third element to take into account in assessing the extent of management instruments' institutionalization is the judge's attitude towards managerial standards enshrined in positive law.

Depending on the instrument, the acuteness of the problem of this attitude's impact differed widely. Thus, such institutionalization soon appeared to be marginal for performance indicators, as the only ruling on the matter by a judge, in this case at the *Conseil Constitutionnel*, was requested in 2016 for the first budget drawn up according to the OLGBL standards. Among the grievances invoked by members of the parliamentary opposition against the promulgation of the finance law adopted by parliament was the inadequacies of the information provided to them by the performance indicators in the annexes to the bill: a lack of information on the indicators, the poor relevance of certain objectives or indicators, and so on. They argued that it was therefore unduly exempted from the accountability obligation introduced by the new organic law. As a result, the quality of parliamentary control over the budget vote was undermined. The *Conseil Constitutionnel* did not side with the applicants, considering that the novelty of the exercise could excuse certain shortcomings (Gibert & Verrier, 2016) which should be remedied in the future. It is not known at present whether this idea of "must do better in the future" signalled that the judge's expectations would be more stringent in the future, or whether it was a symbolic acknowledgement of the provision of the organic law that required "precise indicators" to which the judge would have given only limited consideration. To our knowledge, since that time no appeal against a voted budget has been based on the grievance invoked against the 2006 budget.

There is no case law on ex post evaluation. This is probably because it is not constrained by precise rules and ultimately carries little weight in political and administrative life. The situation is more complex for ex ante evaluation, primarily because there are many cases of institutionalization. As far as legislative impact studies are concerned, the judge, in this case the *Conseil Constitutionnel*, quickly made it clear that it intended to intervene only in a very subsidiary capacity. It considered that, however implicitly, the committee of chairpersons of an assembly had used the documents submitted by the government—including the impact study—to produce its assessment of the satisfactory or unsatisfactory nature of the content of this study. This position of the *Conseil Constitutionnel* was to have a strong influence on impact studies because of the composition of the conference of chairpersons in each assembly and the distribution of voting rights therein, which gives the majority to the majority of the assembly. Only the conference of chairpersons of an assembly opposed to the government can in fact refer a bill to the *Conseil* on the grounds that the impact study is poor and fails to meet the requirements of the organic law. Even when this has happened, the *Conseil Constitutionnel* had thus far not found grounds for censure.

In the field of environmental assessments, there has been a fairly large number of cases where declarations of public utility—which are necessary for the implementation of the projects concerned—have been invalidated following assessments deemed unsatisfactory by an environmental authority. The most widely publicized of such cases related to the closure to cars of the Seine bank road in Paris. However, the city council was able to enforce this closure by changing its motive. It replaced a motive that had to be based on an environmental assessment with one that did not require such an assessment!

Regarding socio-economic assessments, the most famous invalidation of a declaration of public utility necessary to undertake infrastructure works was that of a high-speed railway line between Poitiers and Limoges, a project pushed by then President of the Republic François Hollande. The declaration was invalidated on the grounds, among others, of a poor cost-benefit ratio. It appears that the administrative courts used the cost-benefit analysis here not to impose a truth on the decision-making authorities, but to support their traditional jurisprudence regarding the manifest error of assessment. In terms of Constitutional law, the *Conseil d'État* may quash a decision made by the government in exercising its discretionary power only if the said decision is based on an obvious mistake.

Ultimately, in the third decade of the twenty-first century, what is the situation of these instruments in France? The polymorphic nature of the use of each of the three instruments is striking. This polymorphism manifests very differently from one instrument to the next.

As far as indicators and dashboards are concerned, one cannot be too surprised by the duality between the system set up by the OLGBL, on the one hand, and on the other hand the instruments which the various ministries or public institutions have acquired for their own account. Such duality is commonplace in large organizations. This holds as much for the most aggregated programmes as for their local and regional applications in support of the budgets of programmes and operational units. Another type of duality relates to the difference between the barometer of public action initiated by Emmanuel Macron and the contents of the performance data extracted from the annual reports of the LOLF. The two documents are presented by the government with significantly different orientations. The data presented to the general public and to members of parliament are defined differently from those circulating within the executive, and they have different names (Benzerafa-Alilat & Gibert, 2021): "barometer of public policy results" in the former case, and "performance data" in the latter. This duality clearly reflects the difference between essentially institutional communication with a degree of political euphemism, and communication focused more on government policy news. It suggests a difference, in practice, between a form of accountability that is structured more or less by a public policy approach and the associated abstractions, and accountability regarding objects which more directly affect the citizen-voter and are therefore informed more by a concern to meet social demand. It is not numbers that triumph, but the diversity of ways of using those numbers.

The striking feature of ex ante evaluation is the development of specialized evaluations following the diversification of evaluation obligations, which for the most part have a specific perspective, such as the environment, costs for local authorities, gender equality, or the disabled. In principle, these specialized evaluations shift the focus of the system to analyse before the quantification work of ex ante evaluation. The wide angle used to identify all possible significant effects of a decision gives way to a narrow focus to identify effects of a particular nature or concerning particular types of beneficiaries or taxpayers. Good sectoral knowledge thus becomes all the more important to the success of the evaluator's work. The original cost-benefit analysis is above all an economic instrument, and evaluation focused on particular types of effects is unquestionably technical-economic.

Meanwhile, the forms of ex post evaluation are proliferating. The leitmotif frequently heard in the senior civil service, the claim that evaluation is necessary, seems almost laughable, given how omnipresent evaluation is. The concept remains fashionable, albeit somewhat downplayed, owing to its friendlier-sounding name in the French language compared to "control." Professions that long resisted the term, such as academic economists, have now taken to it. To enter the game, the social sciences have also taken advantage of the participative or plural evaluation trend, which calls for mediation to reduce the contradictions between the claims, concerns and interests of the various stakeholders. For the administration's control bodies, this trend has afforded an opportunity to refresh their image. The luxuriant typology established by Daniel Stuffelbeam (2001) barely suffices to describe all the different exercises which, with reason, by opportunism or out of ignorance, their authors call evaluation.

What is each of the three tools' dominant role today? Do they support decision-making? Do they serve as accountability instruments? Are they used for other major purposes? Or are they much ado about nothing?

With regard to indicators, the importance and visibility of performance monitoring introduced under the OLGBL clearly emphasizes both ex ante and ex post accountability. First, indicators are still to be used to justify budget applications to parliament. Second, they are to support reporting on the effectiveness and efficiency of the use of the funds authorized by parliament. Accountability is also very much present in the many indicators that appear in the contracts between the State and its operators (Gibert & Thoenig, 2019). This requirement added to contracts to define and inform indicators has been seen as a form of renewed oversight. Decision-making support was once a dominant concept of management control, with emphasis on results analysis and the feedback that should ensue on the upstream stages of a management system, namely planning and programming. This is no longer the most visible role of the instrument, despite the systematic reference made by the State to the importance of management dialogue between the national or local levels or between hierarchical levels. In practice, this dialogue all too often resembles more of a ritual than an opportunity for systematic analysis of results over a given period. Decision-making support seems to be provided more by the dashboards that the different rungs of the hierarchy produce at their own initiative.

In the field of ex ante evaluation, the role of cost-benefit analysis, a typical decision-making tool, seems to be changing. Firstly, its decision-making function has been deliberately weakened in several cases. For example, ministries have simultaneously used both multi-criteria analyses and other similar analyses. Their aim was to add decision-making support dimensions not included in cost-benefit analysis. Multi-criteria analysis is easily manipulated when the variables included are subjective and not measurable. Secondly, evaluation requirements, whether they concern all the effects of a decision, as in the case of legislative impact studies, or only specific outcomes, as in the case of environmental assessments, have the effect of signalling a kind of control over the decision maker. With specialized evaluations, the aim is no longer to choose an optimal solution, or even a satisfactory one, but rather compliance with standards, many of which are external to the rationale of the problem at stake. These specialized evaluations are often carried out to avoid undesirable secondary effects in an area that the sponsor wishes to protect or promote. Optimistically, this is the realization of the whole-of-government approach. Pessimistically, we are witnessing a proliferation of constraints weighing on public decision-making, in other words, a constantly reiterated complexification of the management of such decision-making.

In ex post evaluation, the quest for knowledge often seems overshadowed by efficiency and budget-saving considerations, as was evident under the MPA programme. Such considerations underlie the recommendation, by evaluators in charge of assessing non-policies, to develop real policies. They also inform a particular approach to policymaking, when evaluators challenge the objectives of the policy they are assessing and take instead as a point of reference for their work presumed needs of the population, needs which they decide to tack onto the objectives of the policy they are supposed to evaluate.

In the three cases studied, in the absence of a clear doctrine that the central government never really established, due to the agnostic opportunism motivating the use of semantically trendy instruments to solve widely diverse problems, the instruments' overall contribution to decision-making is manifestly weak. A shift occurs, which steers tools towards a control purpose when they should essentially have helped to support management, as Aaron Wildavsky (1979) has pointed out. Moreover, some of these instruments are used in a somewhat mechanical, bureaucratic and ritualistic way when the obligation to use them is unaligned with the lack of belief in their usefulness or appropriateness. This is the case of legislative impact studies and the evaluation of costs for local and regional authorities.

References

Benzerafa-Alilat, M., & Gibert, P. (2016). De quoi l'Etat rend-il compte dans ses rapports annuels de performance ? *Revue Française d'Administration Publique, 160*(4), 1041–1064.

Benzerafa-Alilat, M., & Gibert, P. (2021). A la recherche des causes d'existence d'une dualité système de suivi de la performance pour L'Etat central français. Communication au Xème colloque AIRMAP, 24 pages.

Bezes, P., & Pierrun, F. (2012). État, administration et politiques publiques: les dé-liaisons dangereuses. La France au miroir des sciences sociales nord-américaines. *Gouvernement et Action Publique, 2,* 41–87.

Bono, P. H., Desplatz, R., Debu, S., & Lacouette-Fougère, C. (2021). Le lent développement des évaluations d'impact en France: une approche par les acteurs. *Revue Française d'Administration Publique, 177*(1), 17–28.

Gibert, P. (2010). Contrôle et évaluation, au-delà des querelles sémantiques, parenté et facteurs de différences. *Revue Française des Affaires Sociales, 1,* 71–88.

Gibert, P., & Saussois, J. M. (2014). L'évaluation de politique: des typologies des académiques à la gestion de ses risques par les commanditaires. *Dialogue Euro Méditerranéen de Management Public, MED 7.* Università di Roma Tor Vergata, Italy.

Gibert, P., & Thoenig, J. C. (2019). *La Modernisation de l'Etat. Une promesse trahie ?* Classiques Garnier.

Gibert, P., & Verrier, P. E. (2016). Peut-on discipliner le pouvoir ? Étude sur le contrôle de la rationalité managériale par le juge dans trois innovations législatives françaises. *Politiques et Management Public, 33*(3–4), 165–196.

Inspection générale de l'administration, inspection générale des finances, inspection générale des affaires sociales. (2012). *Bilan de la Revue Générale des Politiques Publiques et Conditions de Réussite d'une Nouvelle Politique de Réforme de l'Etat.* Journal Officiel.

Journal officiel. (1990). *Décret no 90-82 du 22 janvier 1990 relatif à l'évaluation des politiques publiques.* Imprimerie Nationale.

KPMG, & Quadrant Conseil. (2017). *Évaluation de la démarche globale d'évaluation des politiques publiques menée dans le cadre de la modernisation de l'action publique.* KPMG.

Lacouette-Fougère, C., & Lascoumes, P. (2013–2014). L'évaluation: un marronnier de l'action gouvernementale ? *Revue Française d'Administration Publique, 148,* 165–196.

Muller, P. (2000). L'analyse cognitive des politiques publiques: vers une sociologie politique de l'action publique. *Revue Française de Science Politique, 50*(2), 189–207.

Nioche, J. P., & Poinsard, R. (1984). *L'évaluation des politiques publiques*. Economica.

Ould Ferhat, L. (2013). L'importance des approches a-sociologiques en évaluation des politiques publiques. *Construction Politique et Sociale des Territoires, 3*, 19–34.

Stufflebeam, D. (2001). Evaluation Models. *New Directions for Evaluation, 2001*(89), 7–98.

Thoenig, J. C. (2000). Evaluation as Usable Knowledge for Public Management Reforms. *Evaluation, 6*(2), 217–229.

Vedung, E. (2010). Four Waves of Evaluation Diffusion. *Evaluation, 16*(3), 263–277.

Viveret, P. (1989). *Évaluer les Politiques et les Actions Publiques. Rapport au Premier Ministre*. La Documentation Française.

Wildavsky, A. B. (1979). *Speaking Truth to Power*. Transaction Publishers.

PART V

Indirect Reforms

CHAPTER 8

Well-tempered Agencification

Agencification has often been considered one of the main manifestations of NPM (Christensen & Lægreid, 2007).

Agencification refers to the State's delegation of the implementation of its policies to autonomous bodies, whether they are legal entities or not (Overman & Van Thiel, 2016). The term includes agencies that operate in a specific field, delivering goods and usually services to the population (Moynihan, 2006). By extension, it can also refer to agencies responsible for regulating an economic sector on behalf of the State or alongside State regulation (Chevallier, 2010).

Distinguishing between these two types of agency, this chapter studies the links that may exist between their respective developments. At first, the proliferation of both types of agency may seem to reflect a trend towards the dismembering of the State. However, it seems necessary to distinguish between the two, particularly in the French case, if only because of the discrepancy between the length of existence of productive agencies and the novelty of regulatory ones.

8.1 Productive Agencies

At international level, the proliferation of productive agencies is conventionally attributed to the series of benefits they presumably afford in performing their functions, compared to a standard State administration.

© The Author(s), under exclusive license to Springer Nature Switzerland AG 2022
P. Gibert, J.-C. Thoenig, *Assessing Public Management Reforms, Understanding Governance*,
https://doi.org/10.1007/978-3-030-89799-4_8

The first such benefit is that agencies are generally assigned a well-defined field of competence, and the autonomy they enjoy allows them to focus on fulfilling their missions without being disrupted by concerns relating to other State policies. In other words, their distance from politics avoids the blurring of objectives and protects agencies from becoming passive agents of the State (Anastassopoulos, 1985).

The second benefit is the expected professionalization of these agencies' staff in the areas of expertise required for their activities. Appropriate, non-bureaucratic staffing is presumed to guarantee both the effectiveness and efficiency of the organizations thus formed. This requires that the agencies have the freedom to recruit and manage their own staff, and that such freedom be extended to their financial management. The clarity of the objectives assigned to agencies within the framework of a principal-agent relationship facilitates the establishment of an effective system of accountability that allows the State to assess the performance actually achieved. To consolidate this real autonomy, it is often stated that the managers, and especially the chief executive officer, should be given a long-term mandate.

All this reasoning is underpinned by fairly optimistic assumptions. It involves the political powers-that-be agreeing to the long-term ringfencing of a sector entrusted to an agency. This agency is moreover not expected to do anything other than perform in its field. This hypothesis implies that public policy could be sectorized without having undesirable effects on the State's capacity for action. In this respect, it appears to be rather unrealistic.

Strangely enough, empirical verification of the supposed virtues of agencification is often lacking. Some studies have however partially confirmed certain feared or expected tendencies. In Norway, for example, agency senior managers pay less attention to political signals than do their counterparts in ministries. Their stance is fairly independent of the prevailing doctrine of the time, whether it is informed by NPM or not. On the other hand, they give greater consideration to the interests of users and clients (Egeberg & Trondal, 2009). Egeberg and Trondal also point out that, within ministries, the presence of duplicate departments working in similar areas to the agencies tends to make agency managers more sensitive to political developments.

If we are to estimate the real degree of agencification of the State in the French case, we must assess it against this doxa.

The definition of the term "agency" assuredly points to the conclusion that a multitude of agencies exist in France. This concept is said to refer to an administrative body characterized by five properties:

- it is formally and organizationally separate from a ministerial department or cabinet level,
- it carries out public tasks at national level on a permanent basis,
- it is staffed by public servants,
- it is financed mainly by the State budget, and
- it is subject to public legal procedures.

In France, a mechanism of so-called functional or technical decentralization has existed for many years. This mechanism entrusts a specialized activity of the administration to a legal entity different from the State. Usually, this legal entity will be a public institution, generally administrative and subject to public law. It may however involve other legal forms, such as not-for-profit organizations or public interest groupings. Another form of public institution with a more flexible status, the industrial and commercial public institution, is generally used only for economic activities.

The growing functional decentralization of public management has been likened by some to an agencification of the State. It attracted the attention of two of the most prestigious and influential central government authorities almost simultaneously. Each authority produced a report: the *Inspection Générale des Finances* in 2011, and the *Conseil d'Etat* in 2012. The publication of the two reports highlighted the different possible meanings of a term borrowed from abroad that has no legal embodiment in French law.

As the *Conseil d'Etat* pointed out, until the 1990s there had been no call for the extension of agencification. Moreover, new agencies had been created without an identified overarching plan. The *Conseil d'Etat* identified 103 agencies on the basis of two criteria, which it deemed cumulative. The first pertained to autonomy. The second was the fact of having a formative responsibility in the implementation of a national public policy. Their combination is not insignificant, quite the contrary. In essence, the two criteria limit the qualification of agency to bodies with a monopoly on a specific area of competence. This excludes universities, for example, which can be created in unlimited numbers. Perhaps more important in the report by the *Conseil d'Etat* is the foreword signed by its vice-president, acting as president. The *Conseil d'Etat* stated that it did not endorse the idea that agencies constituted a risk for the State and led to its dismembering—a dismemberment which would be both uncertain in its legal consequences and questionable in terms of the management and conduct of public policies. Agencies do not mean less State, but a different kind of State. Therefore, from the *Conseil d'Etat*'s point of view, agencies are not independent, they are autonomous. Although the executive branch is not to interfere in their day-to-day management, it should define the policy guidelines they implement.

As for the *Inspection Générale des Finances*, it was mandated to study legal entities which, controlled by the State, implement public policies on its behalf. Compared to the *Conseil d'Etat*, its field of reflection and study was considerably broader, for it took into account entities without a legal personality. It thus counted 1244 agencies that qualified as materializing a dismemberment of the State, in other words 12 times as many as those identified by the *Conseil d'Etat*. Two very different and even incompatible definitions were thus juxtaposed at central government level. The administration's internal assessment nevertheless reveals two constants.

The first is the shortcomings observed in the oversight exercised by the State: it was too focused on detail, and it was not strategic enough. The State's central administration therefore had to put an end to both these dysfunctions affecting the development of contractualization between the State and agencies.

The second constant was a recommendation. Agencies, at least those considered as State operators, had to be subject to financial obligations similar to those applying to the State services themselves under the OLGBL, as introduced by parliament in 2001.

An organization is considered a State operator mainly based on three cumulative criteria (Cour des Comptes, 2021):

- it exercises a public service activity within the framework of the implementation of a policy defined by the State and classified in the budget nomenclature structuring actions in terms of mission-programmes,
- it is funded mainly by the State, either through subsidies or through earmarked taxes, the latter accounting for 29% of operators' total public funding in 2020,
- it is supervised by the State, in terms of both strategic orientation and financial or economic control.

In this context, organizations that play a role with crucial implications for the State can be considered as operators, even if they do not meet all three criteria (Premier ministre, 2015).

There has been a sharp decline in the number of operators in recent years. It fell from 649 in 2008 to 437 in 2021. These decreases are due to operator mergers, to consequences of the transition to the creation of large territorial regions, and to the removal of certain organizations without significant activity, considered obsolete. With some exceptions, they are not due to a de-agencification or reintegration of agencies' activities or missions into the State administration per se. The operators nevertheless remain an important economic sector. In 2021, they account for a total of 405,152 jobs, and jobs financed by the operators with their own resources are not included in this tally.

Public universities offer an interesting case.

Higher education bodies make up a particularly large share of the agencies—as defined by the *Inspection Générale des Finances*—and operators. In 2021, of the 437 State operators that existed, 270 or 56% concerned the mission of higher education and research. Universities and similar bodies account for 39% of subsidies for public service costs, and the CNRS (National Centre for Scientific Research) 9%. If agencification is indeed at play in France, it seems to primarily affect this field. A brief review of these operators' development is necessary to properly understand the reasons for their quantitative significance.

Before 1968, each academy—which at the time was a territorial administrative district of the Ministry of Education roughly covering a region—had a university. The academy was headed by a rector, who was also responsible for primary and secondary education. It was organized into four main faculties: science, literature, law and medicine. A framework law of 12 November 1968 on higher education, known as the Edgar Faure law after the minister in charge of education at the time, overhauled the organization of this system. It prescribed a process of fragmentation and recomposition. The faculties were split up into more focused teaching and research units. They were then grouped together into universities, which were to become multidisciplinary. The universities thus formed were given a new status, that of "scientific and cultural public institutions." The *Conseil d'Etat* soon categorized this status under its generic label "public administrative institution."

This process led to the replacement of the old universities by a number of new universities, based on a variety of considerations. Real attempts to actually implement multi-disciplinarity, strategies informed by disciplinary corporatism, and standardization to align with the international stage, following the example of the economic sciences that had just separated from law, coexisted in highly variable proportions (Aust, 2005).

In addition to the multi-disciplinarity that was supposed to inspire the recomposition process, other values were emphasized by the Faure law. The one was autonomy, a value which the status of "scientific and cultural public institution" was intended to exemplify. The other value was democracy. This involved all categories of both staff and students being able to sit on the board of each university, following elections by an electoral college. This democratic participation replaced a governance regime in which only professors participated.

The Faure Law of 1968 was amended several times without fundamental structural change. The number of universities then increased through the creation of new institutions in many middle-sized towns. For the State, this was a way of addressing the rise in the number of students, of responding to pressure from local councillors wishing to have academic facilities deemed necessary to attract highly qualified workers, and of democratizing higher education by avoiding the additional expenses involved for students to move to a university town.

Important changes were introduced in 2007 by the so-called Pécresse law. It involved a certain reconcentration of power in the hands of university chancellors and increased the presence of teachers on the boards. Above all, it authorized universities to create foundations in order to increase their own resources.

A law enacted in 2006 had however provided for the creation of bodies for cooperation between higher education institutions, called "research and higher education clusters." This law started a game of musical chairs with new institutional statutes of such complexity that they confused and disconcerted even the least critical analysts of government policy.

The new superstructure was presented by the Ministry of Higher Education in 2007 with a view to helping universities become more autonomous and at the same time become competitive on the international stage. These research and higher education clusters were granted the status of "scientific cooperation institutions," which allows them to award degrees in their own name according to the mandate granted to them by their member universities.

The inter-university form of cooperation and more generally cooperation between higher education institutions thus chosen was reminiscent, *mutatis mutandis*, of inter-municipal cooperation institutions. Once again, the State's governing bodies opted for a "soft" grouping: a research and higher education cluster could be established not only to remain a federal or inter-federal structure, but also as a step towards a merger of the member institutions. Unlike inter-municipal cooperation institutions, which never took the name of the municipalities within their ambit, some research and higher education clusters immediately named themselves as forming a single university. This integrated approach created confusion that was rather troublesome for students but was viewed favourably by the Ministry. The latter was striving for significant effects, not so much to benefit from economies of scale as to enable the new groups to feature in international university rankings, particularly the Shanghai ranking, and if possible to achieve a better ranking than the individual universities under their umbrella. This statistical ambition was openly embraced by the Ministry's services. Improving international reputation thus took precedence over the search for efficiency or savings, which then became priorities in the groupings created in other areas of public policy (Projet de loi de finances, 2021).

More generally, several arguments were put forward to justify the opportunity to create groupings. One argument often invoked was the need to reach a critical mass of students or academic researchers, in the name of "big is beautiful." Another argument was the pooling of resources. A third called for streamlining the education offer in a geographical area, particularly through the coordination of institutions. A fourth emphasized the need to make it easier for the ministry to have single or special points of contact. A fifth advocated a site-based policy, the geographical scope of which varied over time. The latter argument followed an approach that was contrary to agencification, insofar as it prioritized a territorial logic over an organizational one.

The hopes placed in this federalism, or confederalism, whether permanent or to facilitate the transition towards institutional mergers, were revived when a law enacted in 2013 replaced the status of "research and higher education cluster" with a new status, that of "community of universities and institutions." Legally, a community of universities and institutions is a "public institution of a scientific, cultural and professional nature." Except in the case of real institutional mergers, this still involves an interlocking of heterogeneous legal entities. Although governments have ultimately shown a preference for mergers, pressure for strong governance in federative organizations has come from international circles, including the European Commission in Brussels, which has made these organizations' eligibility for research contracts dependent on the credibility of this governance (Guiselin, 2019).

Most recently, the main features of policy surrounding agencies in the field of higher education have not fundamentally changed.

Thus, in support of the bill passed in 2018 that bore the name "For a State at the service of a trusting society," the associated impact study stated that institutional groupings, whatever their form—merger, association or community of universities, institution—were conceived as a tool for structuring the national higher education and research landscape, particularly to remedy its fragmentation across the French territory. The bill's stated aims were to enhance institutions' international visibility and appeal, and to foster coordination between the training offer and research programmes in a given area. The same impact study provided to parliament to review the bill made a rather symbolic reference to the principle of efficiency which, as we have seen, was only secondary in this policy. It stressed the intention that, by facilitating the creation and functioning of groupings, the implementation of experimentation with new organizational methods would eventually result in economies of scale, although it was not possible at that stage to put a precise figure on such economies. They were expected to be induced primarily by the numerous forms of synergy and pooling resulting from the mergers and/or simplifications of governance and support functions such as financial management, information system costs, documentation, procurement, and student life. In other words, quantification would be carried out at a later stage, as this was a different matter.

As for the dependence of universities and similar bodies on the State, it is quite evident from the percentage of jobs involved, that is, financed by State resources. In 2019 these accounted for 86.6% of all full-time equivalent jobs in this sector, a figure very close to the average rate of 86.9% for all operators.

It is important to note that French universities are among the least autonomous in Europe in terms of managerial control. A ranking by the European University Association in 2017 placed them 21st out of 29 countries for their organizational autonomy, 21st for their financial autonomy, and 22nd for their autonomy in terms of human resource management. This ranking is virtually the same as the one established back in 2010 by the same association (Estermann et al., 2011).

8.2 Regulatory Authorities

The development of regulatory authorities, known in France as "independent administrative agencies"—more precisely independent public agencies for those that are legal entities—is far more recent than that of productive agencies. The first of these authorities was the *Commission Nationale Informatique et Libertés* (French data protection authority), founded in 1978.

In international doxa, the existence of these authorities is justified by a series of presumed benefits (Christensen & Lægreid, 2007). From this perspective, it is useful to have bodies with analytical capacity in the various types of expertise needed to regulate the different economic sectors concerned. A separation from political power is necessary to ensure that a rational approach to regulation prevails over often short-term visions which are overly prone to compromise, or are too sensitive to pressure from stakeholders who are quick to lobby the administrations traditionally in charge of their regulation. Collegial decision making is also advocated, and has become a standard feature of authorities responsible for ensuring that various points of view are taken into account. In addition to these considerations, which are essentially informed by a quest for decision-making relevance and/or optimization, are considerations of a more opportunistic kind. Regulatory authorities are said to avoid a posture such as that exhibited by governments: they avoid having to make decisions on problems where there are more hits to be taken than recognition to be gained. In the event of stakeholders being dissatisfied with a decision to be made or already made, the existence of an independent authority could also allow for the criticism of those stakeholders to be directed at the experts rather than at those in power. This lightning rod or umbrella function enables politicians and senior civil servants alike to find scapegoats and, more generally, to appear more conciliatory than the agencies.

The development of regulatory authorities in France has been largely linked to the European policy of deregulating and opening up to competition those sectors of the economy where State monopolies often reigned, for instance railways, electricity, postal services, telecommunications. Given the size of the country's public sector—particularly as a result of the nationalizations of 1945 and to a lesser extent those of 1982 when non-monopolistic sectors were targeted—major work was required to tease out the productive function of the companies which had previously enjoyed a monopoly. At the same time, it was necessary to ensure a regulatory function was in place for the sectors in which these companies would henceforth face competition. A fragmented organization was to replace the varying degrees of symbiosis that existed between public monopoly companies and the ministry providing oversight.

The creation of regulatory authorities has only partially transferred competence from the State to these authorities. First, none of these authorities have a legal basis superior to ordinary law and their existence remains at the discretion of parliament, subject to the provisions of European directives. Second, they have to contend with problems that did not exist in the monopoly situation. This is the case, for example, in the telecommunications sector, where one operator continues to provide a universal service and the additional costs generated by this mission must be shared among all the companies operating in the sector. It is thus necessary to calculate this additional cost as objectively as possible, or to establish best practice rules for all the players in the sector. Other factors explain the development of independent administrative authorities. First of all, there is a concern, across all economic sectors, for preserving competition and combating de facto monopolies, dominant positions and cartels. Here again, European Union legislation has been superimposed on national legislation.

The number of independent administrative authorities has risen to over 40. This situation has been a source of concern among members of parliament, who see their development as anarchic.

A report by a Senate committee of inquiry noted the extensive variety of reasons for creating independent administrative authorities (Mézard, 2015). Some appeared to be primarily symbolic actions set up following a political scandal, when the executive wished to provide a legislative response. Another reason put forward was the creation of such an independent administrative authority in response to a problem deemed sensitive, or to make it take the heat of the unpopularity of difficult decisions. The members of the Senate committee identified divestiture in two respects: divestiture of the judiciary, since independent administrative authorities had a power of sanction, and divestiture by the executive and even the legislator, since these authorities' accountability to it was deemed to be too weak.

In its report, the senate also deplored the presence of too many members of the major central government ministries in the agencies' governance bodies. It feared that this could trigger some sort of capture process if State representatives were tempted to increase their control over the agencies. It even considered that authorities such as those regulating competition, the audio-visual sector, information technology or the financial markets, among others, formed a State within a State, forcing the political authorities to work with them without democratic control in return. The report therefore called for the establishment of a general statute for independent administrative authorities that would open up their governance, guarantee the independence of their members, and ensure genuine parliamentary control. A 2017 law largely met the senate's demands. With some exceptions, it prohibited concurrent membership of multiple independent administrative authorities, and established incompatibilities with political functions that might be exercised by their members. More generally, it set out a code of ethics.

As for the monitoring of independent administrative authorities, it is materialized in several forms.

These authorities are required to provide an annual report to both the executive and parliament, and to report to the relevant parliamentary committees on request. They must also allow the government to present parliament with a report on the management of independent administrative authorities and independent public authorities, in the form of a general appendix to the draft bill for the year. This document must include for each independent public authority, a strategic presentation including the definition of performance objectives and indicators, a presentation of the actions carried out, and a presentation of expenditures and employment, with detailed justification. It is also to set out the forecast distribution of jobs paid by the authority and a justification for variations from the existing situation. It shall include an analysis of variances between forecast and actual data for funding, resources and jobs, as well as objectives, expected and actual results, indicators, and associated costs. The information required by the independent administrative authorities is therefore similar to that required for the different programmes of the State administration.

In practice, most independent authorities have a relatively short and turbulent life. Mergers abound. Changes to areas of responsibility, whether in connection to these mergers or not, are frequent. The authorities' names vary accordingly. There is sometimes a clear trend towards the broadening of their powers. This is reflected in the evolution of the French competition regulator, for instance.

The current competition authority has been in existence since 2008. It is the distant heir of a modest technical committee on cartels that was created in 1953, itself a provisional conclusion to debates with a long and eventful history (Chatriot, 2008). This committee was responsible for examining infringements of antitrust law and communicating its opinion to the Minister of the Economy, who could then refer the matter to the public prosecutor. Its competence was extended in 1963, to abuses of dominant positions. In 1977, a law turned the body into a competition committee with the authority to advise the government in all matters relating to competition and to issue opinions on mergers and proposed mergers. It was transformed again by an ordinance in 1986, when price control was abolished, and renamed a competition council. At this stage it was given the authority to impose sanctions under the control of the judiciary—authority which until then had been held by the Minister of the Economy. This council was to be consulted on certain bills.

The early 1980s saw a standardization of the work methods and competences of the competition council under European law. Its powers were strengthened in 2001. In 2008 it became the competition authority, and at the same time gained more powers previously held by the Ministry of the Economy, particularly with regard to mergers between companies. It was also granted additional modes of intervention, and in 2015 was given further powers.

In 2021, there is a total of 25 independent administrative authorities in France. Only six are public, that is, endowed with legal personality. The other 19 are organically integrated into the central government administration, despite being recognized as independent.

Most regulatory authorities have a college whose chairperson handles the general management of the authority. The college makes non-individual decisions, which are often called technical decisions so as not to appear to compete with regulatory power, which is the preserve of the government alone. The majority of authorities have the power to sanction. However, they must exercise this power while respecting the principle of separation between those who prosecute and those who decide on the sanction. This principle requires either the specialization of the members of the college, or the existence of a sanctions committee that is autonomous from the college. Despite the fact that they are bound by principles inherited from judicial procedures, none of the authorities has the status of a court; the sanctions they impose are administrative sanctions. As such, like most of their other decisions, they can be referred to the *Conseil d'Etat* for a full review, and not just for cassation.

Overall, independent authorities account for a very small share of the State budget. Their expenditure amounts to approximately €520 million, for a State budget of about €400 billion. They employ just under 3500 of the State's 2.5 million employees. Three of them have fewer than ten employees.

These independent administrative authorities can be divided into four categories.

Ten of them can be considered as economic regulatory authorities working in sectors opened to competition: electronic communications and postal services, antitrust regulations, transport, gambling, financial markets, energy, the audio-visual sector, renewable energy, the dissemination of works, and the protection of intellectual property rights on the Internet. They are larger than average in terms of both budget and number of employees, and because of their expertise needs, they make extensive use of contractual employees.

Four independent administrative authorities provide sectoral regulation with a primarily non-economic focus. They deal with nuclear energy, health, higher education, and the fight against doping.

Seven deal with public liberties in different ways: compensation for victims of nuclear testing, information technology, classified defence information, airport noise pollution, the various places in charge of depriving individuals of their freedom, the defence of rights, and the monitoring of intelligence techniques.

Four authorities' competence relates to public governance: access to administrative documents, political campaign and finance accounts, public debate, and transparency in public life.

Our detailed analysis of documents relating to parliamentary processes shows that there is very little compliance with the provisions for independent authorities to report on their performance as required by the budget law. Only five of the 25 authorities produce even one monitored objective or performance indicator. To make matters worse, in no case are the results of their action detailed. Instead of listing objectives and indicators, one of the authorities—the one covering health—even refers on its website to its programme, which is no more than a list of works. In times of Covid-19, this is particularly surprising. We can assume that this indifference to the requirements of a law stems from the fact that, as a public authority, it is financed by social security and not by the central government. As far as the application of the cardinal principles of new public management is concerned, there is certainly room for improvement!

How independent are these independent authorities?

Taken to the extreme, the independence of a regulatory authority, whether administrative or public, would achieve what Max Weber—echoed many times (Ansaloni & Smith, 2018)—called political expropriation, thus justifying the expression "dismemberment of the State" far more than do the productive agencies. If this truly reflects the situation in France, a question arises about the guardian of the administrative and even constitutional temple that is the *Conseil d'Etat*. Why is it visibly unconcerned about the laws passed by parliament?

A first level of explanation lies in the status of these authorities' founding texts. Most of them are ordinary laws: what one parliament has done, another parliament or the same one can undo. In fact, legislative assemblies do not hesitate to do so, as we show later in the chapter. There is one exception: the authority responsible for the defence of rights has been enshrined in the constitution since 2008; its powers and prerogatives are set out in an organic law. It follows that individual decisions or technical regulations issued by independent authorities can be quashed by the *Conseil d'Etat*, as can any decision of the executive and its administration.

8.3 To Each Their Own Prism

The history of agencification in France over the last few decades reveals a number of convergences that suggest a common doxa shared by the senior civil service and academia (Bézes & Musselin, 2013).

An assessment methodology reveals however that beneath this doxa lies a far more important reality: a wide diversity of prisms used to see and act, shaped by the passions and cognitions conveyed and shared in particular circles. The main features highlighted can primarily be explained by the prism through which they are seen. The appropriation of a function or role by the members of a group or institution can indeed be likened metaphorically to seeing through a prism.

Parliament, oversight bodies and academics agree that the development of agencies and regulatory authorities has taken place without an overarching plan. This would explain why the size of agencies varies from one to 54,500 employees, as in the case of an agency called *Pôle emploi*, responsible for compensating unemployed workers and facilitating their return to work, and advising employers on recruitment. With its 485 employees, the financial market authority is a giant next to the tiny committee for national classified information, which has five employees.

Clearly, these disparities cannot be attributed solely to the need to avoid the coexistence of fundamentally different activities or sectors within an agency or authority. In fact, they support the idea of the undoubtedly hasty creation of bodies to address issues which are expressed by the media or shared by active minorities, rather than seriously considered issues.

The number of State operators decreased by 25% over the 2010-2020 period, largely as a result of mergers. The merger of bodies, agencies or authorities over the last 15 years cannot be reduced solely to the "big is beautiful" trend, though it was an undeniable rallying cry at the time of the GRPP programme. Moreover, the lack of a common framework for the functioning, recruitment, accountability and collegiality of regulatory authorities, along with the avoidance of conflicts of interest among their members, goes quite a long way to explaining the promulgation of a new kind of statute in 2017. The intention was to bring some order to a sector which, though modest in size, has a significant impact on economic actors and on the exercise of public freedom.

A sort of intra-administrative consensus exists that reveals a normative constant. It prescribes reinforcing oversight, particularly around professionalization, in the administrative sense of the term, or when increasing the capacity for strategic steering, in the managerial sense. This kind of recommendation implies that the State's poor grasp of what the term "dismemberment" means is due not to agency managers' independent behaviour, but rather to administrations' limited ability to delegate rather than have the know-how themselves. Separating policy design from policy implementation actually requires work to give policies more meaning. However, this ability is not necessarily within the reach of staff who are more used to setting up systems, that is, an agencing of means, than to guiding with concrete objectives.

Agencification effectively adds to the difficulty of the central administrations' work. It is not enough to enable them to make a particular public policy acceptable and compliant, as their sole capability of bringing legal order to a policy is no longer sufficient or even becomes a handicap. This is happening at a time when strict legal and administrative compliance, which departments feel most comfortable with, no longer suffices to judge the merits of a particular policy. The impact studies that the government is required to submit in support of draft legislation amply reflect this (Gibert, 2018).

Enter contracts, an instrument that all too often may be perceived as a miracle model. This common agreement used within the public sphere appears to boast all kinds of virtues, particularly in terms of respecting the autonomy of the co-contracting agency and the smart modernization of oversight. Even the *Cour des Comptes* has lamented the slow development of contractualization (2021). In 2020, only 22% of operators had an objectives and performance contract, although they admittedly account for half of the State's funding. Excluding universities and other public higher education and research institutions, which are exempt from such contracts in the name of their autonomy, the rate stagnates at 42%. Regrettably, where contracts do exist, they only partially cover the missions of the co-contractor, they have gaps surrounding the operational implementation of the objectives, and the monitoring indicators are inadequate. The *Cour des Comptes* advocates generalizing contracts with operators and transforming them into what it defines as real levers for improving the efficiency of action by strengthening their content. The problem is that contracts in the public sector were meant to play this role since their inception. They were supposed to be the document where the objectives to which the co-contractor committed were made explicit, and where the concept of performance was formalized. However, the contractual instrument's value is contingent on how it is appropriated. No incantation will eliminate its weaknesses.

More original than the concept of contract is the fate of the concept of agency.

Agency is an import that rode the wave of reformers and modernizers (Overman et al., 2014). As noted earlier in this chapter, the concept took on two fundamentally different understandings in two major State bodies, the *Conseil d'Etat* and the *Inspection des Finances*. Admittedly, both focused their criteria on participation in the implementation of public policy. However, for the *Conseil* only one-of-a-kind bodies qualified, whereas the *Inspection* included groups of bodies carrying out the same activities, whether competing directly, in cases such as universities, or each in their own territory, as with regional health agencies.

The problem is that the agency was and still is a concept that the State administration has great difficulty defining, and the boundaries of which are still somewhat blurred and not very compatible with the State's constant distribution of rights and duties. The fate of the agency was therefore sealed. It had to take a back seat to administrative categories that were less vague than concepts, better aligned with the prevailing mindsets in the world of senior administration, and capable of differentiating between beneficiaries of rights and those subject to constraints.

This transition from the use of the concept to that of administrative categorization has occurred in the last 20 years with the rise of the "operator" category and the formalization of the "independent authority" category.

The category called "State operator" has budgetary roots. Its legitimization is somewhat convoluted. The budget directorate of the Ministry of Finance justifies it with a statement in the budgetary procedure for public service subsidies. It makes receipt of such subsidies a major criterion for inclusion in the category of operators. However, the only thing stated on the subject in organic law is that these subsidies fall under State operating expenditure. There is no mention of the budgetary constraints applicable to the bodies which the budget directorate qualifies as operators, namely those that receive these public service subsidies.

More specifically, operators are considered as bodies with a legal personality that meets three cumulative criteria, which are expressed in legal terms as follows:

- a public service activity that can be explicitly linked to the implementation of a policy defined by the State and identified in the budget nomenclature according to its purpose, following the mission-programme-action breakdown;
- funding provided mainly by the State directly in the form of subsidies or indirectly via earmarked resources, particularly tax resources. This does not preclude the operator from carrying out commercial activities as well;
- direct control by the State, which is not limited to budgetary or economic and financial control but must fit within the exercise of oversight, with the capacity to guide strategic decisions, whether this is coupled with participation on the organization's board or not (Projet de loi de finances, 2021).

Organizations that do not present all these characteristics but are considered to handle critical matters for the State can however also be classified as operators.

The ambiguities of this definition are evident.

Identifying the link between an agency's activity and a budget programme makes for a reductive understanding of the effects produced by this activity, to say the least. The ability of an oversight authority to steer strategic decisions is only partly a legal problem. It means that independent administrative authorities may be considered as operators. The problem lies above all with the expertise of this authority, for which the agency is in no way responsible. As for the loophole around organizations that handle critical matters, it can give the impression that any organization that the central services of the Ministry of Finance considers to be a State operator is ultimately a State operator.

Inclusion of specific agencies in the category of operators has been and still is used for other purposes, namely to impose constraints that had not been foreseen by the legislator. This is the case of the employment ceilings for each operator as regards jobs paid out of State funding. It is also the case of accountability concerning their debt levels, of their own resources, and of the jobs financed with those resources. The principle of systematic contractualization with the State remains poorly respected, as mentioned above. This extension of accountability constraints from a legal field defined by organic law to the field of operators appears justified, however, in view of the volumes at stake: the 437 State operators mentioned in the 2021 budget received €63 billion in public funding, with 46 billion provided through budgetary allocations and 17 billion through taxes. The ceiling of public jobs they can use is set at 405,000.

As for independent authorities, the 2017 law established a list. Until further notice, an independent administrative or public authority is a body that features on this list.

An in-depth assessment shows that the French doxa conceals a wide variety of prisms. One point is fundamental in this respect.

The major entities of the French senior civil service are clearly in a situation of coopetition (Gibert & Thoenig, 2019). Their high levels of specialization lead them to cooperate in resolving the dysfunctions they identify in the administrative system. At the same time, however, their desire for power is insatiable, which leads them to avoid being confined to technical roles, for instance as legal, accounting or financial experts. Although the fact of remaining a simple expert, whether in administrative law, public accounting or procedural knowledge, is certainly an honourable social status, it is considered limited. To be recognized as a generalist is something else altogether; it is the ambition of a successful life and the competence that affords access to management positions. Generalist bodies are indeed more valued in the public system. These entities are therefore eager to pitch themselves as advisors to the prince or to play such a part when it is effectively recognized. This tendency puts these large entities such as the *Conseil d'Etat*, the *Cour des Comptes* and the *Inspection des Finances* in competition. The stakes are twofold: the management positions that the entities' members can obtain in the central administration and at the head of agencies and regulatory bodies; and their production of more or less innovative reports and recommendations.

The two above-mentioned reports on agencies illustrate this coopetition. What is striking in comparing them is the serenity of the *Conseil d'Etat* in the face of this trend, in contrast with the concern that seems to emerge from the report of the *Inspection Générale des Finances*. This difference in tone cannot be reduced to the one's desire to counter the position of the other.

The serene approach of the *Conseil d'Etat* when it states that there is no dismemberment of the State underway, while also noting the existence of serious problems with the proliferation of agencies, stems from the fact that none of this really challenges the legal order of which it is the guardian. With very few exceptions, agencies and independent administrative authorities are public law bodies under the control of the administrative judge. The main principles of public law apply to them in the same way as they apply to the State administration, under the control of the *Conseil d'Etat*.

From a financial perspective, however, which is that of the *Inspection Générale des Finances* and the directorate of budget and finance, agencies can appear as threats. First, resources could be misused when the legislator allocates a tax to an agency, thus making it independent of the annual budgetary decisions endorsed by parliament. Another threat identified is long-term financial risks associated with agencies using their own resources for recruitment not covered by the State. While such recruitment is legally possible, its reversibility is not guaranteed in the event of a reduction in the agency's own resources. A third type of perceived threat relates to debt, when an agency's level of debt risks forcing the State to provide it with exceptional assistance. All these risks are seen as causes for concern at a time when the rise of internal auditing within the administration is being systematized, at least from a budgetary and accounting perspective. This rigour reflects aversion to the risk of administrative financial excesses, which is particularly pronounced given the impossibility of seriously combating such risks inherent to political decisions. It follows that many of the recommendations made by the *Inspection des Finances*, as well as many of the practices adopted by the budget directorate to reduce these risks, are actually designed to bring the financial regime of the agencies—and even their staff regime, in terms of its financial consequences—as close as possible to that of the State administration itself. It is therefore the quest for flexibility in the establishment of agencies that are challenged.

De-agencification does not necessarily involve the reintegration of agencies into the State apparatus itself. It can occur by imposing on agencies an operating regime that is similar, if not identical, to that of administrations. To draw an analogy with the concept of *publicness* (Bozeman & Bretschneider, 1994), we could apply *agenciness* to State operators. This concept would certainly retain the characteristics of the ideal-typical agency. But an assessment approach would examine the mix achieved, for a given operator, between its agency features and its traditional administrative features. *Agenciness* would be a version of *publicness* applied to a particular type of public organization, at least in its French version. The financial administrations of central government, for their part, are pushing for a reduction of operators' *agenciness*.

In addition to the two legal and financial prisms, there is a third prism: that of the territory.

One of the criticisms levelled at agencies is that they promote public policies which are not implemented under the authority of the regional or *département* prefect, the territorial representative of central government. The integration of the agencies' function into the broader policies of a specific territory therefore requires cooperation between the devolved State administration and the agencies. To fulfil their missions efficiently, State agencies have two alternatives. Either they receive firm directives from their national leadership, if not from the central government headquarters, or they build up strong cooperative relationships with local government institutions. In the first case their autonomy is next to nothing; they are bureaucratic machines. In the second case they become active local partners and their autonomy is much greater. They are able to adapt general policies as defined in Paris, to fit local particularities. In other words, bureaucratization and co-optation are incompatible.

REFERENCES

Anastassopoulos, J. P. (1985). Les entreprises publiques entre l'autonomie et la dépendance : une analyse des divers instruments de régulation des entreprises publiques par l'Etat. *Politiques et Management Public, 2*(3), 73–98.

Ansaloni, M., & Smith, A. (2018). Une agence au service d'une stratégie ministérielle. La crise du Mediator et la concordance des champs. *Gouvernement et action publique, 1*(7), 33–55.

Aust, J. (2005). La loi Faure, une rupture avortée ? Effets de policy feedback et application de la loi Faure à Lyon. *Politiques et Management Public, 23*(1), 53–69.

Bézes, P., & Musselin, C. (2013). Le New Public Management : Entre rationalisation et marchandisation ? In L. Boussaguet & al. (Eds.), *Une 'French Touch' dans l'analyse des politiques publiques ?* (pp. 128–151). Presses de Sciences Po.

Bozeman, B., & Bretschneider, S. (1994). The "publicness puzzle" in Organization Theory: A Test of Alternative Explanations of Differences Between Public and Private Organizations. *Journal of Public Administration Research and Theory, 4*(2), 197–224.

Chatriot, A. (2008). Les ententes : débats juridiques et dispositifs législatifs (1923-1953) La genèse de la politique de la concurrence en France. *Histoire, Economie et Société, 27*(1), 7–22.

Chevallier, J. (2010). Le statut des autorités administratives indépendantes: harmonisation ou diversification ? *Revue Française de Droit Administratif, 5,* 896–900.

Christensen, T., & Lægreid, P. (2007). Regulatory Agencies—The Challenges of Balancing Agency Autonomy and Political Control. *Governance, 20*(3), 499–520.

Cour des comptes. (2021). *Les relations entre l'Etat et ses opérateurs.* Report commissioned by the public policy evaluation and control committee of the Assemblée Nationale. Assemblée Nationale.

Egeberg, M., & Trondal, J. (2009). Political Leadership and Bureaucratic Autonomy: Effects of Agencification. *Governance: An International Journal of Policy, Administration, and Institutions, 22*(4), 673–688.

Estermann, T., Nokkala, T., & Steinel, M. (2011). *University Autonomy in Europe. II.* The European University Association.

Gibert, P. (2018). Réflexions sur l'appropriation française de l'analyse d'impact de la réglementation (AIR) dans le cas de la mise en œuvre des études d'impact des projets de loi. *Politiques et Management Public, 35*(3-4), 243–272.

Gibert, P., & Thoenig, J. C. (2019). *La Modernisation de l'Etat. Une Promesse Trahie ?* Classiques Garnier.

Guiselin, E. P. (2019). Les regroupements d'établissements dans l'enseignement supérieur et la recherche : enjeux politiques et cadres juridique. *Revue Française d'Administration Publique, 1*(169), 37–50.

Mézard, J. (2015). *Rapport Fait au Nom de la Commission d'Enquête sur le Bilan et le Contrôle de la Création, de l'Organisation, de l'Activité et de la Gestion des Autorités Administratives Indépendantes.* Paris: Sénat, 126(1).

Moynihan, D. P. (2006). Ambiguity in Policy Lessons: The Agencification Experience. *Public Administration, 84*(4), 1029–1050.
Overman, S., et al. (2014). Resisting Governmental Control: How Semi-autonomous Agencies Use Strategic Resources to Challenge State Coordination. *International Review of Administrative Sciences, 80*(1), 172–192.
Overman, S., & Van Thiel, S. (2016). Agencification and Public Sector Performance: A Systematic Comparison in 20 Countries. *Public Management Review, 18*(4), 611–635.
Premier ministre. (2015). *Circulaire n°5798/SG relative au pilotage des opérateurs et autres organismes publics contrôlés par l'Etat*. Légifrance.
Projet de loi de finances. (2021). *Annexe sur les Opérateurs de l'Etat*. Imprimerie nationale.

CHAPTER 9

From Espoused Theories to Theories in Use

With the exception of the revised version of the OLGBL, the major government programmes launched since the end of the 1960s have not brought about any significant changes. The promises made have yielded limited results. The same goes for the instruments used: their appropriation has been modest, sometimes biased and even counterproductive. This observation is not new. As mentioned in the academic literature decades ago, the comprehensive approach to public sector reform, which is grandiose and head-on, often accomplishes very little (March & Olson, 1983). In the case of the central government in France, can we however draw definitive conclusions?

The starting point for this chapter is an observation. The major programmes aimed explicitly and directly at overhauling public management represent only the tip of the iceberg. The rest consists of developments that are fuelled by measures and initiatives with a different apparent purpose but which, through a series of halo effects, lead central government to adopt significant changes. Things move but quietly, even unintentionally. In other words, espoused change theories are those that the general government in Paris claims to follow when it defines comprehensive programmes. Theories in use are those that can be inferred from its action (Argyris et al., 1985). These are not called State reforms.

Three such measures or initiatives at national level are discussed below:

- on 7 January 1983, a law was promulgated titled "Distribution of competences between the *communes, départements, régions* and the State,"
- on 21 July 2009, a law on "hospital reform, patients and territories" was published, and
- in January 2010, a "reform of the territorial administration of the State" was launched, followed by a law passed in January 2014, for the modernization of territorial action and the institutionalization of metropolises.

These three types of measures affect different but essential areas, namely: public health; decentralization and intergovernmental relationships; and the coverage of the territory by the field agencies of the central government. They have demonstrated a certain continuity, surviving the political changes at the head of the State. They are driven by a management approach which, for each of the stakeholders, is becoming more complex and significantly changing their governance (Thoenig, 1979).

We devote a section to each of them, and conclude the chapter with a comparison of their assessment.

9.1 Devolution

Within the general government of a State in the broadest sense of the term, international organizations distinguish four main components: central government, federated States, local government, and the social administration (Thoenig, 2006).

France, a country that sees itself as a unitary structure, does not have any federated states, but the other three components are strongly present and their differences are clearly perceptible. Three civil service functions coexist: the State, local authorities, and hospitals. They are governed by a general statute and are subject to common rules of conduct, although some of their specific features are recognized, linked in part to the constitutional recognition of local authorities' autonomy and the particularities of hospital institutions. The differentiation between the three types of administration also involves specific methods of financing, with a distinction between taxes collected for the State, those collected for local authorities, and the financing of social administrations through compulsory social contributions.

As far as local and regional authorities are concerned, the developments that have affected them have been characterized by greater public policy freedom gained, in contrast however with the growing financial constraints imposed on them by the central government.

France may be an indivisible republic, as stated in Article 1 of the constitution, but it is now also a decentralized State, as its Article 72 stipulates: territorial authorities may take decisions in all matters arising under powers that can best be exercised at their level. This cautious and somewhat cryptic recognition of decentralization and of the so-called general competence clause dates from the constitutional reform of 2003. It enshrined a process set in motion by decentralization laws transferring competences to pre-existing local and regional authorities, a policy that had begun about 20 years earlier. The absence of a hierarchy between the local authorities, namely the *régions, départements* and *communes*, is also enshrined in the constitutional order, as no territorial authority is legitimate in exercising authority over another.

The decentralization laws passed in the early 1980s thus afforded local authorities with certain freedoms which had previously been subject to strong State control. The oversight exercised until then by prefects, the representatives of central government in the *départements* and *régions*, allowed the latter to oppose any of the authorities' decisions that they considered illegal. This decentralization led to a form of control requiring prefects to go through the administrative court or the regional audit office set up for this purpose, for their opposition to succeed. Until 1981 the *département* as an institution had very little autonomy. Although its deliberative assembly, called the *conseil général*—since renamed the *conseil départemental*—was democratically elected by the local population, its decisions were implemented by the prefect, the representative of the State, and his services. In other words, the *conseil général* did not have its own services. In 1981 the prefect's role was abolished. The *département* has since been governed by the elected representatives of the people under the presidency of one of these representatives, appointed by their peers. More importantly, the *conseil général* was given its own administrative capacity and did not have to rely on the services of the State. The State moreover transformed a previously purely administrative institution, the *région*, into an autonomous political and administrative authority, like the *département*. This decentralization was fuelled by transfers of competencies and authority.

The *régions* acquired their own competences in various fields such as economic development, culture, occupational training, and so forth. The *départements* were granted their own competences for social assistance and school transport, and the *communes* for urban planning documents. Primary and secondary school premises were transferred to the three types of authorities: primary schools to the *communes*, middle schools (*collèges*) to the *départements* and high schools (*lycées*) to the *régions*.

This first wave of decentralization was followed by a second wave in 2004. For example, most of the national roads were transferred to the *départements*, and individual economic aid was transferred to the *régions*. Technicians, blue-collar workers and service staff in schools were devolved to the local and regional authorities, which had previously become responsible for school premises.

These transfers of competences and staff were carried out with financial compensation from the State to meet local authorities' new expenditures. The volume of these transfers was however deemed too low and sparked major disputes. For the State, this compensation system had the benefit of avoiding restructuring of the tax system, which would have required it to reduce national taxes and increase local taxes. It therefore opted for the opposite of an increase of local authorities' fiscal autonomy, which strongly signalled the limits placed on generalized autonomy.

Since then, several reform laws have been passed successively.

These were mainly driven by a twofold idea. To curb the local authorities' rising spending, which reduced the central government's chances of coming close to meeting the Maastricht criteria, it was necessary to tackle the perverse effects of two characteristics of the system, namely the multiple levels of authority involved, and the excessive number of authorities at each level, on the grounds that this plurality creates redundancies. Decentralization was said to allow each level to set up policies in a same field, for example cultural affairs, without consulting with other authorities. This was believed to generate additional costs due to local authorities' small scale of production, particularly in the country's 35,000 municipalities, the vast majority of which are in rural areas and do not have the necessary financial resources. This desire to increase the size of municipal as well as regional authorities was evident under the presidential five-year terms of Nicolas Sarkozy and François Hollande. Under Sarkozy's presidency, when the GRPP was declining, some spoke of a policy of mergers within the central government, in reference to a real adage, "big is beautiful," the antithesis of the traditional managerial aphorism "small is beautiful." The superiority of larger-sized authorities was consecrated in 2011 during President Hollande's term in office, when the 22 *régions* that had existed until then in metropolitan France were replaced with 13 new ones. The value of increasing their size was then pitched not so much as a way to achieve economies of scale in the running of the *régions*, as a way to give them a greater capacity for action and the ability to effectively exercise the new functions that may be assigned to them. The example of the German Laender was often cited.

Unable to follow through with this approach, however, the government of the time resorted to increasingly sophisticated and confusing contortions. Thus, the idea once envisaged of abolishing the *département*, an institutional territorial level considered to be the weak link in the system, was abandoned. Likewise, the forced merger of small *communes*, a solution once seen as essential to tackle the lack of resources available to their councillors, was given up in favour of strengthening inter-municipalities, followed by a more or less authoritarian grouping together of these inter-municipalities.

The general competence clause, a legal concept which in France, as well as in the United Kingdom and Germany, translates the possibility for a local authority to intervene in a field of competence beyond those explicitly attributed to it, on the basis of its territorial interest in the matter, was even done away with for a time. Intergovernmental relationship studies have rightly emphasized the importance of this clause (Rhodes, 2018). In France, it is currently blamed for creating policy redundancies between different levels of local authorities. However, faced with strong opposition from local elected representatives, successive governments have given up on repealing it, but not without inventing a new solution, which consists in imposing forced inter-level cooperation. This has led to the creation of the legal concept of the lead local authority.

In each *région*, a body called the *conférence territoriale de l'action publique* (territorial public policy council) has been instituted. Paris once again resorted to an institution-building approach. In principle, this body is responsible for fostering the concerted exercise of the competences of local authorities, their groupings and their public institutions. As stated in Article 1111 9-1 of the territorial authorities code, its purpose is to debate and issue opinions on all matters relating to the exercise of competences and the conduct of public policies requiring the coordination or delegation of competences between the local authorities and their groupings. A coordination instrument, called a territorial agreement for the concerted exercise of a competence, is also provided for by the law of 16 January 2015 on the delimitation of *régions*. The territorial agreements must set out streamlining objectives and the methods of joint action for each of the competences concerned. They must be drawn up by the *région* and the *départements* for each of the areas for which they are lead local authorities. They may also be drawn up by the *communes* or their groupings for the areas for which they are lead local authorities. Each agreement must be examined by the territorial council and its observations must be taken into account. It is then submitted for approval to the deliberative assemblies of the authorities or groupings concerned. It is binding only on those that are signatories.

Such absurd arrangements suggest how difficult it is for central government to encourage local authorities to cooperate without resorting to exhortation or undermining their autonomy. The Gulliver of central government is an idol with feet of clay (Hoffmann, 2013).

Increasing decentralization is almost permanently on the government's agenda. In early 2021, a bill called "Decentralization, devolution, differentiation and decomplexification" provided for new transfers of competences or responsibilities to local authorities in the areas of roads, non-teaching staff in schools, and so forth. We shall see.

Local authorities' policy-making competence in the widest range of fields triumphed with the central government giving up on the removal of the general competence clause. This clause allows a local authority to act in all areas of interest to its territory. The massive transfer of staff from the central government to regional institutions reinforced this capacity for action while at the same time weakening that of the State, particularly in the engineering professions.

Together, the transfers of specific competences, the maintenance of the general competence clause, and staff transfers, along with a fairly broad recruitment policy, have given local authorities far greater leeway for action than they had in the 1970s. From the 1980s, training programmes led to the widespread acceptance of the new public policy management paradigm by the upper echelons of the local civil service. This greatly increased capacity for action enabled municipal, *département*-level and regional public policies to flourish, while at the same time ensuring the success of the idea of shared public policies. The implementation of many public policies would henceforth associate central government and local government in increasingly intertwined ways, making it difficult to identify the exclusive competences of one level or another, or even areas of competence.

The methods chosen to consolidate decentralization however caused a proliferation of contracts of all kinds between the national and local levels. As a result, public policy became increasingly complex and far less legible. This was clearly the opinion of senior public officials in Paris, as expressed in 2020 by the *Cour des Comptes*. It is evidenced in the fact that the call for the evaluation of these shared policies does not seem capable of providing a credible solution to the problem (Accar & Guiguet, 2020).

The other side of the distribution of competences between the central government and local authorities paints a very different picture. Local and regional authorities appear to be increasingly constrained.

To be sure, the decentralization laws explain most of the increase in the share of local expenditure in the overall mass of public expenditure: from 16% in 1980 to 19% in 2018. The financing of expenditure linked to the transfer of competences was covered by transfers of the income from various taxes. Fiscal federalism, on the other hand, has declined. Taxes for which the quota was set by local authorities have disappeared or are disappearing. This is particularly the case of taxes such as the *taxe foncière*, French version of property tax. The freedom of local authorities' fiscal policies is very limited in the case of land tax. The rates of value added tax for companies, which finances part of local authorities' budgets, are now determined by the State. Moreover, the central government's supervision of the financial management of local authorities, of the evolution of the volumes of their expenditure and of their debt has increased considerably. Paris has decentralized competences but increased its intrusion in local affairs.

9.2 The Public Health System

The hospital system and more generally the health system illustrate a second type of trend: attempts by the central government to exert more control over the sector by hybridizing their management.

In the 1960s, the French public hospital system stood out for the simplicity of its organization, and the way it was financed. There were about a thousand public hospitals which, in the largest cities were grouped together under the State umbrella of a single organization, such as the *Assistance publique des hôpitaux* in Paris and the *Hospices civiles* in Lyon. Elsewhere they were autonomous, had the status of local public institutions, and were managed by a board chaired by a local elected official. Most of the time, they were under the responsibility of a *commune*. Their dependence on this local authority was limited, as their funding was national. Nevertheless, local councillors were in favour of their attachment to the *commune*, for in middle-sized towns the hospital was often one of the primary, if not the primary, employer of the *commune*.

Each hospital was financed through a system known as the *per diem*. It was essentially based on the full cost of a day's hospitalization calculated by major service category: general medicine, obstetrics and surgery. This full cost was equal to the sum of the costs incurred directly or indirectly by the service over the previous year, divided by the total number of hospital days spent in the service during that year (Simonet, 2013). The *per diem* for the following year was set by the prefect of the *département* where the hospital was located, based on this cost price with a few adjustments, for example to make up for a past deficit. Each hospitalization bill was equal to the *per diem* multiplied by the number of days spent in the hospital. For the vast majority of hospitalized patients residing in France, most of the costs were covered by social security medical fund, with the rest paid by the patient or their private health insurance. It is important to note that the French social security system is an institution which symbolizes the benefits of the welfare State. It was set up at the end of the Second World War and is managed jointly by two parties: the trade unions and the employers' unions.

With rising economic strain and hospital costs, however, the pricing system was gradually called into question. It appears that the cost accounting on which it was based was particularly unrefined. The accounting system did not distinguish between different kinds of illnesses and patient treatments. This was the case particularly between patients who, for the same length of stay in hospital, required heavy or light care depending on the case. Worse, the system was suspected of encouraging hospitals to keep patients longer than necessary: the *per diem* charged was independent of the length of hospitalization, whereas it was generally accepted that, for a given pathology, a patient required more care and therefore incurred more costs during the first few days of hospitalization. With a constant daily rate, the patient's profitability for the hospital increased with the length of hospitalization. Thus, French women spent eight or nine days in maternity wards, incurring what the advocates of change called unjustified costs, since women in the US stayed in hospital for only three or four days after giving birth.

Replacing the system was put on the political agenda in the early 1980s.

The central services of the Ministry of Health became convinced that the implementation of the system of diagnosis-related groups in other countries offered many benefits. It was adopted in France under the name of "homogeneous patient groups." The idea was to finance hospitals by applying a standard rate for each patient, based on the homogeneous group into which they fell. The rate was to be determined according to the national average cost calculated for each group.

This initiative was not insignificant. First, it represented a major intervention by central government in the hospital sector. Second, it upset the bipartite management of social security. This made waves and triggered an outcry, particularly among local councillors who voiced their fears regarding a reform designed by Parisian technocrats.

This solution, which was too innovative, was however postponed in favour of a system known as the comprehensive budget. Under this system, hospitals received a lump-sum payment from the social security, which was essentially based on that of previous years and was not informed by the number of nights spent in hospital. The system was deemed to encourage hospitals to push people out as soon as possible, since a night's stay as such did not earn the hospital anything.

Ultimately, a pricing system based on the homogeneous patient groups was adopted, but under a different name: activity-based pricing. The name was justified by the fact that the acts performed for the benefit of a hospitalized patient were a key determinant of patients' categorization in a particular group.

The reform of hospital financing went hand in hand with a series of other reforms of the general health system. They are significant, for they shared a common trait: all reinforced the weight of central government. First, an organic law of 1996 created financing laws for the social security system, which determined the general conditions of its financial balance. Based on revenue forecasts, the financing laws set expenditure targets. The organic law also created what it called a national health insurance expenditure target. A warning committee was responsible for informing the government, parliament and the national health insurance fund when the target approved by parliament was on track to be exceeded.

At the same time, the financing of health insurance, which was based on employer and employee contributions, was diversified to reduce the burden of contributions on companies. It was partly financed by the general social contribution (CSG), a disguised additional income tax levied across the board. A corollary of the increasing reliance on taxation to fund social security and of the growing disconnect between benefit payments and employment was the publicization of social security finances, which had previously been separate from public finances per se. In short, the parity between trade unions and employer organizations in the governance of social security was waning, while governance by the State, its elected politicians and its central administrative services was gaining ground.

A second major step in the rise of central government through financing was taken with the organic law of 2 August 2005.

Following the example of the OLGBL passed in 2001, this financing law would henceforth have to include in an annex what the organic law called quality and efficiency programmes relating to social security expenditure and income. These programmes were to include a diagnosis of the situation of the French population, objectives associated with precise and justified indicators, a presentation of the resources deployed to achieve these objectives, and a statement of results achieved over the last two financial years. The performance rationale thus made its entrance at the highest level of accountability of the various branches of the social security system governing health, family life, disability and pensions. The publicization of social security finances could also be seen in the contracts of the national funds of the various branches, each of which had the status of a public institution. Each branch was required to sign multi-year agreements with third parties, such as the 128 funds that handled health insurance operationally at the sub-national level.

The State and the social security administration in the field of health moved closer together in two stages. In 1996, regional hospitalization agencies were created. In 2010, they were replaced by what were called regional health agencies. The instrument of agencification found very fertile ground in the health sector. The State was creating a real parallel administration, the scientific cornerstone of which was officially called the *Haute Autorité de la Santé* (high authority for health). The regional agencies were public administrative institutions that reported to the Minister of Health and which, in each *région*, steered the application of policy defined by the Minister at national level. The central government thus added a new network of field agencies working on the periphery of the other networks operating on behalf of the State at sub-national level. This agencification was to be heavily criticized by many for its lack of responsiveness during the Covid-19 crisis in 2020 and 2021.

The staff of these public institutions come from both the State administration and the health insurance system. They are responsible for modernizing and streamlining the healthcare offer in their *région*. To this end, they are in charge of the unified regional management of healthcare in both hospitals and the rest of the health system, particularly private practice. Their mission is to ensure efficiency. The Covid pandemic has proven to be a major test, not only of their operational capacity, but also of their function. Are they services external to the Ministry of Health in the strict sense of the term, or are they a kind of prefect covering the hospital and health sector as a whole?

9.3 State Field Agencies

For a long time, the diversification of the State's areas of intervention also involved a diversification of ministries and the corresponding proliferation of local State services. The latter were formerly referred to as external services, as opposed to the central administrations, which were meant to hold expertise and hierarchical authority.

This language spoke volumes about the status given to the departments responsible for implementing national policies across the country, compared to the departments responsible for developing them. A new ministry could only feel complete if the implementation of its policies did not depend on a body such as a *préfecture* or a field agency of another ministry. Hence the proliferation, from the 1960s, of devolved services placed directly under the remit of the central administrations, at both *département* and regional level.

In 2009, under the aegis of an appendix to the PPGR called the reform of the territorial administration of the State, and very discreetly in relation to the general public, local State services underwent a major reorganization. While the duality of levels between *département* and *région* services was maintained, the grouping of authorities was however imposed by the central government. It reduced the number of regional directorates from 13 to five. Together these five directorates' portfolios covered the environment, land development and housing, food, agriculture and forestry, youth, sports and social cohesion, business, competition, consumption, work and employment, and finally cultural affairs.

Moreover, in each *département* and depending on its size, seven directorates were grouped into two or three inter-ministerial *département*-level directorates. However, the latter were far from grouping together all of the State's decentralized administrations. When they were created, they brought together only 32,000 employees. For various reasons, they did not include directorates such as those of public finance, public security, national education, or the legal protection of the youth, not to mention the services of the army and the justice system. In other words, a major part of the government sector, along with the services of the Ministry of Education, escaped inter-ministerial grouping.

At *département* level, the organic distinction between the central ministries and their respective devolved services was thus affirmed. The ministries could of course continue to send instructions to their services, which had become a simple subset of an inter-ministerial directorate. But two new intermediaries now stood between a ministry and its field service. One was the prefect, whose already long-standing and at times somewhat theoretical authority over all central government services in the *département* was reasserted. The other was the director of the inter-ministerial *département*-level directorate, a State official who could belong to a ministry other than the Ministry of the Interior.

The ministries, however, held onto a key strength, which stemmed from the budget structure established by the OLGBL. Their touchstone was the necessarily ministerial programme within which funding was fungible, when there was no fungibility between the programmes of different ministries. The ministries kept control of their local staff by grouping all the funding in that area and by centralizing their staff funding in support programmes which allowed them to maintain their role in the local management of staff. The other types of funding, on the other hand, were delegated to the prefects, who in turn sub-delegated them to inter-ministerial *département*-level directors. In principle, the latter could not transfer these from one programme to another, and were therefore required to maintain the allocations as voted by parliament. The consequence of such processes was clear. It made the territorialization of public policies difficult. Central government was struggling to meet the challenges of the new times.

9.4 A Comparative Assessment of Theories in Use

The transformations, over the last 50 years, of the three fields which we very briefly presented—local authorities, hospital management, and the territorial grid of the central State—did not follow a linear path. Political changes at the head of the State as well as the recognition of the

Table 9.1 Major developments in central government action: a comparison

	Dominant development	Status challenged	Activated principle	Role assigned to the financial structure
Local authorities	From local authorities to shared policies	Unity and indivisibility of the Republic	Democracy Proximity	Limiting the effects of decentralization
Health	From the local public institution to the hybrid organization	Local public service Joint management by trade unions and employers Autonomy of social policy Separate management of social security branches	Rise of the central government Driving through a systemic vision Hybridizing hospitals Rationing Territorializing	Centralizing
Devolved State services	From organizational control to the territorialization of State action	Corporatism of organizations	Unity of the State across a territory	Creation of head-on opposition to organizational structure

Source: Authors' own

counterproductive effects of certain reforms sometimes led to long pauses in these transformations, or even to a sense of backtracking. However, some general features can be distinguished in each of the three areas (Table 9.1).

Concerning territorial government, France has evolved from a situation where one type of authority, the *commune*, largely held centre stage, generally handling the affairs of a territory modest in size and with a small population—38,000 communes in the 1960s—to a tetrarchy of authorities or groupings: *communes*, inter-municipalities, *départements* and *régions*. This evolution suggests a growth of the power of the local councillors who steer their territorial public policy. The fact that the general competence clause, which at one point was threatened, was ultimately confirmed is significant. It contributes to all levels of government having a stake in a wide range of public policy areas, and therefore to the emergence of competing or redundant policies, and of co-financing, whether shared or not.

A policy is considered by the central government to constitute a shared policy when it entails the intervention of at least one of the four local entities mentioned. This does not imply that they have identical roles. One actor may have initiated and developed the policy, while the other merely implements it. However, because the actors are autonomous, the shared nature of the policy involves a minimum of consultation and coordination to execute it. Success is moreover meaningful only in relation to the objectives pursued. Yet it is not certain that these objectives will be spontaneously shared by all the local authorities involved. In other words, the sharing of policies, an inevitable corollary of the growing structural complexity of general government, makes public policy far more complex. This state of affairs is accepted on the grounds that democracy is more accomplished when it is exercised as close as possible to the citizen-subjects, limiting the risks of technocratic excesses by a distant power relying on a long decision-making chain. The definition of France as a single, indivisible republic has thus been upset, as the addition of the adjective "decentralized" to the French Constitution attests.

The main limitation of the shared-policy and co-sovereignty model of local government relates to the evolution of the financial macrostructure of the general government, which has not increased the decision-making latitude of local authorities. On the contrary, the central government has removed or reduced their fiscal powers by eliminating the taxes on which they had leeway in setting rates. The State has chosen to finance the competences transferred to local authorities not by granting new fiscal capacities, but through subsidies or tax transfers, the amount of which it sets on a more-or-less discretionary basis. Decentralization has therefore not been attended by the development of fiscal federalism, quite the contrary.

In the field of healthcare, private-practice medicine originally coexisted with a hospital system comprised of a multitude of institutions considered as local public services. This set of institutions was financed by a social security system created after the Second World War and placed under autonomous joint governance. This form of governance was born out of a clear intention to differentiate between nationalization, which was desired, and State control, which appeared to constitute a counter-model.

The current situation is very different.

First, as we showed in the previous section, the choice to finance the social security system through specific contributions—paid in part by employers—is at odds with the wish to reduce social security contributions, which are claimed to harm the international competitiveness of companies. This has led to the financing of health insurance through taxation, and thus to a reduction of joint management, which has increased the role of the State.

Second, we are witnessing a rise of the State, built on a systemic conception of the health system. This approach is close to systems analysis reasoning. Prevention, the work of family doctors, the care pathway, and hospitalization are all parts of a whole that constantly need to be balanced.

Third, activity-based pricing, which aims to ensure that institutions comply with national standard costs, constitutes a complete departure from the old system, which was based on the old budgetary principle that if there are costs, they must be covered. The transformation of the financing system has reduced the publicness of hospitals (Bozeman, 1987). It has made each hospital dependent on an implicit market of average performance assessed according to the average costs of treatment of each homogeneous patient group and the case mix they treat. The institutions have thus been put under pressure, much to the discontent of medical or paramedical staff. However, publicness has not disappeared. Hospitals' qualifications as such are issued by the regional health agencies of the central government, which also decide on the opening and closing of beds.

A dependence on political authority that makes hospitals hybrid organizations continues to exist, especially as the State, through its regional health agencies, interferes in determining the means operators are to use to reduce health expenditure. Combined with the imperative directives issued by the regional health agencies concerning the number of beds available in each hospital, this system paints a picture of rationed health. This expression, which is always refused by the government of the day, has nevertheless been openly embraced by one of the main promoters of this system (Kervasdoué et al., 1980).

Finally, the creation of regional health agencies reflects the central government's recognition of the importance of territorial proximity. Yet the consequences of this measure remain ambiguous: having more agencies means less bureaucratization and control by the State. The public authorities' management of the COVID pandemic through the agencies supports this idea. The fact that these regional health agencies' constituencies were mapped onto the new large regions when the latter were created suggests that a new administrative silo has been added to the already fragmented network of silos that the State's field agencies constitute.

As stated in 2007 during the PPGR operation, the State's devolved regional services are the locus of national public policies' territorialization.

The services of the *départements*, on the other hand, are defined as specific local entities. This formulation is certainly elegant, yet it lacks clarity. First, it implies that the *région* is the relevant territory for territorialization and therefore that it is sufficiently homogeneous for this purpose. Second, it gives the impression that the services of the *départements* are essentially offices to which citizens go, whereas proximity often lies with institutions under the remit of these *département* services but serving a geographical area smaller than the *département*.

The redeployment of State officials from *département*-level services to the services of the *régions* supported the idea of the *région*'s prevalence over the *département*. This perspective was soon tempered, as the *département* authority, which had temporarily been deprived of the general competence clause, regained it. Where public policies are shared, an inevitable link must be established between the modalities of administrative devolution and those of political decentralization. The *département* could provide such a framework, for the political-administrative bodies of the *département* authority needed strong contacts in the government's field agencies located in their *département*.

The 2007 reform mentioned above was seen by some as a revenge by the prefects, who had been upset by the implementation of the OLGBL. They felt that they had been stripped of an important resource which had enabled them to secure their power over the State's other external services in their constituencies. The OLGBL did introduce the fungibility of funds within each programme, allowing programme managers to transfer funds from one type of expenditure to another and from one action to another. However, it prohibited transfers from one programme to another, that is, essentially from one policy area to another. In other words, it followed a vertical approach, with programmes subdivided into operational budgets and operational units at execution level so that they could be spread across the whole national territory, at the expense of a horizontal territory-based approach. The result was a clash between the territorial organizational structure of the State and its financial structure.

In early 2021, the prime minister sent prefects a roadmap. They were given a three-year inter-ministerial mandate to strengthen their role in the steering and leadership not only of State services but also of public operators. This extension to operators was certainly a victory for the prefects. It also amounted to a negation of the concept of public operator, which challenged the agencies' specificity and autonomy. The management procedures governing the administrations became references for the control exercised by the prefect over State services, which differed from the references used by the State to control production agencies. Corporatist behaviour on the part of prefects broadened their role, at the expense of the autonomy that the status of agency had nevertheless granted to the public operators. This was a consequence of intensified territorialization, which undermined the process of agencification.

The link was maintained between each devolved *région-* and *département*-level service and the directorates and ministry from which they originated, from which their staff came and from which they received their funding. However, the fact that the prefects were the secondary authorizer for all the directorates under their remit nevertheless gave them a right of review over these services' functioning. That being said, it did not allow them to modulate the distribution of funding based on what they considered to be the hierarchy of needs and policies to carry out in their *région* or *département*. On the other hand, two special budgetary programmes were made available to prefects to carry out territorial policies in their *département*.

The most recent developments in the organization of devolved services are savings-driven. This is reflected in the merging of support services inherited from the former directorates, such as staff, finance and procurement, and the eradication of duplicate services across those of a prefecture and those of the directorates under its remit. At the same time, managing an increasingly dense inter-ministerial system favours the use of a solution that has already demonstrated its limitations in the past. This solution mobilizes a theory of inter-organizational integration that is based on the capacity for coordination through hierarchical centralization. The more differentiated and compartmentalized an institutional unit's components, the more centralization is needed. The less direct cooperation there is between them, the more coordination is needed through the hierarchy of authority. The miracle solution is the prefect. This theory in use has been appropriated by both the leaders of the executive and many local elected officials.

There is somewhat of a vicious circle at work. The more Paris advocates or even demands devolution to its field agencies to set up a network in the country that is symmetrical to that of decentralization for the benefit of local authorities, the more the governance of the administrative sphere, which is so clear on paper, gives rise in practice to a complicated if not disorganized and contradictory coverage of the territory by the State, and the less spontaneous cooperation between its multiple field agencies occurs at local level. The more autonomous a ministry's field agency is, the more influential it is, particularly in relation to local elected officials and in the game of intra-administrative competition (Crozier & Thoenig, 1976). Many *département*-level directors who previously received their powers from a ministerial delegation now receive them from a prefectural delegation, a fact of which they are not always aware. Depending on the *département* and the *région*, the respective competences of the State and local authorities do not cover the same areas or the same responsibilities.

For the central government, managing inter-ministerial relations is like rolling Sisyphus' boulder up a hill. The France of local authorities is moreover becoming increasingly diverse in institutional terms—with at least four levels of authorities—and in terms of population distribution—metropolitan areas, medium and small towns, and rural areas. Applying the same devolution model to all *régions* and to each *département* is a sweet illusion.

Ultimately, one key observation arises from this comparison between the three areas just covered and the way in which central government contributes to their development in a discontinuous or even chaotic way.

In two of the three areas, local authorities and State field agencies, organizational structure is clearly the determining factor. Financial structure, which is established by the rules of the budgetary game, the criteria for allocating funds and fiscal power, acts as a brake on the dynamics at play. It is also a reminder of the centralization of a central government responsible for the sustainability of the financial balance of the State budget and, internationally, for the financial balance of the general government.

In the third area, health, the situation is different, although changes in organizational structure also play a role. The modification of financial structure has been used as a powerful lever for the evolution of the local actor that is the hospital. Reform has been more destabilizing than in other sectors. The search for efficiency has been experienced as undue managerialization. It remains an unacceptable prospect in the eyes of many professionals in the medical sector.

Health is also somewhat of a textbook case for new public management. First, because of the importance of measuring in this field. While indicators are multiplying in other areas of public policy, they are most often of little importance. This is the case of the indicators included every year in the documents supporting the finance laws submitted to parliament. Despite their mediocre quality, they shock very few people, simply because *central government* services are not financed according to the performance they measure. They determine the funding of institutions and therefore the resources available to them.

All in all, while the previous chapters show that explicit programmes do not lead to significant developments in practice and that the appropriation of instruments is also very limited, this chapter highlights more significant developments, both good and bad. These are generated by actions that do not fall under the banner of specific reform programmes although governments call them reform programmes. These developments are not linear; they allow for advances, just as they cause setbacks. The measures implemented apply to issues that may seem essentially administrative or sectoral, rather than institutional or pertaining to the sharing of power. Last but not least, the evolution of the relationship with the citizens is in this case, as in the case of the programmes, largely a secondary concern.

References

Accar, B., & Guiguet, X. (2020). *L'Evaluation des Politiques Partagées entre l'Etat et les Collectivités Territoriales*. Inspection Générale de l'Administration.

Argyris, C., Putnam, R., & McLain Smith, D. (1985). *Action Science: Concepts, Methods and Skills for Research and Intervention*. Jossey-Bass.

Bozeman, B. (1987). *All Organizations are Public: Bridging Public and Private Organizational Theories*. Jossey-Bass.

Cour des comptes. (2020). *Les finances publiques: pour une réforme du cadre organique et de la gouvernance Rapport public thématique*. La Documentation Français.

Crozier, M., & Thoenig, J. C. (1976). The Regulation of Complex Organized Systems. *Administrative Science Quarterly*, 547–570.

Hoffmann, S. (2013). *Paradoxes of the French Political Community. In Search of France*. Harvard University Press.

Kervasdoué, J., Kimberly, J., & Rodwin, V. (1980). *La santé rationnée ?* Economica.

March, J. G., & Olson, J. P. (1983). Organizing Political Life: What Administrative Reorganisation Tells Us About Government. *American Political Science Review*, 77(2), 281–296.

Rhodes, R. A. W. (2018). *Control and Power in Central-Local Government Relations*. Routledge.

Simonet, D. (2013). New Public Management and the Reform of French Public Hospitals. *Journal of Public Affairs*, 13(3), 260–271.

Thoenig, J. C. (1979). Reform Policies of Local Government in France. In J. Lagroye & V. Wright (Eds.), *Local Government in Britain and France* (pp. 83–109). George Allen and Unwin.

Thoenig, J. C. (2006). Territorial Institutions. In R. A. W. Rhodes, S. A. Binder, & B. A. Rockman (Eds.), *The Oxford Handbook of Political Institutions* (pp. 281–302). Oxford University Press.

CHAPTER 10

Human Resources: A Keystone Structure

The previous chapters point to one major observation: the capacity for change and flexibility of the structures governing the organization and finances of the public sector are limited and variable, but they do exist. The same cannot be said for the structure of human resources, which organizes public servants into a set of categories according to the types of occupation to which they give access and the associated duties and rights. This structure creates inertia, with major consequences on public management.

This chapter assesses this structure in four steps. First, it examines the foundations underpinning the structure. Second, it shows how it consolidated, if not ossified, over almost half a century, particularly by extending to institutions beyond the State civil service. Third, it reviews initiatives that have been taken to address its lack of flexibility, but which have done little to change its foundations. Finally, it examines a far more radical approach that has been on the government agenda since 2017.

10.1 The Creation of the Basic Structure

The immediate post-war period was a crucial founding moment. On 2 October 1945, the provisional government presided by Charles de Gaulle signed a decree creating a national school of administration (*École Nationale d'Administration*, ENA).

© The Author(s), under exclusive license to Springer Nature Switzerland AG 2022
P. Gibert, J.-C. Thoenig, *Assessing Public Management Reforms, Understanding Governance*,
https://doi.org/10.1007/978-3-030-89799-4_10

Its stated mission was to democratize the recruitment of senior administrative civil servants and to professionalize them. As a public administrative institution, it was placed under the remit of the ministry in charge of the civil service, and not the ministry in charge of higher education. Its students were to be recruited through a competitive entrance examination, as were those of the *grandes écoles* that had been training the engineers recruited by the State, sometimes since the early nineteenth century, the best-known example being the *Ecole Polytechnique*.

On 19 October 1946, a law was promulgated that concerned all State employees, not just its senior managers. It is considered one of the great progressive texts inspired by the authorities that had led the resistance against German occupation. After the liberation of France, Charles de Gaulle, president of the council of ministers, entrusted the portfolio to Maurice Thorez, leader of the Communist Party. Thorez acted both as vice-president of the council and minister of state in charge of the civil service. The law was adopted by parliament thanks to a coalition ranging from the far-left to the centre-right.

This 1946 law set out rules applicable to all civil servants belonging to the State civil service, in other words, to the agents of the central government. It institutionalized a *statut général* (the general civil service regulations) that applied to all levels of the hierarchy, from junior employees to senior management, and from local services to the offices of the ministries in Paris. As for the major administrative corps that pre-dated the *statut général* of 1946, such as the *Conseil d'État* created in 1799, the *Cour des Comptes* created in 1807, and the *Inspection Générale des Finances* established in 1816, their particularities would be included in the principles governing the *statut général* applying to civil servants, with a few exceptions such as magistrates and the military.

To avoid boring or misleading readers unfamiliar with the legal subtleties of the 1946 law, a few specific measures warrant some explanation.

The first is the distinction between rank and post.

A civil servant's rank is a personal attribute that cannot be taken away from them. Their post refers to a position that they occupy at a specific point in time and from which they can be removed. This position can be within or outside the administrative scope of the corps to which they belong. In this sense, rank and post are not strictly linked. For example, a public servant may be transferred to another function or post, or even no longer hold one, without losing their original rank or salary, and without being penalized as regards promotions. Their original corps or status serves as protection.

Rank and post may however be linked. Not all posts can be held by anyone with any rank and from any corps. Some functions, the list of which is established by administrative law, prohibit unrestricted access. They are reserved for civil servants of a particular rank and from a particular corps.

One type of position escapes the *statut général*. It comprises senior posts at the highest level of the civil service administration, which are left to the government's discretion. They are therefore subject to a different regime. About 500 individuals are concerned: for example, prefects, ambassadors, directors general and central administration directors. The list is not exhaustive, although a decree issued in 1985 did determine the number and type of such roles. The government is free to appoint both civil servants and non-civil servants to these positions. If civil servants are appointed, they are generally placed in a position known as a secondment. If a non-civil servant is appointed to such a position, they are not granted a permanent appointment in the civil service; they are therefore not entitled to tenure and cannot rely on being able to find another position in the civil service. Moreover, the individuals holding these positions are revocable *ad nutum*, that is, at the full discretion of the government. In practice and as stipulated by the 1985 decree, only 5-7% of these positions were to be filled by contracted staff from the private sector, who had however for the most part transitioned via a position as advisor to a minister. The turnover rate did nevertheless remain high (Eymeri-Douzant, 2021). Between May 2017 and September 2019, 83% of these senior managers out of a total of 194, were not renewed by the new president, Emmanuel Macron.

The second particularity of the 1946 law relates to the way in which public servants are categorized. It regulates a system based on the concept of a corps.

A corps is comprised of one or several ranks. Corps group together civil servants subject to the same special status and entitled to the same ranks. The ranks between which promotion proceeds by selection are divided into grades between which promotion proceeds by seniority. Each grade is associated with a pay index, which defines the civil servant's remuneration. In principle, the set of indices associated with the ranks and grades of a corps therefore determines civil servants' pay. Most of them spend their entire career in this corps. Their careers are then characterized by both a more or less rapid succession of ranks or classes and, within these, of grades, all of which are subject to procedures that are often complicated. The idea underpinning this system is to prevent favouritism and clientelism. The legal concept of *statut général* therefore covers a set of provisions that determine the situation of those who benefit from it and that of their employer, in terms of recruitment, career and retirement. In the case of civil servants, it is theoretically unilateral, not contractual. This concept is supported by the fact that very precise pay scales replace the goodwill of the hierarchy. Thus defined, the *statut général* is supposed to protect public servants from the arbitrariness of their superiors. Moreover, civil servants at all levels of the hierarchy, irrespective of the ministry, are recruited through competitive entrance examinations, not through co-opting or on a discretionary basis. Merit, as measured by success in an impersonal recruitment examination, is the only thing that counts.

A normal career depends on the stratum or corps to which one belongs. Normal, in terms of staff management, is defined as spending one's entire working life in the same corps. However, there are exceptions to this normality. For example, it is possible to move from one corps to another through special competitions or direct procedures, but the number of people recruited in this way remains limited. Additionally, contractual staff can be hired for types of jobs not found in these corps, although such exceptions are limited by restricted quotas allocated cautiously.

Through the combination of two formal frameworks, the corps and the *statut général*, the 1946 law distinguishes France from other countries, particularly those which have the statutes but not the corps, such as the United Kingdom and Australia. In these countries, civil servants must meet two requirements: they must have common senior manager skills, and be suited to the post. Except for those operating in expert fields, they must demonstrate management skills, for example in the areas of leadership, reporting, communication and adaptability. In France, these priorities are far less important, as membership of a particular corps is what makes the difference in terms of remuneration, retirement and access to positions. It is no coincidence that French civil servants' pay is referred to not as a salary but as a *"traitement,"* that is, an index-linked salary, based on rank. The State does not remunerate a job or a professional skill. Basically, their *traitement* is supposed to enable each civil servant to hold their social rank.

The *statut général* provides the basic structure, which is the same one for all civil servants. But it is fitted out internally by a series of detailed statutes. Each level has its own particularities that distinguish it from the others, in terms of the hierarchical rank of its members and of their ministry. The architecture underpinning the 1946 law, the features of which we have just outlined, points to at least four major remarks from a management assessment perspective. These relate to a certain number of deadlocks that future human resources management may be faced with.

The first relates to mobility between the levels of the building.

The statutes provide predictable prospects and job security guarantees, but they also limit most civil servants' career prospects. In theory they do indeed give each civil servant the possibility of obtaining a very senior position, but in practice a civil servant has to be very lucky to be able to climb to the top levels of the administrative building. In reality, those from a better social or education background are favoured (Thoenig, 1987). For most people, the wait to ascend can be long, and the psychological toll becomes heavy to bear as the aspirant becomes older and more senior. The prospect of retirement sometimes takes over quite early as the reference timeline. In short, human resource management does not value experience and mobilization through motivation.

The idea that the *statut général* is an advantage because of it offers protection and a minimum career guarantee is in itself not wrong. It is however oversimplified. The average civil servant, who belongs to corps with short careers and a relatively narrow wage scale, may feel routine setting in fairly early on in their career and grow weary of the difficulty of accessing mobility that is generally not imposed on them. They may also consider that they are paying dearly for the benefits of the *statut général* if they compare their remuneration with that of friends or relatives working in the private sector. At the same time, the protection granted by the *statut* creates little incentive to migrate to the private sector. This is compounded by de facto impossibility of doing so when civil servants age without acquiring the skills that would give them a marketable qualification to work for companies. They then become effectively captive of their membership of the administration. As a result, mobility from the public to the private sector mainly concerns senior civil servants. In addition to their own qualities, they can boast about their network of contacts in the world of government public institutions to their new employers, as these networks are a highly sought-after business asset.

A second key feature revealed by the overall assessment of the *statut général* is the function served by the competitive entrance examination.

The competitive entrance examination (*concours*) has been enshrined as a means of ensuring equality. It defines normality. Other forms of recruitment and promotion remain exceptions, admittedly tolerated but with vigilance, or very sparingly. A civil servant derives legitimacy from the entrance examination they sat, the lived experience of which constitutes their identity. For example, an administrator recruited through what was previously the postal and telecommunications service entrance examination and who completed the full syllabus of the ENA did not however become an ENA alumnus. Likewise, an engineer who joined the telecommunications corps after graduating from the *Ecole Polytechnique* and who attends the *Ecole des Mines* in Paris, which trains engineers, will not be a "true" civil engineer. Identity is not just a reflection of an administrative artefact; it is experienced as a branding that one bears for life. The education completed after the entrance examination does not produce any legitimacy, even if for some people its length justifies differences in positioning in the strata of the system. In other words, this upstream branding, which is supposed to create equality, creates inequalities that are perpetuated throughout the working life cycle.

A third point concerns independence from politics.

The *statut général* and its variations by strata ensure independence from politics. The 1946 law and the parliamentary debates that preceded it made ample reference to the need to put an end to two practices: clientelist recruitment by elected officials, and co-opting by administrative corps favouring recruitment from their members' social circles. The solution adopted by the government was drastic: to limit the intrusion of politics and politicians as much as possible, including in the recruitment and appointment of tenured staff. In other words, the labour market accessible by the State risked being closed off, and the use of new professional skills would become more difficult. The range of specializations would depend more and more on an administrative world which, through the training and experience of its members, was based on narrow, generalist, procedural and dated administrative know-how.

One exception was however tolerated: a small number of positions escaped the hegemony of the civil service and remained subject to the discretion of the executive. The executive could appoint whosoever it wished to in these positions, irrespective of whether the person was a civil servant or came from the private, civil-society or political sector. The list included director general positions and the chair of the board of public institutions, public enterprises, and national companies, which are appointed by the council of ministers. It varied from one year to the next. Politicization was the threat to be avoided.

A comparison is often drawn between the spoils system, exemplified by the United States, and the French system of a statutory framework guaranteeing a lifetime career. However, this opposition is not as radical as either side claims. As we already pointed out above, in France, the government retains considerable discretion to appoint and dismiss those in positions such as prefects, ambassadors and central administration directors, to name but a few. It can appoint members of corps other than those under the remit of the ministry to which their corps is normally assigned. If a civil servant appointed to a position on a discretionary basis is dismissed, they return to their parent corps. They thus have a comfortable safety net. While functionally subject to arbitrariness, they are statutorily protected. This is not the case of their colleagues from outside the civil service.

Finally, a fourth feature pertains to the actual income hierarchy and its differentiation effects.

Civil servants are placed in a stratification system based on qualities largely beyond their control and performance. The indices that define positions provide a very flat pay range compared to the private sector. This is due partly to the idea that one cannot really get rich in the service of a State financed by taxpayers, and partly to the weight of trade unionism that does not favour opening up the pay index scale too much. These indices also define the hierarchy between corps. But all this applies only to the indexed salaries themselves, which can be supplemented by bonuses and allowances. The latter may be very low or even close to zero or, on the contrary, they can account for about 80% of remuneration in a small number of corps and ranks, thus considerably modifying the hierarchy of remuneration compared to that of the indexed salaries. This double hierarchy significantly widens the actual pay scale. It differentiates financially between civil servant corps with the same indexing levels, and consequently makes it possible to discreetly change their hierarchy. Bonuses' share of total remuneration therefore generally increases with the status of the corps in the hierarchy of indices: it is higher for civil administrators than for attachés, higher for attachés than for administrative secretaries, and so forth. On average, managers receive twice as much in bonuses as employees lower down in the hierarchy.

10.2 The Extension and Deepening of the Structure

Over the years, the framework drawn up by the 1946 law became an absolute frame of reference for managing the human resources in charge of the administrative public service. Far from being treated as a bureaucratic relic to be confined to the shelves of history, it evolved and was amended somewhat, particularly by a government order of 4 February 1959. The aim was to adapt it to the constitution of the Fifth Republic, which had just been adopted by universal suffrage, championed by President Charles de Gaulle.

The persistence and even vivacity of the 1946 model was perfectly illustrated in the early 1980s, after President François Mitterrand and the left wing arrived in power. The new government adopted a policy that could be interpreted at face value as paradoxical.

Gaston Defferre, mayor of Marseille and then Minister of the Interior, launched a spectacular decentralization of power to local authorities (Schmidt, 2007). The *départements* and their general councils recovered a capacity for administrative and political autonomy that had been gradually taken away from them since the late nineteenth century (Thoenig, 1987). The representative of the State, in other words the Prefect, no longer had oversight of the external services of the State or the services of the *départements*. Meanwhile, the *région* became a fully fledged institution with its own political bodies elected by universal suffrage, and its own administrative services. Moreover, both the *régions* and *départements* were given rather broad competences. In short, the relationship between the State and local authorities seemed to be opening up (Thoenig, 2005). At the same time, however, the minister in charge of the civil service, Anicet Le Pors, a member of the Communist Party who belonged to the same government as Gaston Defferre, was preparing a major reform of the civil service. This law, approved by parliament on 13 July 1983, affirmed parity between the three branches of the civil service: the State, local authorities, and hospitals. It also detailed the rights and obligations of civil servants. In fact, it upheld and specified three general principles of the 1946 law:

- equality, which underpins the rule that entry into the civil service requires sitting a competitive entrance examination,
- independence, with the rank as the property of the civil servant, separate from their post,
- responsibility, with society having the right to hold any public official accountable for their administration.

The extension of the *statut général* of 1946, which until then had applied only to State employees, was institutionalized by two separate pieces of legislation. A law of 26 January 1984 dealt with the local civil service. Another law of 9 January 1986 completed the institutionalization of the hospital civil service. France saw the range of corps and statutes grow and become more attractive. In 2017, there was a total of 5.46 million public servants: 2.45 million working for the State, 1.89 million for local authorities, and 1.16 million in the hospital sector. Of this total, 83% had civil servant status.

Not all permanent civil servants are however identical from a legal and administrative point of view. Subtle differences exist. They may appear insignificant, but they are not. Complex differentiation within France's civil service is concealed under a single institutional umbrella. Whereas one legal text defines civil servant's status in general terms, there are over a thousand special national statutes applicable to particular corps of particular job categories. This is the case of provisions, referred to as special statutes, which differ across corps that fall within the same category in a common statutory grid, the *statut général*. The magistrature and the military, for example, enjoy specific provisions. Moreover, there are so-called exceptional statutes which, while they fall within the framework of the *statut général*, enjoy significant exceptions in comparison: this is the case for academic researchers. Furthermore, each of the three branches of the civil service—the State, local authorities and hospitals—takes into account the organizations to which it refers. Thus, local authorities have job categories, not corps. This inversion of the raison d'être and the mechanism is justified by the desire to respect the autonomy of the *régions*, *départements* and *communes*. Yet the fact of there not being a corps for local or regional civil servants means that they do not benefit from the right to transfers from one authority to another, since the decision depends on the authority to which they apply.

At the same time, the significant differences in statutes between the three branches of civil service should not obscure the drive to generalize a model by imitating as closely as possible the *statut général*. This model has been taken to extremes, particularly in terms of the training of senior managers. The ENA serves as a blueprint. Thus, a national institute of territorial studies (*Institut national d'études territoriales*, INET) was formally created in 1997 in the wake of the law creating the civil service of local authorities. Its mission is to select and train the administrators of large local authorities. The INET is not under the authority of any state ministry; it is an autonomous public institution in charge of the training of all territorial civil servants. It recruits through its own competitive entrance examination and produces territorial administrators. Like the ENA, the INET does not have permanent academic researcher staff. It is also under the watchful and conservative eye of its alumni. The INET is a clone.

More generally, and with a few rare exceptions, the training of civil servants in all public services is mostly provided outside universities, without its own corps of lecturers and researchers. It relies essentially on a group of temporary staff, many of whom are practitioners drawn from the ranks of former students. This model encourages reproduction far more than innovation.

Imitating the State model is not straightforward. The decentralization of the early 1980s could have provided an opportunity to develop a new model for both the staff statutes and the training of the management leadership. Reflection on the feasibility and the opportunity of this new approach was overshadowed and gave way to corporatist concerns over comparability. To obtain a statute similar to that of the State civil service and ensure the possibility of transfer from one to the other, it was necessary to advocate a comparable length and type of training and selectivity through competitive entrance examinations similar to those of the cream of the crop in the civil service.

The 1983 *statut* and the subsequent laws and regulations thus attest to a spectacular ossification of the civil service. This is partly ideologically driven, and partly justified by the legitimate desire to remove territorial civil servants from the discretionary power of local executives. It is also partly attributable to an inferiority complex towards the central government administration, spurring the desire to endow the territorial civil service with the apparent signs of a same level of dignity.

As far as the rules of the game for staff are concerned, a process of isomorphism was evident (DiMaggio & Powell, 1983). The decentralization of 1983 did not involve NPM. The concern was not with importing an instrument and a management system from the business world, but with mapping as closely as possible the human resource management structure governing local authorities on that of the central government. This process was not coercive, even though a State law operationalized its basic structure. It was a process of mimicry. It was based not on the reputation of organizational efficiency of the system imitated, but essentially on its effectiveness in acquiring social status as well as limiting the risk that a local spoils system would be implemented by mayors. Avoiding discretionary behaviours by local politicians was expected to protect jobs inside the local public service.

The organizational structure therefore clashed with the staff management structure. It was permeated by the specific statutes of the civil service corps, and its fundamental rules did not evolve. The corporatism that informs this model is widespread. The higher up the organizational hierarchy one goes, the more corporate professional associations take the place of trade unions. Self-perpetuating corporatism.

10.3 The Ineffective Quest for Flexibility

A third stage was characterized by the realization by top executives that the structure managing State staff had become increasingly rigid and restrictive over the past half century, precisely at a time when the organizational and financial structures would have required greater flexibility for the employer.

Various measures appear to have been taken to this effect, organizing the merger of different corps, staff planning, the hosting of temporary staff, and ongoing training (Guyomarch, 1999). These measures however remained modest and failed to effect any radical change to the structure.

A first course of action adopted by the government was to remedy the fragmentation of the civil service by reducing the number of corps through mergers.

An exemplary case of a merger was launched in 2009, bringing together two corps of senior civil servants, namely engineers from the Ecole Polytechnique. The one corps was within the province of the Ministry of Public Works and mainly covered urban areas, while the other one came under the Ministry of Agriculture and covered rural areas. However, the results of the merger remained mixed for many years. The members of the merged corps continued to stand out from each other, and in practice each side retained much of its former autonomy and specificity in terms of the management, placing and evaluation of its members. From the outside, the rationality of certain mergers may also seem questionable. For example, beside for hypothetical financial reasons, the creation of a single corps grouping together rural hydraulics experts with those of roads and bridges was a measure for which the effects excepted by the political authorities—flexibility of action, broader know-how—remain to be proven.

Mergers are both difficult and inflationary. Although they concern corps with fairly similar pay scales, the payment of supplementary remuneration called bonuses, sometimes a significant addition to salaries themselves, follows its own system in each corps and the actual amounts can differ significantly from one merged body to another. In the senior civil service, these supplements can double the basic pay cheque.

Civil service managers are cautious about pay policy. On the one hand, there is pressure from trade unions and, to a lesser extent, public opinion to narrow the pay scale between the lowest- and highest-ranking civil servants. On the other hand, realism and the desire to maintain a high-quality senior civil service require that senior civil servants are paid in line with their responsibilities. The solution adopted to navigate this double bind is to compensate for the levelling effects of a flat salary scale by opening up the bonus scale considerably. The percentage of bonuses in remuneration therefore increases with the status of a corps in the index hierarchy. This salary-bonus duality allows the State employer to differentiate financially between civil servant corps with similar pay scales and thus to discreetly change their hierarchy. Mergers of corps challenge this differentiation between the corps concerned, and demand an alignment with the most favoured corps. They therefore prove costly.

A second measure adopted by the executive in 2015 was a job and skill planning policy. In its own way, this was a ruse by the State.

This management system, a method commonly used in companies and other countries, was designed to harmonize the widely diverse practices of different ministries. The aim was to put an end to the old practice of grading civil servants without a face-to-face meeting between the assessor and the person being assessed. A new practice had been imposed in the meantime, that of the evaluation interview, but this method of human resources management appeared to be insufficient. Although the new so-called planning method was expected to change attitudes while avoiding a legal revolution, it was not made compulsory, on the pretext of facilitating incremental learning.

In 2017, the socialist prime minister, Bernard Cazeneuve, devised a comprehensive strategy that contrasted with the previous incremental approach to human resource management. It was supposed to be implemented by all ministries within two years. A circular dated 16 March 2017 set out the objectives of a State human resources policy and the strategic levers to be mobilized. Its style, its construction, and its mix of what was said and what was not, made it strikingly reminiscent of all the previous strategic documents drafted and made public, particularly in the context of the contractualization and renewal of the oversight of operators.

Nothing, whether essential or accessory, was to be left out of the expression of fundamental medium-term choices.

Some 50 actions were proposed, 15 of which were priorities. The directorate-general for the administration and the civil service would be responsible, at inter-ministerial level, for implementing and monitoring the evolution of State human resources. The document set out rules informed by societal values such as gender equality, support for disabled workers, and the prohibition of discrimination. Yet the civil service continued to be exempt from labour law and remained governed by administrative law. None of this challenged the fundamental structure of human resource management.

The government took a third route, which was also a ruse: the use of contractual staff to reduce the shortage of professional skills.

The *statut général* provides that permanent civilian posts in the State, local authorities and their public administrative institutions are the preserve of civil servants. This principle has no constitutional value, yet it remains well entrenched in practice through numerous decrees for functional positions. A dispensation allows the recruitment of contractual agents when no corps of civil servants is qualified to perform the necessary functions. The recruitment of experts on a contractual basis is treated as a suitable solution because the expertise required meets a transitional need, that is, to ensure the shift from one state of practice to another.

The use of permanent employment contracts in the civil service was institutionalized in 2005. It was treated not as a human resource management tool, but as an emergency measure. Such was the case for computerization, which had become a matter of urgency. It was also a way to address the lack of job security for staff that the administration wished to retain, beyond the six-year period within which fixed-term contracts could legally be renewed. This measure also concerned staff aged over 50, who already had fix-term contracts and had been in the position for over six years. The measure taken in 2005 thus appeared to be a compromise between providing more attractive conditions for staff on contract, and avoiding their integration as tenured civil servants. A further step was taken in 2012 when a new law authorized the integration of contractual staff as civil servants. This law became null and void in 2018. The State could not rely solely on civil servants specialized in a particular field, for their way of thinking was often shaped more by the culture of their field than by the search for innovative solutions. Given the highly competitive labour market and evolving skills, it was faced with the absolute necessity of recruiting flexibly and retaining contractual staff with new expertise. In 2017, an inter-ministerial action plan was drawn up to address all recruitment difficulties across strategic professions, whether old or new, such as those related to management, management control, human resources, and technical professions. Its contribution was to remain very modest.

Ultimately, change was not the result of comprehensive reflection on the nature of the tasks to be entrusted to two main categories of public servants, permanent and contractual staff, but the product of ad hoc reactions.

In the 2010s, some 700 so-called senior posts, such as secretaries-general, directors-general and directors of ministries, had been appointed at the discretion of the government every year. They were open to people from the private sector. In practice, however, only 5-6% of these posts were filled by contractual staff from the private sector, most of whom had nevertheless previously worked as advisers to a minister.

In late 2019, it became legally possible to recruit contractual staff to fill management positions in the three branches of public service: the central government administration, local authorities, and hospitals. This measure concerned considerably broadened the scope of possibilities. For the State, for example, its effect reached to about 3000 positions such as deputy directors, project managers and sub-prefects. Until then, these management posts had been the territory, if not the preserve, of civil servants only. For example, nearly half of them were held by civil administrators who had graduated from the ENA, the crowning achievement of their careers.

More generally, it is doubtful that two types of population with different employment statuses but occupying the same functions in the broad sense of the term can peacefully coexist within the same organization. Enhancing the porosity of the borders between public and private employment remains a goal that will not be easy to achieve.

An alternative often adopted by companies to get their staff's professional skills up to speed is continuous training: endogenous *aggiornamento* becomes a strategic weapon for the efficiency of their action. What about the French civil service?

An in-depth assessment suggests unambiguously that in-service training for practitioners is a weak palliative for State human resources management. Although it is supposed to serve as a lever to change administrative management and broaden the thinking of its civil servants, in reality such training is far from resolving the cognitive delays that are fuelled by the excessive inbreeding in the civil service, that innervate its thinking, and that mitigate the demotivation due to the lack of career prospects.

Assessing the efficiency of ongoing education cannot be reduced to considering the few statistical variables usually displayed by the sponsoring administrations, such as the total number of days provided, the range of subjects covered, or the amount invested. In 2017, professional training expenditure amounted to 3.2% of the wage bill. Training for existing staff takes on many forms, from facilitating the introduction of a new management tool in an administration or service to training undertaken by a civil servant at their request. While initial training remains monopolized by specialized schools of administration, in-service training involves a variety of non-exclusive offers of executive education. A careful assessment reveals three main features of such training.

First, the few major programmes set up since the 1970s by certain ministries have had a short life span. There are a wide range of reasons for taking part in a training programme. For the sponsor, it is often associated with a perceived deficiency, which can only be ascribed to civil servants who benefited from exceptional access or promotions. It is seen as minor added value, purely technical and therefore not worthy of in-depth attention. For the participants, the motivations range from the appeal of a fashionable programme to the obligation to meet a prerequisite in order to access a particular post.

Second, training is not designed to turn the generalist civil servant into a specialist, but to make them aware of a specific skill without forcing them to have the associated expertise. It is expected that this will enable them to identify the contributions of an innovation and to work with it. The dominant training model remains that of the ENA: addressing informed enthusiasts.

Third, the approach most widely used is a-managerial. The evaluation of a programme is most often based on in-training written and/or oral assessments, mainly by applause. These are guided by cross-admiration between three parties: the speaker, the participant, and the sponsor. The participants' expectations and the personal relationship, whether friendly or negative, between the sponsor, the trainer and the audience play a decisive role. However, prioritizing the audience's expectations can cause the trainer to be overly sensitive to them, leading him or her for example to prefer storytelling to constructed and relatively conceptual presentations, at the risk of making excessive inferences.

Two other approaches are used far less. The one relates to the skills of management technicians. The emphasis shifts from an irenic presentation of the novelty and what sometimes resembles an editorial advertisement for the innovation, to an examination of the difficulties encountered in the field by those in charge of implementing it. The key here is to enable participants to overcome these difficulties. The trainer offers less academic and more experiential knowledge of the tools proposed. The other approach is driven more by for the intention to implement management reform. It focuses on the positioning and appropriation of the tool in the service management system. The tool is studied not as an isolated object but as an instrument of disruption. The evaluation of a programme is done cold, to capture how the message heard in class was appropriated, and with what consequences.

All in all, the results of the various attempts listed above to gain more flexibility have been very limited. The structure of staff management remains ossified, even if it has gained a few levers to make up for its lack of flexibility. Despite some non-negligible progress with the ruses and palliatives we have just reviewed, the government authorities ultimately remain powerless to change the foundations of the structure of human resources. For example, establishing a specific mission within the ministries to identify and support high-potential executives is still something of a sword in the water. Instruments to manage jobs and skills remain a superficial initiative.

These bleak findings on continuing education further exacerbate a more general and lasting cognitive trend stifling the capabilities of the public service, and in particular but not only that of its managers: the prevalence of home-grown cultures.

The management of the public sector and its development is largely devolved by politicians to senior civil servants, especially to ENA alumni who graduated top of their class. They hold leadership positions in ministerial cabinets and at the head of the central services that count. The elite of the elite exercising this quasi-monopoly is a very small world. Only about 15% of the students who leave the ENA join one of the three major corps every year, and their members in the central government account for about 400 active members on average.

This is a well-known fact: the State is governed by ENA alumni (Suleiman, 2015). The consequences, however, are less known. Yet they are not insignificant, for the ENA–*grand corps* twosome still constitutes the keystone of the State's human resources.

The members of this small world share a common range of management skills that can be described as essentially generalist, not expert, as discussed in Chap. 5. This generalist profile is decisive in terms of the skills that distinguish a senior civil servant from a corporate manager, and especially from a manager who is a strategy, finance or organization professional and who will have had to prove themselves in practice before hoping to move up the ladder.

For a true professional, competence is legitimate if and when their actions have proven to be effective in the face of facts. In this case, their culture is a professional or expert culture.

For a senior civil servant, the roots of competence lie elsewhere, in the school from which they graduated. They will know how to deal with everything because they have passed a competitive examination and can boast a general culture. They are formatted over the course of identical initial training. The ENA graduates who will join the three major corps are for the most part devoid of any prior professional experience, even if they have to do a short internship during their studies. The programmes they have to follow and which determine their final ranking are often provided by alumni for whom teaching a course at the ENA is a mark of social distinction rather than an academic vocation. "Entre-soi" is a practice learnt very early on when one has a good chance of joining the elite. Many of the seminars skim over content that borders on general culture. The disciplines taught are hardly explored in depth. The disciplinary fundamentals of applied management sciences are barely covered, if at all, and in any case have little weight in the exit ranking. Operational management, accounting, evaluation, human resources, and organizational implementation, to name but a few, are not studied. Socialization and academic performance cultivate distinction and penalize expertise.

Leading and managing a department is not the priority for the exit ranking, nor is it a priority for a graduate's subsequent career. Once they have joined a major corps, novices can remain members of that corps for life. Job security is guaranteed. Moreover, the likelihood of rapidly accessing a leadership position is assured. The elite of the elite can even hope to take up management positions in the private sector and return to the corps if they wish. The head of the corps acts as an employment agency, and risks of political arbitrariness remain very low. The protection afforded by the *statut général* fosters relationships with peers that can be corporatist. The elite corps compete with one another to occupy the best positions, while at the same time being able to form an alliance when their privileges are threatened by third parties. They present themselves as the only ones fit to seriously address anything relating to the pursuit of the general interest and the administrative instrumentation required for this purpose.

Generalists of the highest level share a common cognitive and cultural capital that conveys a particular repertoire of action for the organizational and financial management of the public sector. A top-down managerial approach prevails. The preferred tool for dealing with problems is the inflation of managerial innovations or pseudo-innovations that are institutionalized without being appropriated beyond a small circle, and a concern for budgetary savings prevails over genuine financial streamlining. Technological innovation is favoured as a vector of change.

These pre-established and self-evident truths form the basis of a kind of rationality widely shared by French administrative elites.

This administrative rationality does not result in the rejection, in principle, of the legitimacy of political rationality in terms of conduct (Quermonne & Rouban, 1986). It is however reflected in the conception that senior civil servants convey of their own role and of public interest. Its purpose is to preserve the integrity of their organizational power, whatever reform politicians may envisage. No imperialism is mobilized to defend an option and no principled opposition to willing cooperation with politicians is voiced. Caution is nevertheless required. Administrative rationality is characterized by distance, in the name of general principles such as concern for the general interest and maintaining the civil service's politically neutral stance. In fact, it helps establish a boundary between their organizational competences and those said to be political, which they see as the responsibility of ministers, their cabinets and their advisers.

In the eyes of senior civil servants, the task of political leaders, once they have announced a policy decision, is to obtain budgetary resources and to liaise with external actors such as the general secretariats of the president and the prime minister, other ministries and parliament. On the other hand, putting policy into practice within the ministry is not their concern. Administrative rationality is based on the premise that politicians do not have the necessary know-how to implement policy. In other words, to reform services without causing collateral damage such as a staff strike or affecting the quality of public services, specific knowledge and experience are required, and only the civil servants in charge have these, along with the necessary competences to apply them.

This rationality relies on action geared towards incremental and long-term adjustments. Politicians come and go, civil servants remain. It is reflected in the use of a specific form of instrumental translation of policies: the issuing of instructions, standards and roadmaps for internal services. It acts through procedures, which may be drawn up by the top of the hierarchy and imposed in an authoritarian way, but allow leeway for discretion to the intermediary levels in charge of implementing the details. The top of the hierarchical pyramid is in charge of entities that may often have different contexts and tasks associated with their remit.

In short, the challenge of administrative rationality is to "keep the service running" smoothly and without risk, especially as the policy decreed by the government is committed to producing results within a short space of time and to generating appropriate consequences. The rationality of ministers, prime ministers or presidents of the Republic is and should remain political, even if it is driven by civic, electoral or moral principles of their own. The major stake for them is possible power gain, by distinguishing themselves from their predecessors, paying tribute to fashionable ideas, and hoping to fare well in public opinion. The gain is therefore short-term.

10.4 A Challenge to the Structure?

From the late 1960s, the government authorities announced several times that they were going to reform the keystone that the ENA was said to constitute. Of course, such intentions were all part of the political discourse. When things were bad in France, ENA alumni offered an ideal scapegoat. But in reality, at best these reforms culminated in very limited measures and at worst were abandoned without follow-up. The time frames were too short and resistance from all sides of the political spectrum created unmanageable dissension. The announcement itself had enough of an effect.

It was not until the 2017 presidential elections that the subject was broached in a more meaningful way. One of the candidates, Emmanuel Macron, the future President of the Republic, made firm commitments. This was especially remarkable as he himself was a pure product of the elite factory. Once he arrived at the Elysée, this ENA graduate and former member of the *Inspection Générale des Finances* launched a reform that reached far beyond the ENA. His vision and his stated ambitions fuelled a prolonged and rich debate, both in the media and among the political and administrative leadership. But the president was determined; he forged ahead and made the reform his personal business. A report was commissioned from a former senior civil servant, Frédéric Thiriez, who proposed breaking up the ENA, as well as introducing a basic curriculum shared by the students of the ENA central core and those of several other civil service schools. This was a move that would be highly symbolic of the levelling of these schools' status (Thiriez et al., 2020).

On 2 June 2021, the reform was enacted through an edict which, unlike a law, allows the *Conseil des Ministres* to legislate without having to go through parliament.

From a managerial point of view this reform aims to increase the efficiency stemming from the structure of the civil service staff, the foundations of which are set out in the *statut général* of 1946. It consists of four general provisions.

First, the ENA has been abolished. It has become the national institute of public service (Institut National du Service Public, INSP), with broader missions than those of the ENA. In addition to the training delivered to its own students, the INSP will organize a common core curriculum for students from 14 other schools, all with their own courses, that train future senior civil servants of the State (police, magistrature, etc.) and local authorities (e.g. the INET). The INSP will also be in charge of a new training course for future very senior civil servants, a sort of super-ENA, based on the model of the Ecole de Guerre for the military. The legal status of the INSP, however, will remain that of the ENA: a large administrative institution controlled by the Ministry of Public Administration, and not a public institution of a scientific, cultural and professional nature, governing the world of higher education and controlled by the Ministry of Higher Education and Research.

A second provision abolishes direct access to the major corps upon graduation from the ENA as it existed until now, favouring the very top graduates. Henceforth, they must all have graduated from a new corps called "State administrators." This provision also means that students who are not selected by a major corps and become civil administrators assigned to a particular ministry will join this single, fully inter-ministerial body. Access to the major corps will only be possible after several years of service in the field, followed by a selection and evaluation procedure. Other means of access will also be provided for people who did not graduate from the INSP. A specific provision redefines access to administrative and judicial bodies such as the *Conseil d'Etat* and the *Cour des Comptes*, which will be possible only after two years in A+ posts, irrespective of the school from which a civil servant graduated.

A third provision is even more radical in managerial terms. It is defined as the generalized application of functionalization, the stated aim of which is to switch from a corps-based approach to a function-based approach, through the concept of job status. However, the decree offers few details as to how to implement this reform which raises serious legal problems, as well as problems of accreditation. The statutes of the administrative management corps that would be functionalized are not homogeneous. Some, such as those of the three major inspectorates and control corps, are inter-ministerial, while others are ministerial. The guarantees of independence are not the same either.

A fourth provision is more specific than the previous one. It sets out guidelines and centralizes the inter-ministerial management of senior State officials. A single delegation is to monitor the careers of senior civil servants. The role of the prime minister will thus clearly be reinforced, at least in theory, and the autonomy of the corps, and incidentally that of the ministries, clearly reduced.

Do the provisions set out in the decree of 2 June 2021 suggest a radical transformation of the structure of staff as analysed in the previous sections of this chapter? An assessment approach cannot answer this question. However, it does point to some important observations from a management perspective.

As a legal tool, the June 2021 decree has not put an end to the debate. On the contrary, it has opened it up, especially in the run-up to a presidential election campaign. The decrees defining its application will now be the main battles that are fought. But the devil is in the detail. Active minorities had already mobilized before the decree was drafted, around points that were sometimes crucial to them. The decree was thus revised only a few hours before it was presented to the *Conseil des Ministres*. It reflected a compromise between the highest authorities of the *Conseil d'État* and the *Cour des Comptes*, on the one hand, and the Elysée on the other. It concerned the way in which the committees in charge of recruiting the members of these two institutions operate, pointing towards less discretion for the political power of the chairmanship of these committees.

More fundamentally, the quest for greater administrative efficiency is based on two premises.

The first is functionalization, that is, the transition to the function-based framework. However, as we noted earlier, this alternative already exists, even if it is seldom applied in practice. In this sense, the revolution of 2021 is not a Copernican act.

The second premise is reminiscent of a kind of trickle-down theory, whereby from the top of the hierarchy, through the senior managers and executives, from the *Conseil d'Etat* to the prefect, another way of working and thinking about competence flows down to the grassroots. The gamble is original if not risky: it assumed that changing only the top 1% of the civil service hierarchy without touching the other 99% will be enough. The business world is supposed to serve as a frame of reference. If this were true, we might ask whether the big boss of a company being supervised differently by the board of directors would mean that more efficient behaviours would necessarily be adopted among the staff? This is doubtful.

Public management is also, and above all, a more collective issue requiring adequate organizational, social and political know-how. Change does not happen by force; it requires time and compromises between stakeholders. From this point of view, it is surprising that the June 2021 decree grants special development only to the general inspectorates, namely those of finance, administration and social affairs. From a management perspective, a relative reduction in the number of inspectors compared to managers would be a justified priority.

Finally, it would be useful to consider whether and how the civil service should resemble French society, as hammered home by the government's insistent discourse, relayed by the media, on the democratization of recruitment to the ENA. In any event, definitively answering questions regarding radical change in the structure of staff and avoiding the umpteenth stopgap for this structure remains to be achieved.

References

DiMaggio, P. J., & Powell, W. W. (1983). The Iron Cage Revisited: Institutional Isomorphism and Collective Rationality in Organizational Fields. *American Sociological Review, 1*, 147–160.

Eymeri-Douzant, J. M. (2021). Les hauts fonctionnaires et le Prince dans la France d'aujourd'hui. In E. Aubin et al. (Eds.), *Quelle déontologie pour la haute fonction publique ?* Institut Francophone pour la Justice et la Démocratie.

Guyomarch, A. (1999). Public Service, Public Management and the Modernization of French Public Administration. *Public Administration, 77*(1), 171–193.

Quermonne, J. L., & Rouban, L. (1986). French Public Administration and Policy Evaluation: The Quest for Accountability. *Public Administration Review, 1*, 397–406.

Schmidt, V. A. (2007). *Democratizing France: The Political and Administrative History of Decentralization.* Cambridge University Press.

Suleiman, E. N. (2015). *Politics, Power, and Bureaucracy in France. The Administrative Elite*. Princeton University Press.

Thiriez, F., Méaux, F., & Lagneau, C. (2020). *Mission Haute Fonction Publique. Propositions*. Premier ministre.

Thoenig, J. C. (1987). *L'Ere des Technocrates. Le Cas des Ponts et chaussées*. L'Harmattan.

Thoenig, J. C. (2005). Territorial Administration and Political Control: Decentralization in France. *Public Administration, 83*(3), 685–708.

PART VI

Conclusions

CHAPTER 11

A Review of Developments in France

The French experience over half a century served as a test case in this book to develop a more holistic approach to the assessment of reforms. Without overstating the case, what can we conclude from seven chapters of in-depth analysis?

The French State and its administration have unquestionably changed. However, the changes that have taken place have been largely superficial. What we called the major crosscutting operations announced by successive governments have hardly modified public management by the central government in any direct or significant way. The use of management tools has been disappointing, particularly because it has not been sufficiently refined and has been partially diverted from its primary functions.

Significant developments have nevertheless been accomplished, away from the spotlight, intermittently, indirectly and gradually, sometimes with two steps forward and one step back. They are the result of unnamed reforms, not undertaken under the banner of State reform. These initiatives by political leaders have been more focused and often guided by less abstract objectives.

What can we make of what actually happened? Five major findings emerge from the analysis.

© The Author(s), under exclusive license to Springer Nature
Switzerland AG 2022
P. Gibert, J.-C. Thoenig, *Assessing Public Management Reforms, Understanding Governance*,
https://doi.org/10.1007/978-3-030-89799-4_11

1. The first is that although France has become a State governed by the rule of law, its public service system is not governed by truly managerialized law.

Developments in public management have swayed between striving to consolidate democracy and seeking to make public policy more efficient (Lynn, 1996). In France, the rule of law, which is not the essence of democracy but is nevertheless a precondition thereof, has been strengthened without significantly supporting the search for State efficiency.

Until 1959, at the highest level of legal standards of the French Republic, France proved to be the country of inconsistency. It could boast being the birthplace of the Declaration of Human and Citizens' Rights and of having incorporated a preamble into the 1946 Constitution referring to this declaration and completing it. Yet it remained a country where this was all talk and only talk, insofar as the laws passed by parliament were not liable to be referred to a judge and therefore nullified if they contravened these generous principles. In part of the body politic, this omnipotence of the law was justified on the grounds of the sovereignty of the people, without it seeming shocking that generous or even grandiloquent principles could be reduced to nothing by this said sovereignty.

It was not until the Constitution of the Fifth Republic was passed in 1958 that a *Conseil Constitutionnel* (constitutional council) was established, with the power to nullify laws. At the time, its creation may have seemed to provide more of a safeguard against the legislative encroaching on the executive in the field of regulation than anything else. Thus conceived, parliamentarianism required that laws in the field of government regulations be declared contrary to the constitution before being promulgated or be downgraded with the approval of the *Conseil Constitutionnel* if they were passed after the *Conseil*'s establishment.

The *Conseil Constitutionnel* appeared to provide protection for the executive only. To declare a law unconstitutional, it relied solely on the text of the constitution. Yet this body of text related to the legal competences of the two branches of power, the judiciary and various administrative bodies. It therefore excluded the principles set out in the preamble to the constitution, which referred to the Declaration of Human Rights and the preamble to the 1946 Constitution.

The first major change came with the *Conseil Constitutionnel*'s own jurisprudence. In 1971 it stated that the declaration and the preamble were part of the constitutional standards of reference. These could therefore be invoked within the framework of a constitutionality review. As a result of this decision, the review of respect for public freedoms was added to the review of respect for the limits of the various State authorities' competences and the procedures they had to follow.

A second change occurred in 1974, with an initiative by the executive in the form of a constitutional amendment. This allowed a minimum of 60 members of parliament to refer a matter to the *Conseil Constitutionnel* before a law was promulgated. Until then, such referral was reserved for the President of the Republic, the prime minister and the presidents of the two assemblies. Except in the case of a difference in majority between the senate and the National Assembly, this de facto deprived the members of the opposition of the possibility of having the unconstitutionality of a new law recognized. Finally, in 2008 parliament and the government adopted an additional measure based on the principle of verification of the constitutional validity of a law. In the event of proceedings brought before a court of law or an administrative court, any litigant who maintains that a legislative provision infringes the rights and freedoms guaranteed by the constitution may refer the matter to the *Conseil Constitutionnel*—provided that the *Cour de Cassation* or the *Conseil d'Etat* deem the nature of the issue to be "serious." Thus, a law is no longer considered intangible once it has been promulgated if the *Conseil Constitutionnel* was not already asked to rule on the contested provision before its promulgation.

These new powers therefore guarantee respect for a hierarchy of standards in which the entirety of the constitution is effectively the supreme norm, followed by organic laws, ordinary laws, and regulations, in that order. In principle, this should give real force to managerial standards when they are integrated by legal texts high up in the hierarchy of standards. However, the *Conseil Constitutionnel* has clearly not shown the same vigilance in this area as it has undeniably shown in matters of civil liberties. Even if, with time, the embedding of certain managerial standards has risen in the hierarchy of standards, the same cannot be said of the managerialization of law.

2. A second key finding is that the major crosscutting reform operations have only superficially affected the setting of goals for public policy and consequently its control system.

As emphasized in Part III of the book, political leaders justify the State reforms they launch by the desire to break from the past, without it being clear from what such policy is supposed to break away. Stated aims prove fallacious in practice. The *General Review of Public Policies* (GRPP) did not call policies into question. The *Modernization of Public Action* (MPA) programme had the same objective but with different means. The reason the *Rationalization of Budgetary Choices* (RBC) was never attacked head-on is that it was hard to imagine taking a stand against rationality. By brandishing the slogan of a better State, the *Renewal of public service* programme (RPS) had one merit: it wanted to contrast with the call for less State emanating from certain political spheres at the time, and at the same time to reassure those who feared the propensity for more State, traditionally exemplified by the left.

The only commonality between all these proclaimed reforms has been the use of wording that shows off the will to change and does not stir fear of a social upheaval. They oppose reform to revolution and distinguish it from its original religious meaning, namely the split with Rome. As a result, no desire for counter-reform has ever been voiced for half a century! Launching a reform of the State or its administration is first and foremost a way to break with the previous government's approach to State reform. As its proponents present it, it is a reform of reform.

To give concrete expression to their proclamations, political leaders explore the market for possible structural changes and the market for available management instruments at that point in time. They also explore another market, one which concerns the servants of the reform. They call at times for self-change, to be practised by every department, and other times for change imposed from the outside. Depending on the case, they alternate between or combine the use of human resources internal to the administration and of external resources, such as contractors, consulting firms and, more rarely, university laboratories.

As for the effectiveness of the changes brought about by the major crosscutting reforms, it is barely perceptible, judging by the traces they have left. It gives more of a sense of poor capitalization over time, and of an underutilization of the positive or negative lessons that could be drawn from the difficulties encountered by each of these reforms. One example, among others, is the theorization of the structuring of budget programmes. Initiated within the context of the RBC in the 1970s, it was not pursued in the process of structuring the programmes, carried out as part of the OLGBL passed in 2001.

Other features characterize these major crosscutting operations. This includes their external origin. While the RBC penetrated the major technical corps of the State fairly well, it did not truly spread to the senior administrative civil service. The same is true of the innovation experiments attempted within the framework of the MPA: they failed to be generalized.

The RBC did not rationalize the State. The RPA was not perceptible to citizens. The GRPP did not result in any real change. There was not enough time to properly implement the RPS, which was abandoned as soon as the prime minister who championed it left office. However, the time factor is not a valid explanation for operations that remained on the government agenda for a longer period of time, such as the RBC or even the MPA.

To make sense of the poor results of each of these operations, we need to review the four major acts of management: goal setting, organizing, leading and controlling (Tabatoni & Jarniou, 1975; Thiétart, 1980).

The act of organizing is constantly undertaken by the leaders of the public administration, at least in its most visible and not necessarily most important form: the formal distribution of competences between the different public entities and their subdivisions. This work is carried out both in the context of major crosscutting operations and with the support of specific toolkits. The frequency of these interventions influences the visibility of reform. As far as immediate results go, the act of organizing is performative. As marketing teaches us, in order to sell anything, it must be made tangible, even if the impact and sustainability of results is not guaranteed.

Another explanation for the prominence of organizational structure is the hierarchy of the causes of dysfunction identified in the functioning of administrations. The problem of organization is attributed to individuals; hence, a change of leader is supposed to improve things. The second propensity is to identify a problem of organizational structures deemed unproductive, as the result of duplications or ambiguities in the distribution of competences. Then only, in third place, comes the identification of a problem in terms of deficiencies or shortcomings of the management system, understood among other things as the incentive system, with the sanction-reward measures applying to the organization's employees, a more or less coherent set of management instruments, and so forth.

Goal setting, on the other hand, and in contrast to organizing, is continually problematic. It involves everything pertaining to the end goals pursued, their implementation through the organizational structure, and the transition from rather abstract objectives to operational objectives that are understandable and ambitious but achievable by the civil servants who are primarily responsible for contributing to them. Despite their names or stated ambitions, neither the Organic Law Governing Budgetary Laws (OLGBL), nor the GRPP, nor the MPA have afforded any significant improvement of public policy goal setting.

Moreover, the choices made have reflected a betrayal of these operations' stated objectives. In the division of programmes, the OLGBL prioritized the organizational dimension over the intentional goal-setting dimension, on the understandable grounds that money has to be given to someone. The GRPP and the MPA focused on generating savings without addressing the problem of the side effects of the quest for efficiency on the outputs and even less so on the outcomes of the savings achieved.

These deviations are not actually surprising. There is a point at which the ambiguity and vagueness that can be identified in public policy can no longer be attributed solely to imperfections in State management. The social sciences have sufficiently demonstrated that vagueness and ambiguity are to a large extent linked to the political rationality omnipresent in State management. Whether to win over a sufficient number of voters or to build coalitions of parties with different ideas and agendas, ambiguity and vagueness are rational responses by those in power and those who aspire to be. Precision can prove politically dysfunctional.

Thus, all operations striving for better public policy goal setting can leave a bitter taste. This includes presenting objectives that are convoluted because they seek to communicate clearly different ideas within a single statement. It also includes pitching abstract objectives of which the significance is not well understood by the average reader. Concretely, proclaimed public policy goal setting often results in the statement of pseudo-objectives, that is, statements that are supposed to be guidelines, the vagueness and imprecision of which do not reflect real choices, and which are virtually mere reminders of the missions entrusted to the services. This weakness of proclaimed goal setting is all the more shocking, given that unpublished objectives or crypto-objectives—such as reducing staff costs per student in higher education in order to provide mass education—significantly guide the actions of some ministries or programmes.

In proclaimed goal setting, the model whereby objectives are structured, in other words positioned in relation to one another with final objectives and, as one moves down the structure, increasingly instrumental objectives, is rarely followed. The simplification of this structure into a binary distinction between strategic objectives on the one hand and operational objectives on the other is not always convincing. The shift from objectives to indicators to monitor them without any bias or obvious reduction in scope adds to the imperfections or even the illusory nature of proclaimed goal setting (Gibert & Benzerafa-Alilat, 2016).

Learning of these unconvincing attempts at setting goals for organizations or public policies can be unsettling. While technical causes may not help, basically the main reason for this obstacle relates to the real strategic issue: the way in which the goals that a policy is supposed to address are expressed and communicated. The implicit corollary of that is what could be done but is renounced in order to focus on the priorities selected and to allocate resources—human, budgetary or other—to those priorities. Yet while politicians like to advertise priorities, since they cannot usually display renunciations, their list of priorities is generally extensive and resembles more of a catalogue juxtaposing statutory missions than a real strategy. It may therefore seem preferable to reverse the goal-setting approach, to replace a top-down structuring process with one that is bottom-up: starting from the concrete objectives pursued formally or de facto by the lowest levels of the hierarchy and working up by aggregation towards the objectives of the higher levels. While this substitution is theoretically unsatisfactory, when properly practised it at least has the merit of putting pressure on the administration's productive apparatus (Gibert, 2009).

In any event, progress around goal setting and control is or should be closely linked. Management control is the process whereby managers influence other members of the organization to implement an organization strategy (Govindarajan & Anthony, 1998). In France the way in which control is handled and managed at central State level is a major problem, for it is left to the discretion of each ministry, or even of each branch within the various ministries, with the exception of the control associated with budgetary programmes. There is no overall doctrine regarding the management control of the State.

Seen optimistically, this points to a recognition of the contextualization of control in a group which, because of the variety of domains it addresses, resembles an immense conglomerate. The State public administration as such does not have the solution to aggregate its outputs in terms of their monetary value, as do other organizations that are conglomerates assembling heterogeneous businesses. Seen pessimistically, it signals the lack of maturing of a function, a shortfall that should come as a surprise in an administration that is supposed to have transitioned to a performance-based approach since the introduction of the OLGBL in 2006.

3. State reforms not presented as such have abounded in recent decades. They are more focused, address less abstract problems, and are more effective.

Although they were not part of the major crosscutting operations, they all had in common that they significantly modified or were able to modify, if not the entire functioning of the general government, at least significant parts of it. They generally stand out from the major crosscutting operations in two ways: the absence of explicit reference to the theme of State reform, and more precise identification of the problems they aim to address.

The crosscutting operations identified the problems they sought to tackle summarily, to say the least: the State is too bureaucratic; technocracy reigns; the decisions made are irrational; the portfolio of policies developed so far is too large and therefore too costly. These sweeping judgements are matched by slogans that alone seem to solve the problem: a rational State, a strategic State, a new-world State. One might in fact wonder why previous governments did not adopt these miracle cures sooner: due to backward ideology, ignorance, or malice? The excessive nature of each major crosscutting reform's claims contains the seeds of rapid decredibilization. On the other hand, unnamed reforms, aimed at more targeted changes, are based on forms of identification of problems that may be somewhat basic, questionable, and incomplete, but they are also more credible, as Chap. 9 of this book has shown.

Decentralization is based on the idea that local elected representatives are better able to understand the problems experienced by their constituents and therefore to respond to them. Strengthening local democracy is seen as strengthening national democracy, without this being opposed to better management. This constitutive policy is guided by a theory of action.

In the hospital sector, the reform of activity-based pricing is grounded on a business model aimed at containing the explosion in hospital expenditures. To this end, it has put hospitals under pressure and provided for their remuneration on the basis of an average efficiency. The idea is that they should achieve this efficiency for the different homogeneous groups of patients. This more grounded way of identifying problems for unnamed reforms than for major crosscutting operations does not however guarantee the success of the measures implemented. In fact it gives rise to unintended effects. In the case of local authorities, for example, the layering of levels—*commune, communauté d'agglomération, département, région* and State—and the complexity it creates generate costs and slow down public policy progress.

4. Management instrumentation adds bureaucratic formalism more than combatting it.

Are management or public policy instruments—the difference does not matter here—artefacts that generate added value only when they are appropriated properly and implemented in the middle and lower levels of the hierarchy (De Vaujany, 2006)? Are they fads which, through isomorphism, are deceptively adopted by the public sector and lumped together under the same umbrella when their practices have nothing in common (Oliver, 1991)? Reductive views of management are widespread in both academic and practitioner circles. One perspective equates management with the sole management of people. This is the view implicitly held by those who claim that what has been missing from attempts to reform the State in France is management (Cannac & Trosa, 2007). Another is the instrumental view. It formerly equated the transition to management with the conversion to modern management methods, and today it equates it with the intensive use of management tools that are said to have proven their worth in the private sector.

Chapters 6 and 7 of the book presented the fate of three instruments: indicators and their compilation into a dashboard, ex ante methods of policy evaluation and more particularly cost-benefit analysis, and ex post evaluation. In the process, the assessment also highlighted the intensive use of another tool, the contract. In practice, many management instruments are used in the French public administration.

It would be a serious mistake to equate the use of instruments solely with the import of private sector instruments. Many of these instruments are indigenous. This includes cost-benefit analysis, as well as a wide range of technical tools suited to the complexities of human resource management, budgetary management and accounting management in the public sector. Yet the debates on the contributions and perverse effects of management instruments in the public sector generally focus on tools that are imported or believed to be imported, as in the case of cost-benefit analysis. Some public sector modernizers give excessive credit to these tools, considering that their adoption *ipso facto* solves the problem being addressed. If a local authority appears to be poorly managed, the *Cour des Comptes* advises it to implement cost accounting. In other words, the prescription to implement the tool seems to prevail over in-depth reflection, not only on the choice of concrete modalities for this cost accounting, which are in no way self-evident in a public sector environment, but also on how to approach the problems at hand and appropriate the tool (Gibert & Thoenig, 2019).

The concept of performance is clearly successful. It is as though it were used as a new way of legitimizing the public sector. "We are legitimate because we perform well" often competes nowadays with "we are legitimate because we follow the instructions of our legitimate rulers." In other words, legitimacy through performance competes with rational legal legitimacy. The modernization of management comes to be interpreted de facto through a triple lens: making objectives explicit; formalizing with plans, projects and contracts; and quantifying with indicators.

The value of this triptych is in itself hard to challenge. However, it overshadows another threesome, one that raises the questions of the implementation of the triptych and of the chances of a productive appropriation, that is, a form of appropriation that adds value to the management of services or to public policy. This second triptych consists in considering: whether the political rationality explicitly endorses the appropriateness; the difficulties of articulating objectives and indicators; and the capacity to regularly inform the selected indicators with basic data.

5. The reform of the State or its administration is only a myth with little creative potential.

The key characteristics of the State and its administration are the result of a multitude of decisions and texts enacted at different times, a significant number of which during the revolutionary and Napoleonic eras in the case of France, or even inherited from the monarchy. These texts were drawn up for a wide variety of reasons: ideological, opportunistic, redistributive and, more recently, performative.

Depending on the perspective, one will perceive advances, steps back, or faltering. The sedimentation of texts can seem messy, guided by contradictory rationales that in no way point to an orderly state of affairs. The vast majority of the laws were enacted not with a view to reforming the State but for more focused purposes. State reform is a paradigm that emerged between the wars, at a time—the Third Republic—when the country was experiencing exceptional longevity in its political regime, after the instability of its predecessors, onset by the 1789 Revolution, when no regime lasted more than 20 years.

Genuine State reform, in the sense of a quest for deep and lasting change, is in fact conceivable only in three ways.

The first, and most unlikely, would be to find a primary factor, which if changed would lead to more or less rapid change in all the other factors. This is a monistic solution.

The second would be to build a model aimed at linking the different levers of change, in other words to build a seemingly robust theory of action for reform. To our knowledge, this has never happened.

The third is to remove those features of the State or its administration that are most displeasing to citizens and their representatives and to rebuild the structure, not systematically and according to predetermined plans, but along the way, trying to address as they arise the problems generated in turn by deconstruction. This would probably be more akin to a revolutionary rather than a reformist approach.

What has been called new public management—however questionable the ex post categorization that gave rise to it and its use by academics, which has been excessive to say the least—fits within the first approach. It saw politics as noise that hindered managerial rationality, which had to prevail essentially at implementation level. It was therefore necessary to ward off contamination by politics. The creation of agencies managed as much as possible like companies, or failing that, quasi-agencies characterized by isomorphism with private management, was the instrument used to maintain a distance from politics. This was for the good of politics, or more precisely for that of the public policies over which, for the sake of legitimacy, political authority was maintained. This separation between the elaboration and implementation of policies goes against most of the social sciences' established theories. It was a simplifying hypothesis that overlooked the incompleteness of the terms of reference governing the action of the leaders of these agencies or quasi-agencies, the shifting nature of these policies, and the sense of dispossession logically experienced by those in power.

As discussed in Chap. 8, agencification has been very mild in France. This type of presumed solution to the conflict between political and managerial rationality has not been used to any great extent. Attempts to managerially discipline power as an alternative way of dealing with the conflict of rationalities, where managerial rationality is supposed to rub off on political rationality or hybridize it, have had a very limited impact.

In addition to the example of the impact analysis of draft laws mentioned in Chap. 7, we could also cite the budgetary field in this regard. To mitigate the consequences of annual budgeting and to combat budget deficits, the 2008 constitutional reform introduced programme laws to define the multi-annual orientation of public finances, a real invitation for the government and parliament to define budgetary trajectories. Yet these programming laws—one for central government finances, the other for social security financing—have not been effective because they have not been respected. They have not been respected because they are not binding on the finance laws voted each year. The inclusion of a virtuous principle in the constitution has therefore not really been supported by positive law.

A policy of State reform poses the same broader ontological problem as the policy of administrative simplification sometimes included in the major crosscutting reforms, which is virtually always on the political agenda. Such policy posits that the law ought to be simplified. The complexity of the law is seen as a burden on businesses, an obstacle to France's attractiveness to foreign investment, a source of additional costs for local authorities, and a source of inconvenience for citizens who are subject to a multitude of obligations and risk finding themselves unknowingly in contravention of increasing numbers of legal standards.

Whatever the indicators used, be it the number of texts, the number of pages or the number of characters of legal texts, they attest to the persistence of what can only be called the inflation of standards. Both the flow and the stock of texts, whether legislative or regulatory, are increasing. Operations to remove standards every time a new standard appears have had minimal impact on this trend: it is like trying to save the Titanic by bailing out the water with buckets!

This is an area, however, where the causes of inflation have been identified by the Conseil d'Etat (2016, 2018). A classification was drawn up, distinguishing between factors relating to: the growing complexity of the world; the multiplicity of societal expectations; the power of the producers of standards; the fact that the standard is seen as the preferred vehicle of public policy; the fact that it is the subject of political struggles; the fact that it is a channel for expressing political messages; the growing constraints shaping the hierarchy of standards; the self-sustaining nature of the production of standards; and the fragmentation of the producers of standards of different types and content. This classification, itself subdivided into basic factors, is certainly interesting but has two key limitations: it fails to rank the factors by attempting to establish each one's contribution to the inflation of standards; and it does not indicate—explicitly at least—which factors would be relatively controllable, and which ones would be beyond the control of any authority genuinely interested in putting an end to such inflation. For these two reasons, it is difficult to move from this analysis to effective action.

A policy of State reform *mutatis mutandis* resembles a policy of simplification. Short of setting one's sight on the highest institutional level and seeing the solution as the transition to a Sixth Republic, the reform of the State understood as a comprehensive operation is in fact marginalized by virtually uninterrupted reforms of the distribution of competences, of the three structures that are organizational, financial, and human resources, and of the adoption, more or less embedded in the law, of management and public policy instruments.

This state of affairs seems very difficult to change.

References

Cannac, Y., & Trosa, S. (Eds.). (2007). *La réforme dont l'État a besoin. Pour un management public par la confiance et la responsabilité*. Dunod.

Conseil d'Etat. (2016). *Simplification et qualité du droit. Etude*. Conseil d'Etat.

Conseil d'Etat. (2018). *Mesurer l'inflation normative. Étude présentée en assemblée générale le 3 mai*. Conseil d'Etat.

De Vaujany, F. X. (2006). Pour une théorie de l'appropriation des outils de gestion: vers un dépassement de l'opposition conception-usage. *Management Avenir, 3*, 109–126.

Gibert, P. (2009). *Tableaux de bord pour les organisations publiques*. Dunod.

Gibert, P., & Benzerafa-Alilat, M. (2016). De quoi l'État rend-il compte dans ses rapports annuels de performance? *Revue française d'administration publique, 4*, 1041–1064.

Gibert, P., & Thoenig, J. C. (2019). *La modernisation de l'Etat. Une promesse trahie ?* Classiques Garnier.

Govindarajan, V., & Anthony, R. N. (1998). *Management Control Systems*. McGraw-Hill.

Lynn, L. E. (1996). *Public Management as Art, Science, and Profession*. Chatham House.

Oliver, C. (1991). Strategic Responses to Institutional Processes. *Academy of Management Review, 16*(1), 145–179.

Tabatoni, P., & Jarniou, P. (1975). *Les systèmes de gestion: politiques et structures*. Presses Universitaires de France.

Thiétart, R. A. (1980). *Le management*. Presses Universitaires de France.

CHAPTER 12

Assessing Public Administration Reforms

This book discussed State administration reforms, examining the capacity of programmes and initiatives launched by public authorities to reform the entirety of its civil service, its structures, and the instruments used for its management.

It tested a more general hypothesis. The administrative changes brought about by policies that we refer to as unnamed reforms are more significant and lasting than officially announced reform programmes, which are crosscutting insofar as they involve all or a large part of the central government public sector.

Compared to comprehensive reform policies, measures that remain unnamed bring about more marked changes. The corollary hypothesis is that if real change does occur, it is not the result of voluntarist, tailor-made comprehensive programmes designed to overhaul the system. In other words, the path to change, modernization and efficiency in administrations is a discontinuous process, a succession of steps forwards and steps backwards. Medium- and long-term planning and implementation have unrealistic expectations. Reforms advance where they are not expected. They get lost in the ground where they should have taken hold. They also come up against limits and the unspoken.

The demonstration of this more general hypothesis is based on a full-scale test. The case we chose covers half a century of government efforts

© The Author(s), under exclusive license to Springer Nature Switzerland AG 2022
P. Gibert, J.-C. Thoenig, *Assessing Public Management Reforms, Understanding Governance*, https://doi.org/10.1007/978-3-030-89799-4_12

to modernize the State in France, roughly from the late 1960s to the present. The detailed results are reported over the course of the book.

Part III reviewed no fewer than eight crosscutting reform policies or programmes launched over 50 years. This government obstinacy contrasts with the widely shared belief that the French State is not at the forefront of administrative reform efforts. Chapter 6 presented a review of these eight programmes, their publicization, their sponsors, their designers, their fate and their impacts. At first glance, they appear widely diverse, particularly in terms of their content and names. However, although none of these programmes resemble one another, some common features do stand out. Their life span is generally very short. They have come and gone increasingly quickly. Each new government promotes its own version that contrasts with that of its predecessors. With some exceptions, the legislature is kept on the sidelines. In short, even partial effects are difficult to identify. Most of the time, sooner or later, bureaucratic routines and established ways of thinking take over.

Chapter 7 looked at the making of these programmes. It is surprising to note that for almost 50 years, identical processes have been employed to translate the will of the government into strategic goals, set out methods and procedures, and supervise concrete implementation. Reform is advocated in the name of users' well-being, the use of high-tech is said to produce miracles, the senior administration elites are the only ones able to supervise these programmes, and so on.

In short, not much has changed in terms of public management. The more change is announced, the less actually happens.

Part IV strengthened the relevance of this finding. It covered the period from 1968 to today from another angle: that of the appropriation of new public management instruments such as the dashboard and indicators, cost-benefit analysis, and policy evaluation. It presented each of these in the same way: its origin, its first applications, the ways in which it has been used over time, the administrative organizations that employ it, and the resulting new professional skills. Understanding the demonstration carried out in this book requires a little technical finesse at times. A summary provides a comparative assessment of these new toolkits and their actual contribution.

At that point, the book confirmed the pessimistic hypothesis. The mountain of reforms has given birth to developments that could diplomatically be described as moderate to poor. Major crosscutting programmes and new techniques can even reinforce established practices instead of changing them. Promises are betrayed.

Part V explored measures that are ostensibly not related to the reform of the State administration system.

Chapter 9 discussed the use of agencification. Chapter 10 analysed three other measures: devolution to local authorities, the financing of public health and hospitals, and servicing the national territory through external State services. The nature of these policies is either institutional, or financial or organizational. However, each of these measures in turn gives rise to internal changes in the central government administration system that are far from negligible. They affect two functions of its management: the financial function and the organizational function.

As Chap. 10 showed, the third core function of a public organization, on the other hand, has demonstrated remarkable inertia and even stubborn indifference to the developments that have shaped the first two functions. The model applied by human resources, the cornerstone of the administrative system, remains firmly anchored in its past, even if it is increasingly facing attempts at reform.

Flexibility nevertheless has been and remains possible, fuelled by measures that are not specifically incorporated into large and ambitious crosscutting reform programmes. Hence, the final finding: far more change is taking place in unobtrusive and unpublicized ways, through what we refer to as unnamed policies.

Superficially, such findings echo the criticisms levelled at the rational-comprehensive decision-making model. In fact, decision makers' actions are not informed by clearly defined objectives and value-maximizing choices based on a precise examination of possible alternatives. This ideal is unattainable (Lindblom, 1959). Reforms of the large crosscutting programme kind are guaranteed to fail.

This book is not intended to be normative, but ontological. It is guided by Robert Dahl's (1947) critical remark to the zealots of the school of public administration. "The effort to create a science of public administration has often led to the formulation of universal laws [...]. There can be no truly universal generalizations without a profound study of varying national and social characteristics impinging on public administration." This remark remains relevant, even if decisive advances in public management knowledge have been made for more than half a century. In the quest for efficiency and effectiveness in the production of public goods, scepticism remains regarding the development of the great and definitive theory of action.

Our research is based on an in-depth approach known as assessment. It encompasses a set of methods for grasping and assessing how and why internal public sector initiatives succeed or fail in bringing about real changes in the way the public sector operates.

The term "assessment" should not be confused with the concept of evaluation, which refers to a different approach. Evidence and analysis used for evaluation purposes seek to draw links between the outputs of the services involved in a pre-established policy framework or area—public health, education, and so on—and the outcomes, effects or impacts that they generate in the societal environment. It also does not fulfil a control function in the financial or regulatory sense, that is, verifying the conformity of actions with pre-established procedures.

We use the term "assessment" as a standpoint from which to better open the black box of the functioning of public institutions faced with internal reform. In this sense, it involves a series of techniques and parameters presented in more detail in Chap. 2.

Assessment is truly multidisciplinary. Formal and institutional processes play such a key role that they require a sophisticated contribution by public law experts, as the previous chapter demonstrated. Actors' discourse must be compared with the reality of their actions and organizational functioning, drawing on the methods developed by sociology and political science. Ethnology facilitates the understanding of the dynamics and permanence of the appropriation of forms of reasoning and instruments. As a discipline sustained by archive work, history makes it possible to establish the veracity of the facts mobilized elsewhere.

A few lessons can be drawn from the observations recorded in the different chapters.

They can be collated into a series of do's and don'ts that can facilitate real change and allow us to gain perspective from common sense. Observing these recommendations should increase the management capabilities needed to generate a more developed capacity for change, an approach that makes sense not only for high-tech companies (Teece et al., 1997) but also for public institutions such as universities (Thoenig & Paradeise, 2016) and State ministries.

This book does not claim to provide an exhaustive inventory of these capabilities. Nevertheless, over the course of the book some clear "don'ts" become apparent, which make sense in any administrative and institutional context where change management is involved:

1. believing that only comprehensive programmes can bring about significant and lasting change;
2. expecting governments to imperatively pay constant attention to the outcome of reforms;
3. adopting a strict isomorphic style of institutional change, whether normative, coercive or mimetic, and precisely mirroring the same approaches and solutions, whether advocated by professions, suggested by authorities within the institution, or implemented elsewhere, for example by other States;
4. relying on a single source of know-how, whether endogenous or exogenous;
5. imposing short implementation deadlines or no deadline at all;
6. creating new organizations and outsourcing reform to them;
7. not anticipating in detail the ways in which innovations will be adopted by the services on the ground;
8. not making human resource management and innovation processes compatible;
9. decreeing innovation in an authoritarian way and driving it from the top down;
10. confusing monitoring and evaluation.

Ultimately, the book is an invitation to think outside the box in the field of public management, whether to produce knowledge or to make a public system evolve. Thinking differently about change and reforms is not necessarily straightforward. The forms of reasoning applied and the responses implemented are often likely to be inadequate from a management point of view. Both academic circles and practitioners in the field should gear themselves towards satisfying a decisive imperative: making the quest for efficiency and effectiveness a powerful lever for the production of collective goods and democracy. We agree, this is certainly a huge challenge.

References

Dahl, R. A. (1947). The Science of Public Administration. Three Problems. *Public Administration Review, 7*(1), 1–11.

Lindblom, L. C. E. (1959). The Science of "muddling through". *Public Administration Review, 19*(1), 79–88.

Teece, D. J., Gary Pisano, G., & Shuen, A. (1997). Dynamic Capabilities and Strategic Management. *Strategic Management Journal, 18*, 509–533.

Thoenig, J. C., & Paradeise, C. (2016). Strategic Capacity and Organizational Capabilities. A Challenge for Universities. *Minerva, 54*(3), 293–324.